PRAISE FOR *WHERE THE FALCON FLIES*

"Epic. . . . Fighting gale-force winds and plunging into freezing water . . . this trip was like no other." *THE HAMILTON SPECTATOR*

"Adam Shoalts has famously explored the Arctic, created *A History of Canada in Ten Maps*, and now in *Where the Falcon Flies*, reveal[s] the interconnectedness between landscape and nature." *TORONTO STAR*

"For most of us, the expression 'as the crow flies'—or, in this case, peregrine falcon—is usefully descriptive. Not so for adventurer-historian Shoalts." *THE GLOBE AND MAIL*

"An exceptionally fine writer as well as adventurer, Shoalts knows how to keep you turning the pages, whisking you along, every paddle stroke of the way." NATIONAL OUTDOOR BOOK AWARD JURY

"A tremendous trek. . . . Shoalts has perpetually melded history, geography, anthropology, and storytelling to bring Canadians into his canoe. . . . The charity and kindness of complete strangers Shoalts meets along the way becomes an enduring theme in the book. It is inspiring to read how, in these days of great division in our society, a single adventurer paddling down a river or tromping down a logging road can bring out the best in people." *WINNIPEG FREE PRESS*

"Adam Shoalts has hit the mark again with his latest book. . . . My favourite portion of Shoalts's writing is the way he stitches moments of Canadian history into his book. A high school kid can skip every history class, but still gain more knowledge just by reading *Where the Falcon Flies*." KEVIN CALLAN, *EXPLORE* MAGAZINE

"*Where the Falcon Flies* takes readers along, vicariously, on this incredible journey—prepare to be wowed!" *HORIZON MAGAZINE*

PRAISE FOR *THE WHISPER ON THE NIGHT WIND*

"[*Whisper on the Night Wind*] is a spooky read, and after finishing it you might want to take a few days off before heading back into the wilderness. . . . A page turner for sure." *EXPLORE* MAGAZINE

"Modern-day explorer Adam Shoalts reminds us that our world is full of mystery, possibility, and awe." CBC

"A fantastic, fun, and chilling tale." *CANADIAN GEOGRAPHIC*

"[Adam Shoalts] continues to go where his curiosity pulls him—often into uncomfortable places we might not go ourselves—and is more than happy to bring us along in the recounting. Spine-tingling . . . captivating." *SUDBURY STAR*

"The place they end up is so isolated and untravelled that it could give the yips to even the most seasoned explorer. Shoalts is precise in his descriptions of setting and his writing is filled with . . . a clever, intentional use of language that heightens tension and lets a creepiness seep into the narrative." *QUILL & QUIRE*

"Like something out of Lovecraft. . . . [Shoalts] writes like an explorer of old . . . thrilling." BOOK CITY

"He's a great writer . . . enthralling . . . his use of language keeps you glued to the page." *MYSTERIOUS UNIVERSE PODCAST*

"Shoalts takes us deep into the heart of Labrador. Chock-full of immersive prose and captivating details, I felt as though I truly was in that canoe, ready to solve an eerie, century-year old mystery. I was left goosebumped and utterly captivated." ERIN A. CRAIG, *New York Times* bestselling author of *House of Salt and Sorrows*

PRAISE FOR *BEYOND THE TREES*

"*Beyond the Trees* is a remarkable tale—and a staggering feat. . . . It's mesmerizing to be guided through Canada's wilderness through Shoalts's eyes. . . . Shoalts also wields a wicked wit." *ATLANTIC BOOKS TODAY*

"[*Beyond the Trees*] might just soothe your need for adventure . . . wonder-filled . . . [a] beautiful book." *BUZZFEED*

"A wild adventure . . . riveting." *MONTREAL GAZETTE*

"Adam Shoalts takes readers across the rugged Canadian landscape . . . the trek was considered to be a near-impossible feat to achieve on one's own. . . . [*Beyond the Trees*] offers a beyond riveting adventure memoir that'll keep readers hooked until the very end." CNN

"Adam Shoalts does what most of us would never dare to do. . . . *Beyond the Trees* is a very readable homage to the wilds of the Canadian North." *RICHMOND NEWS*

"[A] rousing adventure story." CANADA.COM

"Adam has a magic way of writing and making you feel like you are hiking through the wilderness with him." BOOKS WITH COOKE

"The adventure of a lifetime [told] in thrilling detail." TVO

"[Shoalts] brings us along on his solo journey across the Arctic, infused with the wonder of seeing this majestic land and the urgency of making it back before winter sets in." *TORONTO STAR*

"His journey took him . . . across the terrestrial world's largest expanse of wilderness outside Antarctica . . . [an] engaging, hazard-strewn account." *NATURE*

"If you love an outdoor adventure, *Beyond the Trees* is for you." *KAMLOOPS MATTERS*

PRAISE FOR *A HISTORY OF CANADA IN TEN MAPS*

"It's an epic journey. . . . Shoalts has done an elegant job of . . . reminding us of the vast and brooding influence of geography on our history." *THE GLOBE AND MAIL*

"Adam Shoalts's book is a must read for anybody with interests in Canadian history, geography, and exploration." CANADIAN GIS

"Shoalts analyzes early maps in order to paint a picture of the land that would become a nation, bringing its earliest stories, voices, and battles to life. Combining geography, cartography, history, and anthropology, Shoalts leaves no stone unturned." CBC

"A brilliant book." *CANADIAN GEOGRAPHIC*

"[A] marvel. . . . If you like maps, you'll like this book; if you like both maps and crisply recounted Canadian history, you'll love it. Shoalts . . . takes you inside [explorers'] heads as they face fear, doubt, and despair in tandem with cold, starvation, and rebellious wanting-to-turn-back companions. . . . Canadian history writ well." *WINNIPEG FREE PRESS*

"A masterful approach to mapping Canada." *TORONTO STAR*

"One fine book perfectly written for the armchair adventurer." POSTMEDIA

PRAISE FOR *ALONE AGAINST THE NORTH*

"Rare insight into the heart and mind of an explorer, and the insatiable hunger for the unknown that both inspires and drives one to the edge. Adam Shoalts . . . calmly describes the things he has endured that would drive most people to despair, or even madness." COL. CHRIS HADFIELD, astronaut, International Space Station commander, and author of *The Apollo Murders* and *The Defector*

"As gripping to read as it must've been exciting to live!" LES STROUD, Survivorman

"Adam Shoalts's remarkable solo foray . . . is the kind of incredible effort that fosters legends." *WINNIPEG FREE PRESS*

"Shoalts's love of nature, cool professionalism, and almost archaically romantic spirit draw us into his adventures. . . . Shoalts is a knowledgeable and observant guide." QUILL & QUIRE

"Anyone who thinks exploration is dead should read this book." JOHN GEIGER, author, CEO of the Royal Canadian Geographical Society

"The more layers you peel away, the more you begin to see the quick mind and quiet intensity that helps propel Adam Shoalts." BRIAN BANKS, *CANADIAN GEOGRAPHIC*

"It is a story of brutal perseverance and stamina, which few adventurers could equal." *LIFE IN QUEBEC MAGAZINE*

"Shoalts is a fearless adventurer . . . *Alone Against the North* is a rip-roaring yarn." THE GREAT CANADIAN BUCKET LIST

"While the book is a nail-biting chronicle of polar-bear encounters, brutal swarms of black flies, and surprise tumbles down waterfalls, Shoalts also vividly describes an area of the country most of us will never witness." *METRO* (TORONTO)

PRAISE FOR ADAM SHOALTS

"One of Canada's greatest modern explorers." CBC

"Adam Shoalts is the consummate adventurer/explorer of our time." FIELD GUIDE OUTDOORS

"Adam Shoalts is Canada's Indiana Jones—portaging in the north, dodging scary rapids, plunging into darkness, and surviving to tell the tale." *TORONTO STAR*

"Adam Shoalts is one heck of a paddler." POSTMEDIA

"Explorer Adam Shoalts's monumental 4,000-kilometre journey . . . calls to mind the likes of Vilhjalmur Stefansson and Joseph Tyrrell." *CANADIAN GEOGRAPHIC*

"Move over Jacques Cartier, Christopher Columbus, and Sir Francis Drake—Adam Shoalts is this century's explorer." *HAMILTON SPECTATOR*

"Adam Shoalts . . . [has] finished an incredible journey through Canada's Arctic." *GLOBAL NEWS*

"Shoalts is a skilled woodsman and naturalist, able to survive the northern wilds with rudimentary equipment." *CANOE AND KAYAK MAGAZINE*

VANISHED BEYOND THE MAP

VANISHED BEYOND THE MAP

THE MYSTERY OF LOST
EXPLORER HUBERT DARRELL

ADAM SHOALTS

ALLEN
LANE

ALLEN LANE
an imprint of Penguin Canada, a division of Penguin Random House Canada Limited

Canada • USA • UK • Ireland • Australia • New Zealand • India • South Africa • China

First published 2025

Allen Lane, an imprint of Penguin Canada
A division of Penguin Random House Canada
320 Front Street West, Suite 1400
Toronto, Ontario, M5V 3B6, Canada
penguinrandomhouse.ca

The authorized representative in the EU for product safety and compliance
is Penguin Random House Ireland, Morrison Chambers, 32 Nassau Street,
Dublin D02 YH68, Ireland, https://eu-contact.penguin.ie

LIBRARY AND ARCHIVES CANADA CATALOGUING IN PUBLICATION
Title: Vanished beyond the map : the mystery of
lost explorer Hubert Darrell / Adam Shoalts.
Names: Shoalts, Adam, 1986- author
Identifiers: Canadiana (print) 20250161532 | Canadiana (ebook) 20250161621 |
ISBN 9780735236868 (hardcover) | ISBN 9780735236875 (EPUB)
Subjects: LCSH: Darrell, Hubert, 1874-approximately 1910. | LCSH: Explorers—
Canada—Biography. | LCSH: Northwest Territories—
Discovery and exploration. | LCGFT: Biographies.
Classification: LCC FC4172.1.D37 S56 2025 | DDC 917.19/202—dc23

Cover and book design by Dylan Browne
Typeset by Erin Cooper
Cover images: (sky) © evannovostro / Adobe Stock;
(mountains) © Design Pics / Shutterstock

Printed in the United States of America

3rd Printing

Penguin
Random
House
ALLEN LANE

To Thomas, Adrian, and Owen

"With men like him [Darrell] I could go to the moon."

NORWEGIAN EXPLORER ROALD AMUNDSEN, first to the South Pole

CONTENTS

PREFACE

Mist hung about the silent spruce-covered hills enclosing the river. September had brought colour to the ancient land, transforming the slender arctic willows along the banks into golden blazes, while further up the misty hills scarlet patches of bearberry flourished. But the lingering mist and grey skies gave the landscape a somewhat eerie feel. The sombre spruces seemed to stare at us as we drifted on the swift current. We'd broken camp shortly after dawn that morning, and now after five hours of paddling we were thoroughly chilled by the autumn air.

From my place in the canoe's stern, I scanned the mist-shrouded hills for any hint of something out of the ordinary. Somewhere in all this vastness, this immensity of trackless forest and windswept tundra, the haunt of grey wolves, moose, and grizzlies, the remarkable and mysterious Hubert Darrell had vanished in 1910. A restless prospector and expert guide, trapper, and explorer, Darrell was said to have built his humble cabin on the isolated river we were now paddling—it was our mission to find it. That fall of 1910, he was to rendezvous with a couple of fellow prospectors at an agreed-upon point, but Darrell failed to show up and apparently was never seen again. Since he was a lone man in a location utterly remote from civilization, no rescue party was ever dispatched to find him. A planned search was called off due to the difficulties. His disappearance was never explained, nor the site of his lonely cabin ever found.

But I'd spent the last several years tracking down old breadcrumb trails, sifting through forgotten records, running down leads . . . and I felt my searching hadn't been in vain. The clues suggested that somewhere in this vicinity had once stood Darrell's cabin, and given the subarctic location in the Northwest Territories, there was a chance it might still stand. We'd come a long way to find it: weeks of bushwhacking, paddling, and portaging had gotten us this far. But it was a bit like searching for a needle in a haystack.

We beached the canoe on a pebbly shore, then climbed out. Large wolf tracks led along the bank, then disappeared into a willow thicket. My companion slung his gun over his shoulder; besides the wolves, numerous grizzlies roamed the area, and not much farther off were certain to be wandering polar bears. My curiosity led me ahead up the steep slope inland toward the sparse forest cover. I climbed at a brisk pace, turning over in my mind as I did so how this high bank would command a perfect view of the river below. I also noted that the spruce groves—increasingly rare at these far northern latitudes—would have provided both suitable building material and ample firewood. In other words, about as likely a spot as any for an old trapper's cabin.

Coming up over the ridge, suddenly something loomed up in the mist. It was the vague outlines of a structure . . . A chill ran down the back of my neck. I could barely believe it: there, right in front of me, stood the crumbling ruins of an old cabin.

PART I

THE START OF A MYSTERY

WORD FROM LOST EXPLORER.
YUKON INDIANS REPORT MESSAGE
ON TREE FROM HUBERT DARRELL.
—NEW YORK TIMES *HEADLINE*, *September 1912*

It was the fall of 2011 and I was busy reading old historical records, as one often does on a Friday night. My interests lay primarily in fur traders, explorers, and adventurers from days past. I would amuse myself for hours by reading through the entries under the heading "Explorers" in the ponderous fifteen-volume *Dictionary of Canadian Biography*, which I'd been introduced to as a student. Sometimes, in the course of reading one entry, another name would come up, and I would then meander down an unexpected pathway to read that entry too. It was while engaged in this pleasing pastime that I first stumbled upon a name that would later come to haunt my waking dreams: Hubert Darrell.

It was only a very short entry, 941 words in all, that tersely described this obscure figure half lost in the shadows of the past.

Born in England in 1874 or thereabouts (even the exact year of his birth was uncertain), Hubert Darrell had arrived in Canada as a youth to work on a Manitoba farm. The work was presumably hard and dull, and when news erupted of the discovery of gold in the Klondike, like many others he'd headed north. Although Darrell ended up panning for gold along isolated mountain streams in the Canadian North for more than a decade, riches always eluded him. But among those wild mountains and rivers, he discovered his true talent: exploration and map-making—trades at which the self-taught Darrell excelled. In order to support himself in these callings, he worked variously as a guide, trapper, riverboat sailor, and mail carrier between isolated and widely separated arctic outposts. In the process he made incredible journeys alone across windswept mountain ranges, through pathless forest, and over endless miles of frozen tundra that have likely never been equalled. Far more unusual was Darrell's preference for doing without canoes and dogsleds, instead travelling by foot. Darrell guided himself on these undertakings, relying for navigation upon his own maps rather than official charts that were frequently full of errors—errors he often corrected. As he once remarked, official maps were "good to get oneself lost by." Among his most legendary feats was saving the lives of hundreds of American whalers trapped in the ice of the Arctic Ocean. Darrell, alone and on foot, travelled almost eight hundred kilometres to bring news of their desperate plight to the outside world.

His skills led to valuable friendships with Indigenous communities with whom he enjoyed close relations and frequently defended from what he saw as attempts at the time to assimilate them. The author of the brief entry, Peter Lorenz Neufeld, wrote of him, "he came to know the interior of Canada between Hudson Bay and Alaska better than any other white, and he developed an extraordinary reputation for travelling alone in all seasons, living off the land miles from human settlements." Darrell's expertise, uncanny abilities, and staggering feats of endurance led other, more famous explorers to hire him as their guide. In November 1910, Darrell was exploring and filling in blanks on existing maps alone in the western Arctic near the Anderson River when he mysteriously vanished.

The brief entry intrigued me: here was a lost explorer, and not a famous one like Franklin but a true cold case. Following that fateful Friday night when I first stumbled upon this lost explorer, I began—casually at first, then later with single-minded focus—collecting whatever material I could dig up on him. The more I learned, the more intrigued I became. Despite his obscurity today, Darrell had left deep impressions on others who crossed his path. Roald Amundsen, the legendary Norwegian explorer who became the first person to navigate the Northwest Passage and later the first to reach the South Pole, held Darrell in awe, remarking that with men like him "I could go to the moon." Another famous polar explorer, Vilhjalmur Stefansson, leader of the Canadian Arctic Expedition, also encountered Darrell in the North. Stefansson was well-known for his ego and testy relations with his rivals. But for the solitary woodsman Darrell, he had nothing but admiration, stating that he considered Darrell in a class of his own and noting that he was more accomplished than any of his more famous contemporaries. Even the North-West Mounted Police eventually found this enigmatic, lone wanderer indispensable. From 1906 to 1910, the Mounties hired Darrell to guide their dogsled patrols through the Yukon's formidable mountains.

When Darrell vanished, newspapers as far afield as New York and Los Angeles covered his disappearance, but despite clues reported by Inuit trappers and Mounted Police inquiries, his fate remains a mystery. What could have happened to him? One theory was that he'd simply fallen through a patch of weak ice somewhere . . . but there was evidence to suggest that didn't happen, and in any case, for a seasoned traveller of Darell's abilities, it seemed somewhat unlikely. Of course, as I knew from my own solitary expeditions, hazards are a fact of life alone in northern wilderness: an ill-chosen campsite wiped out in a landslide, a sudden storm while crossing an open stretch, a careless swing of an axe, a mistake in an unforgiving rapid, or even a dinner invitation from a polar bear. Though perhaps what had happened to Darrell was something darker: in the lawless expanse of the far North at that time, with witnesses few and far between, violence among trappers who were invariably armed and isolated was not uncommon. Tensions, too, between prospectors who chased after rumours of fabulous gold-filled streams could easily become strained. Strangely, shortly after Darrell disappeared, among his former associates several murders took place in the Northwest Territories. But perhaps it was all a coincidence. Maybe Hubert Darrell, the lone wolf, simply made up his mind to turn his back on the world.

In tracking down traces of Darrell's life, I often felt as if I were chasing a ghost. He'd vanished not only literally, but from the pages of history. Darrell was so little known that no one had ever written a book about him; he didn't even have a Wikipedia page. And since he never married nor had any children, Darrell left no descendants to recall his tale.

Yet what I soon found was that Darrell had left behind a trail of sorts in the form of letters, journals, and hand-drawn maps. To piece together the fragments of his forgotten life, I relied heavily on these unpublished archival documents scattered in odd corners, as well as my own retracing of his routes through the wilderness from long ago. It felt very much like detective work—tracking down leads, making inquiries, sifting through old water-stained journals and faded letters, digging up newspaper records, finding the ruins of abandoned cabins or forgotten campsites, and seeking out elderly individuals who might by chance remember someone who'd known him. Gradually the picture of Darrell's life came into clearer focus, and I began to feel, as I read and reread his diaries and camped where he had once camped, paddled where he'd paddled, broke trail where he had once done, that I knew him—at least as well as anyone can know someone who'd disappeared more than a century ago.

This feeling of kinship spurred me on to find out what had happened to him and to solve, if I could, the mystery of his disappearance. After retracing parts of Darrell's routes, I began organizing expeditions to search for evidence of his last camps, hoping to bring his tale to light. This is the story of what I found.

2

BEGINNINGS

The early details of Hubert Darrell's life are sketchy, but from what can be known it seems his background was thoroughly ordinary, with nothing much that would suggest his future adventurous career. His family tree, in so far as I could untangle it, didn't contain any adventurers, explorers, or other surprises. His father, Charles, came from a humble farming background in northern England, but like many others in 1800s England, he'd left the farm as a young man to seek better prospects elsewhere. After settling in London, he found a job as an insurance clerk. There he would meet Darrell's mother, Emily Elizabeth Jones. She was one of seven children: the daughter of a Royal Navy paymaster, a position in Britain's navy tasked with accounting. This modest middle-class background would have put Darrell lower down the social scale than many 1800s era explorers, several of whom came from prominent families, notably Sir John Franklin. When Franklin disappeared in the Arctic, numerous ships and expeditions were dispatched to find him.

When Darrell vanished, no rescue party was ever sent and his name was soon forgotten.

Not much else about the early lives of Darrell's parents is known, but in any event, the two were married in 1870. Their marriage was apparently a happy one, and together they would have nine children in all. Hubert was their third child, born, according to a baptism record that I found, in Kent in 1874. That the family was close-knit can be guessed from the many affectionate letters Darrell wrote to them, which still survive.

In at least one respect, though, the Darrell family was unusual: they were uncommonly long-lived and healthy. In an age when child mortality was very high (in England in the 1870s about one-quarter of all children died before age five), remarkably all nine of the Darrell children survived to adulthood. Hubert's father lived to be eighty at a time when male life expectancy was barely sixty (the equivalent of living over a hundred today), while his mother lived to be ninety-six. Darrell's siblings were similarly long-lived, with his sister Violet living to be a hundred and five. So although he may never have had riches, Darrell's later extraordinary feats of endurance seem to have reflected his iron constitution, which he apparently inherited from both sides of his family.

At first, the Darrells lived on the outskirts of London in Chislehurst, then a rural part of Kent with rolling hills, ancient woods, and quiet farms. While Darrell was still a child, they moved a short distance away to Sidcup Hill, another community in bucolic Kent. At the time, both places would have afforded plenty of forests to enthral and entice the imagination of a young boy. Even today, the visitor to these areas might be pleasantly surprised by the relative profusion of woods, fields, and nature parks otherwise smothered among noisy urban sprawl. They seem to stand as silent reminders of a landscape that not so long ago had been much wilder.

England today might not seem like fertile breeding grounds for a legendary arctic wanderer, but when Darrell was born it was not quite the densely populated place it is now. In the 1870s, England's population numbered only a third of today, leaving an abundance of quiet countryside where fishing and hunting were still popular, including around the Darrell home. The country's encircling seacoast, too, like all seacoasts, held out the prospects of mystery and adventure for any travel-inclined dreamers. I often wondered if Darrell in his youth had engaged in these rural pastimes, or perhaps on holidays wandered off from home to stare longingly out at the sea. No records from his childhood exist to tell us one way or another, but given his later life it's hard to believe he didn't.

Yet at the time of Darrell's childhood, this age-old landscape was also in the throes of transformation. The Industrial Revolution was gathering steam at a rapid pace. Railroads and factories seemed to be springing up everywhere, with more and more workers setting aside pitchfork and plow for the cotton mill, iron foundry, or coal mines. Forests were cleared, farms built over, sleepy villages transformed into bustling towns, towns into booming cities, and cities into Dickensian landscapes of gaslights, electric trams, skyscrapers, noise, and smog. It was the dawn of modern industrial civilization, the very thing Darrell seems to have turned his back on. While some looked eagerly on the new and dazzling array of technological inventions transforming society, which included the first electric lights, wireless telegrams, indoor plumbing, phonographs, and combustion engines, Darrell instead embarked on a very different path that would lead him to a life of hardship and isolation in Canada's northern wilderness. In 1890, youthful Hubert Darrell, just sixteen years old, left his family home to make his own way in the world—setting out for wilder places in far-off Canada.

3

MANITOBA FRONTIER

Exposed to the natural world in its all beauty and brutality, life as a frontier homesteader on the Canadian prairies helped harden Darrell for the adventurous path ahead of him. Among the woods and rivers of his new home, Darrell began to exhibit unusual abilities in hunting, fishing, and trapping, as well as a prodigious ability for strenuous work. But I've gotten ahead of myself, so allow me to back up for a second to provide some context.

In 1890, Darrell emigrated from the only place he'd ever known to work on a farm in remote Manitoba. His brother Charles, who was three years his elder, had already immigrated there to farm. Now some might think teenagers in those days were always running away from home to take up farming in Manitoba, but this doesn't seem to have been the case. Since the Darrell family wasn't wealthy, luxuries such as attending university were never on the table. With lots of mouths to feed at home, the older boys, Charles and Hubert, had to grow up quickly. By

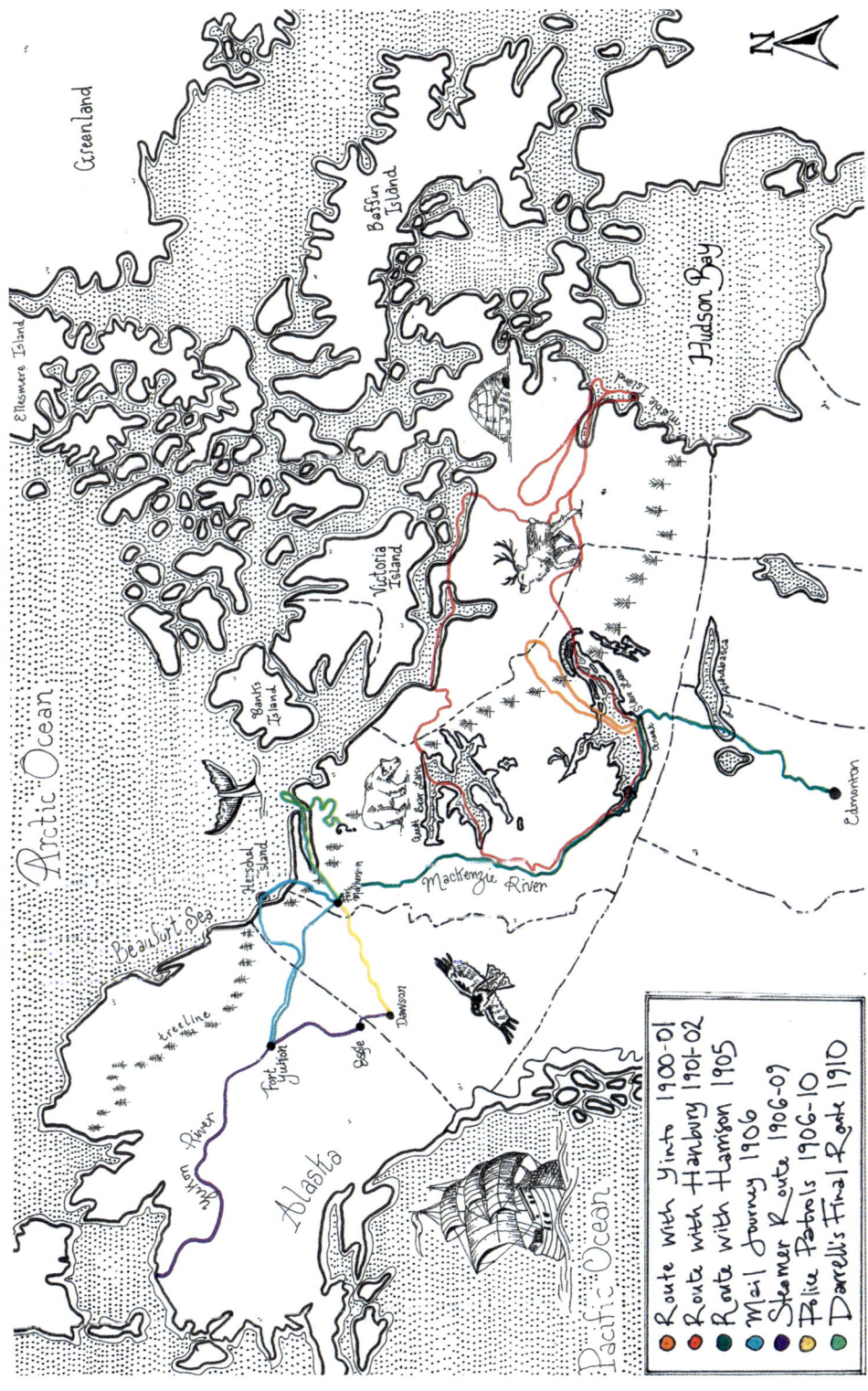

N

Greenland

Baffin Island

Hudson Bay

Ellesmere Island

Victoria Island

Banks Island

Arctic Ocean

Beaufort Sea

treeline

Herschel Island

Great Bear Lake

Great Slave Lake

Lake Athabasca

Mackenzie River

Edmonton

Yukon River

Fort Yukon

Eagle

Dawson

Alaska

Pacific Ocean

Route with Yunt 1900-01
Route with Hanbury 1901-02
Route with Hamson 1905
Mail Journey 1906
Steamer Route 1906-09
Police Patrols 1906-10
Darrell's Final Route 1910

The only known portrait of Hubert Darrell. It was likely taken in 1905, when he was thirty-one years old. PHOTO CREDIT: Photographer Unknown

The richly forested valley of the Birdtail River just outside Birtle, Manitoba, near where Darrell came of age as a young farmer.
PHOTO CREDIT: Adam Shoalts

The moon rises above the Yukon's snowy peaks. Among these mountains Darrell frequently slept out in temperatures down to fifty below.
PHOTO CREDIT: Adam Shoalts

Hauling a sled across frozen lakes in the Yukon to retrace Darrell's footsteps. PHOTO CREDIT: Adam Shoalts

A river scow on the Athabasca River around the year 1900. Such boats were widely used in the fur trade and gold rush, and Darrell often travelled on them, including with Harrison. PHOTO CREDIT: Alfred Harrison

Comparing notes and studying Darrell's journals while camping out as he did. PHOTO CREDIT: Adam Shoalts

A muskox. These shaggy, prehistoric-looking creatures fascinated Darrell and he hunted them with Chief Yinto and his Dene band.

PHOTO CREDIT: Adam Shoalts

Fort McMurray, 1905. Many northern towns in Darrell's day were little more than a handful of cabins and canvas tents.

PHOTO CREDIT: Alfred Harrison

This photograph, taken by David Hanbury, shows their party dragging canoes up the Coppermine River in 1902. Darrell is almost certainly one of the men in the photograph, but it's not possible to say which one he is.

PHOTO CREDIT: David Hanbury

Retracing Darrell and Hanbury's route in the Northwest Territories.

PHOTO CREDIT: Chuck Brill

A photograph taken by David Hanbury of igloos built by Inuit hunters Uttungerlah and Amer-or-yauk, in which he, Darrell, and other members of their party lived during the winter of 1902. PHOTO CREDIT: David Hanbury

A whaling ship frozen in the ice of the Beaufort Sea in 1906. As part of his epic mail delivery journey, Darrell travelled alone and on foot to this ship and other ones trapped in the arctic ice. PHOTO CREDIT: Alfred Harrison

A Mounted Police dogsled patrol heading to Herschel Island in 1909. Darrell guided several dogsled patrols in the North, including to Herschel Island. Part of his gruelling task was to walk ahead of the dogs on foot, breaking the trail for them.

PHOTO CREDIT: Library and Archives Canada/PA-029622

Even in the Yukon's bitterly cold winters, some rivers can still have open water. Crossing such rivers was just one of the many hazards Darrell faced on his long journeys. PHOTO CREDIT: Adam Shoalts

sixteen, they were considered men and as such had to go off to earn a living one way or another.

Given their robust health, physical stamina, and their father's farming roots, the Darrells perhaps naturally gravitated toward trying their hands at tilling the soil. But in Britain they could never afford to purchase a farm. They had to look elsewhere, somewhere that land could still be had for cheap. Western Canada was one such place, where in a bid to attract settlers the Canadian government offered 160-acre parcels for ten dollars. It may sound like a bargain today, but few at the time took the offer. The remoteness and notoriously cold, dark winters deterred many. The great flood of migration to the West was still some years off, and as of 1890, most prospective farmers who could find somewhere else to settle, did.

How the Darrell brothers should have chosen Manitoba specifically is unclear, but it's a reasonable assumption that the family already knew of someone there. Certainly, if they had money or more promising connections, they would probably have chosen somewhere less remote and frigid to farm, but the Darrells had little of either. For that reason, as much as any other, the teenaged brothers ended up nearly three hundred kilometres outside Winnipeg on the windswept northern prairie.

Winnipeg itself, by modern standards, was only a small town of 25,000 inhabitants, but it was practically a metropolis compared to Darrell's new home. The young brothers settled on the outskirts of Birtle, a little farming community just south of the rugged, spruce-clad uplands known as Riding Mountain. It was a remote and wild place—sparsely populated, cold, hard, isolated country. The bitter winters made for a sharp contrast with the world Darrell had left behind. Even today January temperatures average nearly minus twenty degrees Celsius, and it was colder still in Darrell's day. For every homesteader who managed to eke out a living, another or more folded. Most of the hardscrabble farmers in the area grew wheat for export, as well as vegetables for their own table, supplemented by hunting, fishing, or trapping. In bad years, starvation was not unheard-of, and hunger sometimes had to be accepted as a fact of life.

But the landscape near their new home was not without certain advantages: unlike most of the Canadian prairies, the area around Birtle included significant forest cover. Birtle itself sits nestled in the winding valley of the Birdtail River, where fish could be caught and stands of bur oak, cottonwood, poplar, and Manitoba maple flourished. Farmers in the area could actually construct their dwellings of wood, instead of the tiny sod houses that prevailed elsewhere on the prairie, and the valley afforded a steady supply of firewood to help cope with the bitterness of winter. Elk, moose, mule deer, black bear, and grey wolves as well as many smaller animals were all common. Darrell would soon have ample first-hand opportunities to stalk and hunt each of these, skills his life would later come to depend upon. Extensive marshes also lay nearby that teemed seasonally with vast numbers of migrating waterfowl, while the rivers and ponds sheltered beavers and muskrats. It was here that Darrell spent his formative years as a teenager and young man.

The exact details of his days in Manitoba are hazy, but the 1891 Census of Canada records him as living and working as a farmhand on the homestead of one Robert Collis. Collis, a local farmer originally from Quebec, was known to help train young apprentices in the ins and outs of prairie farming. His farm was in Shoal Lake, east of Birtle. The work would have been mostly drudgery—though just the sort of toil needed to harden and strengthen Darrell for his future arctic wanderings. Charles, too, when he'd first arrived in Canada, had worked as a hired hand on the Collis farm, though he was not listed among the five workers there in the 1891 census. By that point, it seems Charles had already moved on. He'd purchased a 160-acre farm of his own farther west. Darrell, after learning the ropes with Collis and maybe putting away a little savings of his own to contribute to a share of his older brother's farm, soon joined Charles there.

The Darrell farm stood several kilometres southeast of the tiny village of Birtle in the Warleigh district. In this wild and lonely place, the nearest neighbours were a mile distant. But company was provided by the occasional wandering moose or elk, and nightly visits by bears and wolves interested in free samples of the farm's livestock. The farm, as I learned first-hand when I walked the deserted field where it once stood, sat on a low ridge overlooking the surrounding prairie, with scattered bits of woodland, marshes, and ponds. Wild flocks of sharp-tailed grouse were a common and welcome sight, as an addition to the dinner table. Notably, too, the old Hudson's Bay Company trail, the Carlton Trail, which horse-mounted riders and wagons followed, crossed a portion of the farm—but human visitors were few. Here these two young brothers, one still a teenager and the other barely twenty, pitted themselves against the elements, struggling to carve out a living in a land where fierce blizzards, crop failures, and wildlife depredations were all normal occurrences. Such circumstances, endured month after month, year in and year out, undoubtedly moulded any who could overcome them into resilient, resourceful, and strongly independent characters.

Although the Darrells were often referred to as "homesteaders," that term technically denoted only those farmers who'd taken the government's land deal: ten dollars for a 160-acre parcel of prairie, which would have to be cleared and planted. Instead, it seems Charles managed to purchase a farm that had already been homesteaded for a little more than ten years prior to their arrival. This had its advantages, but it also entailed a costly mortgage. This debt to the bank would become a source of stress and pressure on both Charles and Hubert for years afterwards as they struggled to pay it off with their meagre earnings. There were other expenses too: the need for draught animals, whether oxen or horses; various tools; seed; and other supplies. All of which meant more debt, and it is little wonder then that so many of these small-scale farms ultimately failed. In hard years, the entire wheat crop was sometimes lost to insect pests, disease, or bad weather.

Journals are lacking to shed more light on this period of Darrell's life. (This might be because Darrell seems to have later lost some of his in an arctic shipwreck.) But we can infer from indirect sources some of what Darrell's life was like at the time. Besides all the normal chores of farm life—the planting and threshing of wheat, the tending and care of animals, repairs to outbuildings and equipment—Darrell had ample opportunity to hone his hunting and other outdoor skills. That he was highly skilled in this regard there can be little doubt, and the incentive of fresh meat for their table probably kept him out on many a long night on the trail of elk, moose, or deer. Like other farmers,

Darrell probably also trapped beavers or muskrats to obtain furs and supplement his scanty income. When he wasn't busy with these tasks, there was the endless harvesting and hauling of firewood needed to endure the bitter winters. The available wood at or near the farm would have soon been exhausted, and then ever longer trips—normally done in the winter on horse-drawn sleds—would have been required to obtain a supply. Amid such hard labours Darrell grew to manhood, inured to back-breaking toil and deprivation, and accustomed to an independence that nowadays many would find hard to fathom.

Sources who knew Darrell later describe him as strong and energetic, quiet but cheerful, competent, and honest almost to a fault. And despite his eventual reputation as a lone wolf and the greatest of solitary wanderers, there is some indication that Darrell enjoyed about as lively a social life as could be expected from a Manitoban farmer in the late 1800s. He'd readily lend a hand on the farms of his nearest neighbours, especially whenever hard labour was called for, and he'd think nothing of trudging for miles in all kinds of weather to help another. Festive occasions would bring these otherwise isolated, scattered farmers together for cheerful banquets, and Darrell seems to have taken part in these too. His later journals and letters recall fondly his friends from the area: William North, Abe Nichol, Ernest Dudley, and the names of quite a few others. Likely it was their shared struggles and common hardships wrestling a living from the land that bonded them together into a close-knit community.

But Darrell was not destined to remain long. Quiet and reserved as he may have seemed on the outside, deep inside him smouldered a restless wanderlust, an insatiable thirst for adventure, an everlasting itch. Such a restless nature made it impossible for him to stay put. Seven years of relentless toil and heavy labour had strengthened and hardened his naturally sturdy build. Yet during all this time, hard as he and his brother worked, the farm's debts only seemed to grow. So, when sensational news came in 1897 of the discovery of gold in the distant Klondike, it must have felt like the answer to their prayers. Breathless reports spoke of men pulling gold nuggets the size of a man's fist out of the Yukon's streams and of gold to be had with every swish of a pan. Charles, who never quite shared his brother's taste for adventure, would remain behind on the farm, while Hubert Darrell, now twenty-three, would set off to seek his fortune in the wilderness. His hope was that he'd quickly strike it rich and then return able to pay off the farm's debts.

4

THE KLONDIKE

I was shivering inside my tent, trying not to freeze to death. The thermometer I'd packed only displayed down to forty below, and it had reached that hours ago. Now with the sun's rays long gone, and ice forming with alarming rapidness on everything my breath touched, it seemed likely to be colder. I was camped alone among the high peaks of the Kluane Range, deep in the Yukon's mountains. As I shivered in my sleeping bag, the conclusion came to me that I really had been mistaken not to pack a warmer one.

It was the trail of Hubert Darrell that had led me into these avalanche-prone mountains, where the winter solitude and silence felt absolute and all-encompassing. I'd spent many months wandering around the Arctic alone by canoe or on foot, but that mostly was from May to September. In those sunny months, the far North is about as wonderful a place as any I can imagine: as close to heaven on Earth in my eyes as it's possible to be (minus the bugs). But it's a strange, altogether different land in winter, when the shadows lengthen and everything freezes dead silent. In a moonlit, ice-encrusted conifer forest in December, everything appears dark and mysterious. Here in the southwestern corner of the Yukon, the nights last eighteen long hours, and the noonday sun seems weak above the snowclad peaks.

Shivering, I reminded myself that at least in this arctic cold the grizzlies inhabiting these mountains were all asleep, hibernating until the thaw. That was a distinct comfort. Wolves, wolverines, and lynx still prowled the midnight forests, but I didn't fear them. The cold, though, I did fear. I had read too many stories of prospectors freezing to death not to fear it. I knew that at forty below, frostbite sets in within minutes if the skin is exposed to the open air. I knew, too, that sleeping out here alone was an invitation to hypothermia.

But Darrell had done so in a canvas tent, or a brush lean-to, many times, and I felt to fully investigate and tell his story, it was necessary for me to do so too. Of course, Darrell's motivation, at least nominally, was the same one that drove upward of a hundred thousand others to head for the Klondike—to find gold and strike it rich. The Klondike gold rush that he became swept up in proved to be one of the greatest gold stampedes in history.

It had all started in the summer of 1896 when a trio of local prospectors—George Carmack, Skookum Jim, and Dawson Charlie—stumbled upon gold in the clear mountain waters of a small tributary of the Klondike River called Rabbit Creek, later renamed Bonanza Creek. But the country was so remote and isolated that it took nearly a year for word of their discovery to reach the outside world. When it did, newspapers spread it like wildfire, with generous exaggerations about the ease of getting at the gold. The result was a frenzy of gold fever the likes of which the world had never seen. Before it was over, fortunes would be won and lost, lives uprooted, a wilderness ransacked by eager prospectors, and many millions of pounds of gold mined out of the creek beds of the Klondike. Despite this, the vast majority of prospectors never made a fortune—in fact many, overcome by the elements, the hardships, the isolation, and the remoteness, gave up without ever sinking a shovel into the frozen ground.

Just getting to the Klondike was an ordeal. Most of the would-be millionaires who flooded into the Yukon in 1897–98 came north by ocean steamer to the Alaskan panhandle, where they were dropped at the tiny ports of Skagway or Dyea. From there, long and tortuous trails led over the towering coastal mountains. The most famous, the Chilkoot, saw long lines of prospectors toiling up the steep slope under the weight of heavy packs and provisions. The Canadian authorities, realizing the chaos and probable violence that would prevail if tens of thousands of inexperienced prospectors flooded into the Yukon, barred entry into Canada for anyone not equipped with at least a year's worth of supplies. This forced prospectors to undertake numerous trips over snowy mountains to the headwaters of the Yukon River hauling the roughly one tonne worth of provisions required. For those who survived this gruelling feat, a further eight hundred kilometres of dangerous water travel, in any kind of craft that they could construct, buy, or trade for, awaited down harrowing rivers, through narrow canyons and roaring rapids, and across crystalline lakes to reach the Klondike's goldfields.

Here, at the mouth of the Klondike River, a moose swamp was transformed practically overnight from a couple of log shacks into a bustling, boisterous boom town of thirty thousand people. Christened Dawson City, it soon boasted saloons, gambling halls, hotels, brothels, and about as colourful a cast of characters ever assembled in one place. Among these dreamers were the novelist Jack London, gambler and showman "Arizona" Charlie, famed vaudeville dancer "Klondike Kate" Rockwell, veteran prospector Swiftwater Bill, the incorruptible Mountie Sam Steele, and perhaps the quiet, unassuming, but competent Hubert Darrell.

I say *perhaps* because Darrell's time in the Klondike, like much of his life, is mysterious: if he kept a diary of his time in the gold rush, it hasn't come to light. We can be certain of only two things: he did not strike it rich, but he did become deeply infected by the spell of the North and the call of the wild. For the rest of his life, he would remain under that spell and wander all over the vastness of Canada's North, quietly amassing a record of exploration that few individuals could ever match. In the process, he became a legend: a strange, enigmatic figure.

But all that still lay ahead. At the moment, young Darrell was just one of thousands of other penniless prospectors wandering among the mountains seeking to hit paydirt. Like most, he had no luck. In fact, within just a few years of the initial discovery, most of the easily accessible surface gold was mined out, the bonanza faded, and the vast majority of prospectors and others departed the North, leaving in their wake abandoned cabins to moulder and Dawson a near ghost town. Yet Darrell did not return to his farm: he'd been bitten by the wilderness bug, and it would haunt him for the rest of his life.

It was a yearning that I understood: all my life, wild places have held a deep fascination for me, an almost magical charm that draws me to them. It had started with the wild forests surrounding my childhood home in Ontario, continued on with countless journeys to remote lakes and forgotten rivers, then even longer sojourns lasting months. That same stirring had also encouraged me to trek into these freezing, snowbound Yukon mountains. And remorselessly cold as it was, as I looked up, shivering, at the moon through the snow-draped branches of the spruces, I thought I knew what Darrell must have felt, drawing him out here. The strange calm and inner peace in spite of the hardships, the wonder and awe all mixed up with adventure and mystery, the wild independence. Many have tried to explain the appeal of the wild, but to me, the reason is very simple and universal: all humans, for the overwhelming majority of our history, once lived in the wild.

Perhaps no one has better captured this paradoxical appeal than the poet Robert Service. Service happened to be born in the same year as Darrell, 1874, and, like him, had come north to the Klondike. Also like Darrell, he found no gold but would linger in the North, finding riches of another sort—material for his poetry. One of his poems in particular, "The Spell of the Yukon," describes prospectors, like Darrell, who were taken in by the allure of the wild:

> I wanted the gold, and I sought it;
> I scrabbled and mucked like a slave.
> Was it famine or scurvy—I fought it;
> I hurled my youth into a grave.

I wanted the gold, and I got it—
Came out with a fortune last fall,—
Yet somehow life's not what I thought it,
And somehow the gold isn't all.

No! There's the land. (Have you seen it?)
It's the cussedest land that I know,
From the big, dizzy mountains that screen it
To the deep, deathlike valleys below.
Some say God was tired when He made it;
Some say it's a fine land to shun;
Maybe; but there's some as would trade it
For no land on earth—and I'm one.

You come to get rich (damned good reason);
You feel like an exile at first;
You hate it like hell for a season,
And then you are worse than the worst.
It grips you like some kinds of sinning;
It twists you from foe to a friend;
It seems it's been since the beginning;
It seems it will be to the end.
[. . .]
The cold fear that follows and finds you,
The silence that bludgeons you dumb.
The snows that are older than history,
The woods where the weird shadows slant;
The stillness, the moonlight, the mystery,
I've bade 'em good-by—but I can't.

There's a land where the mountains are nameless,
  And the rivers all run God knows where;
There are lives that are erring and aimless,
  And deaths that just hang by a hair;
There are hardships that nobody reckons;
  There are valleys unpeopled and still;
There's a land—oh, it beckons and beckons,
  And I want to go back—and I will.
        [. . .]
There's gold, and it's haunting and haunting;
  It's luring me on as of old;
Yet it isn't the gold that I'm wanting
  So much as just finding the gold.
It's the great, big, broad land 'way up yonder,
  It's the forests where silence has lease;
It's the beauty that thrills me with wonder,
  It's the stillness that fills me with peace.

For more than a decade, Darrell would continue to prospect across the Canadian North, but in truth he seems to have cared less about gold and more about the sheer adventure of it. More than that, it was the land itself that irresistibly drew Darrell, like it has with many others before and since.

5

WANDERER

Darrell's interests soon drifted away from the comparatively crowded Klondike and led him to still more remote places. He wandered alone among mountains and streams while experiencing a freedom, wildness, and solitude even more intense than anything back on the Manitoba prairie. At the same time, the far North exposed Darrell to colder and darker winters than what he'd been accustomed to in Manitoba. It was during this time, too, that Darrell likely discovered he was one of those happy mortals who are born with an innate sense of direction: the ability to wander at will through dense forest, icy mountains, and featureless tundra without losing one's way. During the warmer seasons, his nomadic lifestyle took him by boat across vast lakes and down snaking rivers, while come winter he'd usually nestle into a tiny cabin he built himself in some isolated locale.

Darrell's sparse journal entries and occasional letters, scrawled by the light of countless fires, offer glimpses of his life at this time. These letters, often spaced more than half a year apart and always taking months to reach their destination, were sometimes sent to Charles's farm in Manitoba, and from there, forwarded by his brother to their family in England. Nearly half a century after Darrell's disappearance, another one of his long-lived siblings would collect whatever remained of these, as well as the journals Darrell had mailed home, and donate them all to an archive in England. There they sat largely forgotten for years collecting dust. After learning of Darrell for the first time on that memorable Friday night, I made it my mission to seek out and read these records, which I later did. Relying on these— often faded, yellowed with age, sometimes water-stained, and only half legible—I continued to follow Darrell's trail the best I could, retracing his routes over lonely mountain passes and up winding rivers, trying to experience what he once did.

His letters speak of the hardships of the trail, of trekking in blizzards where the snow was thick as fog, and of sleeping out in temperatures that fell to fifty below. Camping alone in such conditions necessitated waking every half hour to replenish the fire. Even so, frostbite was unavoidable, and Darrell's skin would peel from his face on occasion. (I decided to skip recreating this.) Frequently he'd have to break trail while hauling a hundred-pound sled. In rare cases, the snow froze hard enough that he could walk without snowshoes. But amid all the hardships was the strange, entrancing beauty of the North. Darrell remarked of sleeping outside in the dead of winter: "It was a cold, clear night, with the Northern Lights dancing and I rather enjoyed it."

Summers brought their own rewards and challenges. An August 1899 letter that Darrell penned to his father recounts travelling by boat across Great Slave Lake in the Northwest

Territories. Darrell was struck by the beauty and majesty of this immense lake, the world's tenth largest. Spruce-studded islands in places broke up the crystal waters, while high waterfalls tumbled over granite cliffs that dominated the shore. Across these vast inland waters, Darrell travelled night and day, sometimes out of sight of land, and laconically noted in the same letter that it "would fare ill with the boat to be caught in a storm so far from land." The lake's cold depths, the deepest of any lake in North America, harboured monstrous lake trout. Darrell mentions landing some as large as fifty pounds.

Ringing Great Slave Lake at distant intervals were tiny trading posts operated by the Hudson's Bay Company. These isolated posts, set amid unbroken spruce forests, were usually no more than a handful of cabins. It was at these posts that Darrell would sometimes show up to barter furs or deposit letters for his family. In several letters, he expressed his belief that gold was to be found in the Northwest Territories, likely he thought on the windswept barrens or somewhere equally difficult to reach.

The ebbing of the Klondike gold rush had brought a flood of discouraged miners and prospectors into the neighbouring Northwest Territories with the same thoughts, many of them Americans. Some were simply trying to get back south as easily as they could by ascending the Mackenzie River on steamers; others, desperate for riches, wandered aimlessly about, seeking unknown creeks in the hopes of stumbling on the next bonanza. Of these rough American gold-seekers Darrell took a mostly dim view, regarding them as desperate enough that they likely wouldn't hesitate to draw their guns on anyone who came between them and gold. In one letter he remarked, "There are many rough men here & I heard remarks made by some of them, which if overheard he would not trust himself alone with them unarmed." Before coming north, many of these Americans had roamed the Wild West.

Darrell spent the winter of 1899 living in a cramped log cabin on the banks of a river in the Northwest Territories. With him was an older prospector, a fellow from New York whom Darrell thought little of in terms of outdoor skills, dismissing him as "not knowing an axe from a dinner knife." After this, Darrell would increasingly opt to winter alone—an unusual practice when partnering with other prospectors was the norm. The next winter he relocated farther north, closer to Great Slave Lake.

There he built himself a cozy new cabin, measuring ten feet by twelve. For a floor, he broke up the boards from his flat-bottomed rowboat (he could always build another one later), while he fashioned a chimney with rocks and clay pulled out of a river. Darrell described his fireplace as a "grand thing" since it was big enough to light up the whole room—an important consideration in a place where winter nights could last nineteen hours. The log walls he chinked with moss to keep out the drafts. Despite this spartan simplicity, in one of his letters, Darrell cheerfully noted, "I have everything that goes to make a fellow comfortable."

Christmas Eve 1899 saw Darrell making new boards for his bed, while on Christmas Day he checked his trapline and hunted ptarmigans. Then he had Christmas dinner with his nearest neighbour, an elderly Métis trapper, whom Darrell called an "honest old fellow." For their little Christmas feast, Darrell brought the fresh ptarmigans, while his host baked bannock and offered tea. By a blazing hearth, they swapped what news they had, while afterwards young Darrell, curious as ever, asked his aged host about the more mysterious of local wildlife—the uncanny wolverine, with its abilities to evade even the best traps; the strange, otherworldly muskoxen rumoured to be found farther north on the arctic plains; and the gigantic wood bison that still roamed the northern forests. An old Métis trapper, wise in the ways of the woods, would know of these things—the sort of things people in England and even Manitoba knew little about. Such stories undoubtedly whetted Darrell's appetite for further adventures.

Although Darrell was wary of American mining characters, he got along well with Dene, Cree, and Métis trappers. They seemed to have been his preferred companions, and that they also liked him can be surmised by the fact that Darrell—virtually alone among outsiders—would sometimes be invited to join them for weeks or months hunting. He attempted to learn both Athabascan and Cree, the most common languages in the subarctic, as well as French. Alone in his little cabin on many a winter's night, by firelight Darrell would make simple dictionaries of the words he learned. Of missionaries and the Hudson's Bay Company, Darrell thought very little, expressing the then almost heretical view that the natives would be better off without either of them.

His family, it seems, began to wonder what exactly was keeping Darrell in the North. Since the gold rush had faded, they suggested it might be prudent if he returned to the farm. But communicating with a backwoods denizen wasn't the easiest: letters would have to be addressed to the nearest trading posts, where Darrell might eventually collect them. In a belated reply to his family's concerns, Darrell reassured them that he had no intention of remaining in the North much longer. In another letter he explained, "I am simply now trying to make enough to clear expenses and then I will return." But instead of returning, it seems something would always come up to lure him deeper into the wild.

It might be rumours of a fresh gold strike, but most of the time it was simply hunting and trapping. In fact, Darrell seems to have spent comparatively little time prospecting, preferring a trapper's life instead. His journals note making the daily rounds of the traplines that he laid through the winter woods. When spring came, he'd take off wandering again, sometimes finding work on a fur trade steamer sailing the Mackenzie River, the longest and grandest river in the North, which drains Great Slave Lake to the Arctic Ocean. In his journals, Darrell further evinced a strong curiosity about muskoxen—at the time, a mysterious animal—and a desire to hunt one.

After another winter passed and another five-month interval with no word from him, Darrell reassured his family in a letter dated July 24, 1900, that he would return soon: "I have made up my mind to get home when I can and join Charlie again if he will have me, but you must not be surprised if it is some months yet as there is always a difficulty in getting out accepting in the winter." But once again he couldn't bring himself to actually head south. Instead, snaring snowshoe hares, ice fishing, or tracking caribou filled his solitary days. 1900 was a year when much of the rest of the world was amazed by the new technological marvels of the age, including the first motion pictures, electric trolley buses, escalators, magnetic audio recorders, and even the first cars. These were all exhibited to grand fanfare at the Paris world's fair that same year, which drew nearly fifty million visitors from around the world. But Darrell was more interested in simply sleeping under the stars. That fall, his budding friendship with some Dene families near Great Slave Lake led to an invitation to join them on a journey to hunt caribou and muskoxen.

This Darrell couldn't resist, and so off he went again. The leader of the small band was a respected Dene hunter, Chief Yinto. He gave Darrell a couple days to round up all the supplies he could pack—blankets, ammunition, two rifles, a knife, clothing, and as much food as he could carry. Then Darrell joined Yinto and the other Dene hunters. They first travelled across Great Slave Lake, enduring rough seas and storms. On the lake's far side, the Dene met up with their families, who had been camped there waiting for them. After fishing for a time to build up a food supply, the party split into smaller groups for the "barren lands"—the term they used to denote the treeless arctic plains. Splitting up was necessary, as the harsh arctic environment yields insufficient food resources to support large groups— even for the greatest of hunters, which the Dene were.

Yinto's group numbered four other men and their families, plus Darrell. Together by dogsled they headed north, with Darrell given his own sled to manage. Despite the harshness of the landscape, Darrell admired the beautiful snowbound lakes and wide-open vistas. Acting as Darrell's personal guide was Chief Yinto's brother, and during this time, Darrell lived with him and his wife and children. Darrell remarked on the generosity shown by them, later writing in a letter to his own family that they "looked after me very kindly."

When the party neared the northern edge of the forest, they left the women and children behind to camp by a wooded lake, where ice fishing would provide a sufficient food supply. Darrell recorded that in just two hours in a single net set under the ice, twenty-six fish were caught, providing a hundred pounds of food. But such a haul was necessary to keep the dogs fed. It was also here that Darrell ate the last of the flour and apples he'd packed: for the next two months, he'd eat nothing other than what they hunted or caught. Then Yinto led the five hunters, Darrell included, out of the sheltering spruce forests onto the windswept arctic plains. Wisely, Yinto had them hunt caribou as they travelled, caching the meat for their return journey in case things went badly.

As they ventured farther north, they were at times storm-bound by fierce blizzards that made it impossible for even Yinto to find his way. To escape the howling winds, they crouched behind giant boulders or, if none were available, simply huddled with their dogs in the open. Every few days they tried to shoot a caribou, but when they failed to find any, they were reduced to half rations, and sometimes during longer spells of ill luck, there was nothing to eat at all.

After traversing several hundred miles, they at last came upon what they were after—a herd of fifty muskoxen. These strange-looking, shaggy creatures, almost ice age in appearance, are found only in far northern Canada and small parts of Greenland. As such, few outsiders had ever seen them, let alone hunted them. (In contrast, most northern mammals, including polar bears, wolverines, and caribou, are equally distributed across the northern regions of North America, Europe, and Asia.) One can barely imagine what Darrell must have felt staring at no less than fifty of these mysterious, giant horned beasts. Even in our modern and demystified age, when I had my first encounter with a muskox while exploring a lonely river in the High Arctic, it sent a wild shiver through me that made me feel I was confronted by a creature almost prehistoric—or at least something out of *Star Wars*.

Yinto silently motioned the hunters forward: the muskoxen were tucked down in a sheltered valley. They had to struggle to keep the excited dogs quiet as they sneaked over snowy ridges and crawled forward on their chests to get closer. The Dene were armed with muzzle-loading muskets, practically antiques from an earlier era. This meant only a single shot to try to bring down very large and powerful animals. Darrell had two modern breech-loading rifles. One of these he gave to Yinto's brother. When they were close to their quarry, they loosened the dogs. Then the hunters, including Darrell, sprang from cover and unloaded on the startled muskoxen. By the time the smoke had cleared, they had managed to fell eighteen of them.

Ravenous as they were, in one night between five men and twenty dogs they consumed over four hundred pounds of meat, all from a single muskox. The rest they had to pack and transport back. But to skin eighteen giant beasts with limited daylight was an enormous task. On their first full day they managed to skin ten, but then a blizzard blew in and forced them to abandon the work. Only with the return of better weather could they finish. When all was done, each sled was loaded down with nearly a thousand pounds of meat and hide. On the return journey, severe blizzards again hampered and delayed them, but eventually they reunited safely with their families.

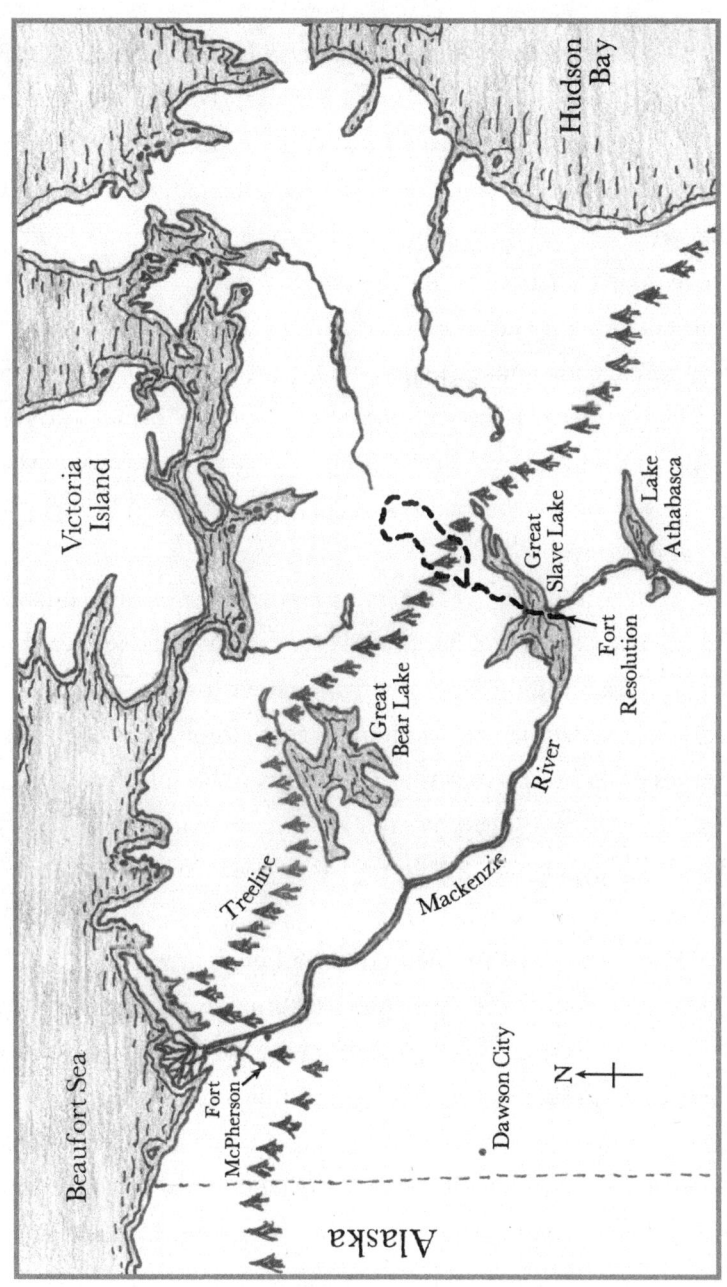

**DARRELL'S MUSKOXEN HUNTING JOURNEY
WITH CHIEF YINTO IN 1900–01**

This three-month journey immersed Darrell in an alien way of life that few outsiders had ever experienced, and taught him much. What he learned would serve him well in the years ahead. This included not only survival on the pitiless arctic tundra, but also the Dene way of stoically subsiding on minimal food at times. Darrell remarked in his notes, "I never felt weak at any moment though starving; a mouthful and tea seems to me to keep strength in most people a long time." More than that, he had learned what Franklin never did: the critical need to travel light in the Arctic in the smallest groups possible to avoid over-burdening local resources, and to adopt local methods of clothing and survival.

After this adventure, Darrell spent the rest of the winter of 1901 alone at his cabin. Meanwhile his family had been sending letters to the trading posts inquiring about his whereabouts. In reply, Darrell wrote back explaining that although he had "fully intended" to return south, circumstances had intervened. Nor could he return just yet, he said, as he had heard rumours of an expedition departing soon for the mysterious Coppermine River, which he hoped to join.

The journey with Chief Yinto had evidently stirred inside Darrell a deep interest in the little-known regions that lay beyond the treeline. The arctic tundra was so vast that their little party of five sleds had practically felt like ants moving across a limitless expanse, and they had only ventured a relatively short distance. As Darrell had learned first-hand, many places beyond the treeline remained unknown to the Dene themselves, let alone known to any outsiders. The Geological Survey of Canada at the time was only just beginning to map these immense areas.

The rumours that Darrell had heard of an expedition were about attempting precisely this daunting task. In fact, several arctic expeditions were about to get underway: one was led by Dr. Robert Bell of the Geological Survey, another by Joseph Tyrrell, both of whom became famous explorers. When these expeditions arrived on Great Slave Lake after a journey north from Edmonton, Darrell hoped they might enlist him. But Darrell's solitary habitats, shyness, and lack of connections didn't make schmoozing his way into an official expedition very likely, and in any case, both already had a full complement of men. His hopes were dashed.

Finding himself out of luck and penniless, that spring Darrell took work again on a fur trade steamer on Great Slave Lake and the Mackenzie River. But as he cruised among the islands and channels of these mighty waterways, his head was filled with dreams of still more distant horizons. As it turned out, much sooner than even he expected, those dreams were about to become a reality.

6

DISTANT HORIZONS

For more than two days Darrell had been trapped in an igloo. Stranded with him were two Inuit companions and a European aristocrat. Outside, a fierce arctic gale raged, making escape impossible. Nearby lay the ice-covered Arctic Ocean, where a few generations earlier Franklin and all his men had perished in their frozen prison. Now they, too, were nearly out of food, with just a few morsels of raw caribou left . . . But I've gotten ahead of myself again.

To understand how Darrell got stuck in an igloo, we have to back up a bit.

In 1898, a British aristocrat named David Hanbury arrived in Canada with the intention of undertaking what he claimed was an arduous wilderness journey for "sport and travel." In reality, Hanbury was trained in surveying and geology and keenly interested in zoology, botany, and much else. He came from a prominent family that had amassed a fortune in the brewery business. Whereas Darrell had to drop out of school at sixteen to earn a living, Hanbury had received the finest education money could buy, and with his inherited wealth had little need of ever working. But instead of living an idle life of luxury, Hanbury enjoyed roughing it. His resulting travels had taken him everywhere from North America to western China and even Siberia.

Oddly enough, Hanbury had developed a profound—some might even say obsessive—interest in Canada's Arctic. Perhaps this came about while sitting in the family mansion and tracing his hand over a globe. If he had done so, he could not have failed to notice that outside Antarctica the biggest blank spot left was the far North. Few outsiders ever visited it. Explorers had not enjoyed much success in cracking its mysteries. Fifty years earlier Franklin had tried and was never seen again, along with every other member of his expedition.

The thought of death by starvation, frostbite, or hypothermia on an ice floe might have deterred some, but not Hanbury. He made up his mind to go off exploring the Arctic. His wealth gave him the freedom to do so, as unlike most explorers, he was not dependent upon sponsors. In 1898 he arrived in Canada, headed for Winnipeg, hired some local guides, and with them canoed 1,500 kilometres north to Hudson Bay. From there, Hanbury hoped to push on right to the arctic interior, but at the little outpost of Churchill he realized (or else was made to see by the local traders) that his plan was doomed to failure given the early onset of winter. Defeated in practice but not in spirit, Hanbury made the most of his time in Churchill—learning all he could— and immediately began making plans for a second attempt. He returned south by dogsled to spend the winter in Winnipeg's finest hotel, brooding over highly imperfect maps of the Arctic and dreaming of penetrating its uncharted regions. He ordered the best expedition gear shipped to him in Winnipeg. Then unable to restrain his curiosity any longer, before even waiting for spring, he dashed off by dogsled with two companions back to Churchill. The fur traders there, hardened veterans, were shocked to see him back again so soon.

Hanbury found himself a willing Inuit guide, Milook, and with him travelled north by dogsled. At Chesterfield Inlet they turned inland, and with the ice melting, they switched to canoe and kayaks. Their route took them across stormy tundra lakes until they reached the main branch of the Arkeleenik (Thelon) River. This mysterious river was unknown beyond its lower reaches even to Milook or the other Inuit, who preferred to remain near Hudson Bay where seals, fish, and other game were plentiful. So, Milook at this point turned back.

Finding himself now without any guide, Hanbury opted to press on anyway. He and his two remaining companions managed to explore and partially map the river for a distance of some three hundred kilometres inland, and then ascended and mapped its northwestern branch another two hundred kilometres. This was no mean feat, given the swift current, rapids, canyons, waterfalls, and other obstacles. After this, the party passed over the height of land, leaving the Hudson Bay watershed. From here, they ended up paddling hundreds of kilometres through unknown lakes and rivers until they at last found themselves in what is now northern Alberta, reaching the tiny outpost of Fort McMurray in the late fall of 1899.

As impressive a feat as this journey was, Hanbury wasn't satisfied. He resolved to undertake another journey, this time

even longer. In total, he now aimed to cover by canoe and dogsled a staggering 4,500 miles—mapping as he went a route spanning Great Slave Lake to Hudson Bay, from there overland to
the Arctic Ocean, and then along part of the Northwest Passage.

Many experienced hands would probably have told Hanbury
that his plan was unrealistic, if not absurd, but Hanbury was
nothing if not determined. In fact, there was more to this eccen-
tric English aristocratic than met the eye: he was fluent in mul-
tiple languages and culturally open-minded, and Hanbury's
intelligence and careful study led him to perceive the weakness
in most past approaches to exploration in the barren lands.
Franklin's doomed expeditions, as well as other British-led ones,
had fallen into the fallacy of believing that there was strength in
numbers. As a result, these expeditions had typically involved
dozens, if not hundreds, of members trying to survive in a harsh
environment with limited local food resources. Hanbury had the
wisdom to see a lighter touch was called for—a small handpicked party numbering only two or three individuals. That way,
they could live off the land and travel flexibly with the seasons.

But above all, Hanbury's approach rested on closely collab-
orating with the Inuit, whose culture he admired and whose
language, Inuktitut, he had learned to speak. His past expedition had introduced him to the Inuit who resided near
Chesterfield Inlet, and with them he had already discussed plans
for a future journey.

After making arrangements in England for the shipment of
his gear, Hanbury set out in the summer of 1901. This time he
made his way first to Edmonton, then only a small farming
town, and from there north to Great Slave Lake. At the main

trading post on Great Slave, Fort Resolution, Hanbury hoped to find suitable recruits to join him. As fate would have it, at the post when he showed up, there just happened to be a young, restless, quiet, and solitary trapper—Hubert Darrell.

Darrell, after meeting Hanbury and learning of his plans, at once dropped everything and signed a contract to join him. At the time of their meeting, Hanbury was thirty-seven years old, a decade older than Darrell, who was still just twenty-seven, though by now an experienced "sourdough" to use the Klondike term. Hanbury provided this description of Darrell:

Tiring of the monotony of life on a farm, this young man had turned his steps northwards at the time of the rush to the Klondike, and like many others over whom the far north had thrown its spell, he had remained in the north. He had accompanied the Yellow Knives [Chief Yinto's band] to the "Barren Ground" on their annual winter hunt after musk-oxen, and was thus well acquainted with the cold and hunger incident to the journey which he now undertook.

Hanbury tended to be a shrewd judge of character, and events would more than vindicate his choice of Darrell. Hanbury also hired a second young assistant, Sandy Turner, whom he had met on his journey north. Besides these two, Hanbury recruited four Dene guides to help transport their supplies eastward from Great Slave Lake. But the Dene would only agree to go as far as their traditional hunting grounds, and not beyond that into arctic lands they were unfamiliar with.

On July 13, 1901, the party embarked in three canoes heading east along Great Slave Lake. For food they planned to rely mostly on fishing and hunting. Given that it was July, mosquito and blackfly clouds swarmed them, but still worse were the big "bulldog flies" that drew blood with every bite. These giant horseflies, still called in northern slang "bulldogs," are indeed much more annoying than any other. Darrell remarked in one of his letters that smoke was the only way to diminish the hordes of biting insects incessantly buzzing around one's head, but that by the time you managed to smoke out the flies, the smoke itself was overpowering. (This, too, I found to be true from my own experiences.) Hanbury noted as they canoed along that the intensity of the swarming bugs seemed to drive even the caribou mad, which ran about trying to escape them, sometimes plunging into the rivers and lakes for relief. On the upside, this made hunting caribou easy, so they had plenty of food.

As the days passed the forests gradually thinned out, until the last scraggly, stunted spruces gave way to arctic tundra stretching to the horizon. Several weeks of travelling had brought them out of Great Slave Lake's vast waters, then through a chain of remote lakes and over rugged portages to the height of land. Beyond this their Dene guides had never been: it lay outside their traditional hunting grounds, and to them, it appeared an unwelcoming environment where they might encounter their ancient foes, the Inuit. They had in fact reached a strange, deserted no man's land that lay between the traditional Dene hunting grounds to the west and the Inuit lands along Hudson Bay to the east. Hanbury had brought with him the most up-to-date and accurate maps available, but these were of no help: the country they had entered into was uncharted. They were now hundreds of miles from any inhabited place or even trading post.

Hanbury, however, had passed through some of this area on his initial expedition two years earlier. He had found it a mysterious, confusing landscape of labyrinthine lakes hidden in thick mists that made it hard to see much of anything. The shores were riddled with long dead-end bays and false channels that led nowhere. Most perplexing of all, compasses would not work, spinning unreliably and refusing to point north—perhaps on account of mineral deposits in the surrounding hills. I found it much the same when I later retraced their route in my canoe.

But Hanbury was nothing if not meticulous: he had packed a sextant prismatic compass, two aneroid barometers, a hypsometer for measuring elevations, several types of thermometers, and a patent log for making observations. He had further equipped himself with the necessary tables and studied the requisite mathematics in order to be able to work out latitude and longitude. Thus armed, Hanbury intended to chart as accurately as he could any route they took.

To reach the Inuit lands, they continued east, working their way down a dangerous river, filled with seething rapids, blind canyons, and hidden waterfalls that required lengthy portages to avoid. Alternating with these hazards were tranquil sections where the river fanned out, and other places where the windswept landscape felt more like an arctic desert, with nothing but miles of barren, blowing sand in all directions. With the Dene having turned back, Hanbury, Darrell, and Sandy were on their own.

Of the three, Darrell had by far the most wilderness experience. Yet he hadn't done much previous canoeing—his travelling

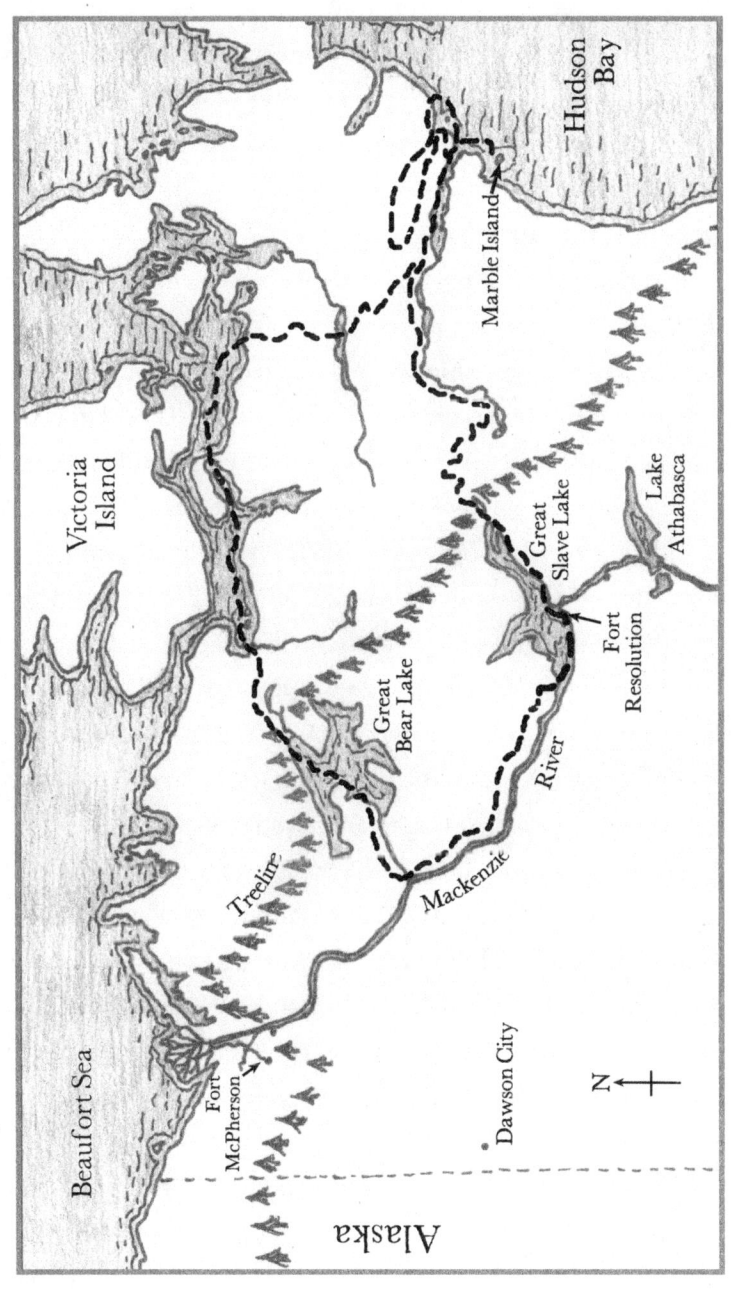

DARRELL'S SEVEN-THOUSAND-KILOMETRE JOURNEY
WITH HANBURY BY CANOE AND DOGSLED IN 1901–02

was mostly done in winter, or else by rowboat. Darrell, however, was a quick study, and he seemed to have picked up navigating rivers by canoe pretty intuitively. Hanbury had paddling experience from his past travels, while Sandy had little but proved adept enough at learning.

The river of mystery that they were descending Hanbury might well have been expected to name. Victorian-era explorers, after all, were in the fashion of naming geographic features they came across. But it was another of Hanbury's eccentricities that he strongly opposed this practice and insisted instead on the use of Indigenous place names for geographic features. This principle eventually led to Hanbury meticulously recording hundreds of Inuit names for lakes, rivers, creeks, mountains, and even particular camping places. Only in cases where there was no existing name for a feature, which in a landscape as sparsely inhabited as the barren lands was not uncommon, would Hanbury name something. Even then, he often tried to use Indigenous-derived names or else simple, descriptive terminology.

With this in mind, Hanbury insisted on calling the river they were now mapping the western branch of the Ark-i-linik River, as this was the Inuit name he had learned two years earlier for the main river draining into Hudson Bay. Ironically, government surveyors would later rename it the Hanbury River in his honour. When Hanbury learned this, he declined the tribute and insisted instead on the use of the original name.

By the end of summer Darrell, Hanbury, and Sandy had covered more than a thousand kilometres and arrived at a chain of big, windswept lakes lying near the Hudson Bay coast. These were the same tundra lakes that Hanbury had spent several weeks camped on in 1899. At that time, he had met and befriended a small band of Inuit hunters, led by a man named Amer-or-yauk. Outside influences had only slightly altered their traditional lifestyle despite the fact that fur traders had been sailing to Hudson Bay for nearly three centuries. They still built kayaks and dogsleds, speared caribou, and wore deerskin clothing and parkas—though they had acquired metal tools, guns, matches, tobacco, and other items from trading ships. Hanbury admired Amer-or-yauk and the other Inuit, describing them as intelligent, strong, brave, friendly, and hospitable.

At the time of their first meeting, Amer-or-yauk had promised Hanbury that, should he return, he would assist and guide him on his proposed epic journey northward to the Arctic Ocean. Whether he and other Inuit ever expected Hanbury to actually return is unclear, but in any case, return he did. It proved a joyous reunion. They celebrated with dancing and feasting, negotiated terms, examined the very imperfect maps Hanbury had brought, and discussed a plan of attack for the winter. As usual, Hanbury was effusive in his praise of the Inuit, noting that although they had never before seen a printed map, they could grasp its meaning at once and with a pencil fill in all sorts of details regarding distances and features.

To pull off the expedition, Hanbury had made arrangements beforehand to have the necessary supplies transported aboard a whaling ship, the *Francis Allyn*, already bound for Hudson Bay. This included not only winter clothing for himself, Darrell, and Sandy, but provisions, ammunition, trade goods, and photographic equipment. At the time, whalers would make the long and hazardous voyage north to arctic waters to hunt whales during the brief summer, then allow their ships to get frozen in and overwinter. Such ships might remain for a year or two before their holds were filled with enough whale oil to return. This made it easy enough for Hanbury to arrange to have his supplies put aboard one. There was just one wrench in his plan: in Hudson Bay's icy immensity, finding a ship might prove much harder than he imagined.

Forecasting in advance where the *Francis Allyn* would overwinter wasn't possible. But based on what he'd been told, Hanbury assumed the likeliest place was Marble Island, a desolate and uninhabited quartzite outcrop lying eleven kilometres out from the mainland. To this distant island they now headed in their canoes. It was well into September, with ice already forming on smaller lakes and violent gales and freezing temperatures. To reach the island, the trio had to first paddle almost one hundred kilometres south along Hudson Bay's bleak coast—frequently finding themselves pinned down by heavy seas or bewildered by fog.

When they arrived opposite Marble Island, they set out on the perilous crossing. Paddling fragile canvas-covered canoes across frigid open seas in the fall might sound dangerous—and it turns out, it is. But capsizing or running into polar bears wasn't what most worried them. Their greatest fear was the walruses that kept aggressively approaching their canoes. In his journal, Darrell noted he was afraid they might attack, as were Hanbury and Sandy. Their fears, it seems, may not have been entirely unfounded: walruses can reach lengths of over eleven feet and weigh in excess of two thousand pounds, and with their ivory tusks have been known to kill even polar bears.

After surviving the crossing, Hanbury's party at last reached the glimmering quartzite rocks of Marble Island—only to have their hopes crushed. No ship was to be found, only the lonely graves of past sailors who'd attempted to overwinter there. Whether the *Francis Allyn* lay safely overwintering in some other spot, or whether it had been wrecked in a storm, they had no way of knowing. Without the ship, their situation appeared dire: winter was almost upon them, and they lacked the clothing, footgear, and provisions to survive it. But there was nothing for it: they had to canoe back the more than hundred kilometres they'd come.

Their return journey up the exposed coastline was a desperate struggle, with snow coming down steadily and their hands suffering terribly from the cold. The ice was now nearly three or four inches thick on the lakes, but saltwater doesn't freeze as easily, so open water along the coast allowed them to painstakingly press on. By the end of September, with winter practically upon them, they had reached Baker Lake, an inland arm of Hudson Bay that, although tidal, is freshwater. Here, at a place called Nell-yuk-yauk, their fortunes improved when they came upon another of Hanbury's past friends, the great muskox hunter Uttungerlah.

Dispensing with a traditional kayak, Uttungerlah instead travelled the coast in a small rowboat with a sail, which he'd bartered from a whaling ship. And now, from his caribou-skin coat, he produced a letter for Hanbury. It was from the captain of the *Francis Allyn*, informing Hanbury that the ship was overwintering at Depot Island. They were in luck after all, well, partial luck—this barren island lay some three hundred kilometres to the north. Given it was nearly October, it seemed exceedingly doubtful that they could journey there before winter. But Uttungerlah assured them that with his rowboat it could be done.

So, stashing their canoes, Darrell, Hanbury, and Sandy joined Uttungerlah and headed north. After a rough and dangerous passage, they finally found the *Francis Allyn*. It was a small vessel with a crew of twenty-four, but safely stowed aboard were all of Hanbury's supplies. These were soon transferred over to Uttungerlah's rowboat. Darrell up to this point had remained unflappable in the face of everything, but their adventures had shaken Sandy. Hanbury made a decision to leave him aboard the ship, explaining in his own words that "I had seen that he found the travelling life somewhat tough. The absence of fire and the diet of meat 'straight' were not to his taste, and, being a newcomer, he could not make up his mind to disregard hardships."

It was decided that Darrell and Hanbury would go with Uttungerlah and also Amer-or-yauk to live in igloos and hunt muskoxen for three months. Then, come mid-February and the increase in daylight, they would return to collect Sandy and resume their long and perilous journey north to the Arctic Ocean, and from there to parts unknown.

Over the following months, Darrell worked hard to learn Inuktitut. In his journal, he scribbled the words he learned, repeating them over and over to himself until they stuck. Meanwhile they survived on muskox, caribou, and fish they caught through the ice—sometimes enduring periods of fasting when hunting failed. Of their diet, Hanbury commented, "The flesh of the musk-ox, in spite of the strong smell of musk . . . is excellent eating, but it is generally pretty hard and requires much cooking." (Personally, when I once sampled it, I didn't find it much to my taste, but then I wasn't starving when I ate it.) Hanbury also mentioned eating wolverine, wolf, and just about everything else they could hunt. Temperatures fell to as low as minus fifty, but Darrell found life in an igloo surprisingly pleasant. It was much warmer and more comfortable than the deerskin tents he had lived in earlier.

With the days finally growing longer, in mid-January the four of them set off over the frozen sea by dogsled for the whaling ship. They found things there had gone well enough: only a single crew member had died when he'd left the ship and become lost in a blizzard. As for Sandy, the three-month rest had done him well. They spent a further month hunting seals around the ice-bound ship, and then judged the time right to embark on their long journey. Once the sea ice melted, they planned to switch to their canoes, so for the time being they carried these lashed lengthwise to the dogsleds.

Their route took them inland from Hudson Bay, westward over frozen lakes and rivers. Along the way, they picked up the adopted sons of both Amer-or yauk and Uttungerlah, as well as their wives and children. Blizzards at times delayed them, and at other times they had to divert course to hunt. But Amer-or-yauk and Uttungerlah were so adept at building igloos that this could be done each night in little more than an hour. These temporary camping igloos were naturally smaller and less roomy than the ones they typically built when remaining longer at a single spot. Inside them every night, they had to attempt to dry their wet socks and clothing with their own body heat.

Meanwhile their dogs slept outside, where prowling arctic wolves were an ever-present danger. Once, after crawling out of their igloo in the morning, Hanbury found his best dog had been eaten by a wolf.

After weeks travelling inland, their course turned north to seek the Northwest Passage. It was now well into April, but temperatures were still frequently below minus forty. They had now journeyed so far that they had reached territory that was unfamiliar even to both Uttungerlah and Amer-or-yauk. As such, they decided to divide the party, with most of the women and children staying behind with Uttungerlah's adopted son Ilartnark at a suitable spot for ice fishing. The rest of them pushed on with the dog teams, deeper into a strange landscape, lacking even frozen lakes and other features. The maps Hanbury carried with him were of no particular use, though with the sun he continued to ascertain their latitude to plot as much of their route as he could. By boiling the thermometers he'd packed and comparing the differences with the air temperature, Hanbury could also work out their height above sea level. Darrell, for his part, endeavoured to learn as much as he could from Hanbury about these sciences, while simultaneously learning from Uttungerlah and Amer-or-yauk more about traditional arctic survival.

They had almost reached the Arctic Ocean when a particularly severe blizzard struck—forcing them into the shelter of a couple of hastily constructed igloos. Their food by this point had nearly run out, with only a few caribou scraps left. Darrell took their situation with his customary stoicism, but poor Sandy found such suffering difficult to bear. Confined inside a dark igloo, Hanbury noted: "Sandy made a remark in the evening to the effect that he found deer's meat most unpalatable and tasteless, and I hinted to him that possibly in a few days the taste of the meat would not trouble him, for there was no sign of deer to be found. He listened to my remark in silence."

But worse than the lack of food was the lack of water. With no fuel to burn and extreme temperatures, melting enough snow wasn't feasible. To obtain water, it was necessary to chisel down through the ice, but it was eight or nine feet thick. On the small frozen streams that they were following, sometimes they would discover, after the intense effort needed to chisel through eight feet of ice, no open water at all —just rock bottom.

Bereft of food and even water, they huddled in the darkness of the igloos, desperately waiting for the blizzard outside to abate.

7

POINTS UNKNOWN

I f during his time stuck in an igloo Darrell questioned his
decision to join Hanbury, he didn't mention it. Even now, his
wanderlust and boundless curiosity, fortitude, and hardihood
didn't abandon him. After more than two cramped, disorienting
days, the blizzard finally passed.

Free at last, the party pushed on for the Arctic Ocean. By
mid-May they had reached it, hitting upon the Northwest
Passage itself. This fabled sea route had for centuries haunted the
dreams of navigators, only to end up luring many to an icy grave,
including Franklin. But with the ocean still frozen solid,
Hanbury's party travelled over the sea ice in their dogsleds, turning westward and following the rock-bound coastline. Along
this ultra-isolated northern coast few outsiders had ever been,
and fewer still who'd live to tell of it. Travelling across the ice,
they eventually encountered small bands of Inuit, amazingly
none of whom had ever seen Europeans before or, for that matter,
any non-Inuit person. It was the early twentieth century, and the

Wright brothers were only a few years away from their world-changing invention, but these few hunters were among the very last Indigenous populations in North America to encounter outsiders, surviving in splendid isolation. Their ancient customs and tools were still intact: they had only instruments and clothing they fashioned themselves. This included bone-tipped harpoons, bows and arrows made of driftwood (other Inuit had long since acquired firearms), stone kettles for boiling water, and stone lamps for illuminating their igloos. Such was their isolation that even Uttungerlah and Amer-or-yauk struggled to understand them, as the dialect they spoke differed greatly from their own.

As might be guessed, Hanbury was greatly impressed by these hunters. He described them as "tall, strong fellows" and "hardy-looking, good-natured and happy." As they feasted together and got to know one another, communication became a bit easier, and soon they were all friends. The names of the hunters they had met were Hun-il-yak and Pun-uk-tuk, and from them Hanbury with his customary thoroughness recorded as many of their names for geographical features as he could. The two of them agreed to guide the party westward to the mouth of a big river—what could only be the legendary Coppermine River.

Through June and into July, they continued by dogsled over the decaying sea ice. At one point, the sun's glare off the ice left Darrell and Sandy both snow-blind for a day. Hanbury, luckily for his sake, had a pair of wooden Inuit snow googles that spared his eyes. But as the season advanced, more and more cracks and open water appeared, making travelling increasingly hazardous. By July 11, the ice had melted so much that it became necessary to abandon the sleds and switch to their canoes. They hoped the dogs would be able to survive by hunting arctic ground squirrels, until Uttungerlah and the other Inuit would be able to pick them up on their return journey.

In another week, they'd reached the mouth of the turbulent Coppermine River. Now began their difficult canoe journey up it, working slowly with ropes affixed to the two canoes to haul them from shore against the ferocious current. Hanbury in his account seldom ever spared a minute to comment on his men, Darrell and Sandy, but in the case of the arduous ascent of the Coppermine, he made a rare exception and noted that both were "excellent." Darrell apparently took the lead in this back-breaking work. At the same time, Hanbury's notes indicate that in the evenings, while the others rested about the camps, Darrell would often wander off on his own, disappearing for long hours on solitary treks. Sometimes he'd return lugging a caribou over his shoulder, a pair of arctic hares, or other fresh meat, while on other occasions he'd bring back fossils, geological specimens, and even butterflies that Hanbury asked him to gather.

After struggling up the Coppermine for ten days, they came upon a smaller river coming in from the west, which they fol-lowed: it led them into a chain of long, curved, and windswept arctic lakes. These lakes were marked on Hanbury's map as the Dismal Lakes, so named by an earlier British expedition that had ventured north in a failed search for Franklin's lost party. Though Hanbury, with his dedication to Indigenous names, noted with satisfaction that he learned from Hun-il-yak and Pun-uk-tuk that the actual name for these lakes was Teshi-er-pi.

Once they had made it through these long lakes, Hun-il-yak and Pun-uk-tuk had reached the limit of the lands they knew and were eager to turn back. The date was August 9, and the time had come for the party to bid goodbye to each other and split up. The Inuit, taking one of the canoes, would retrace their steps back to the dogs, and from there make their way homeward after the sea froze again. With the other canoe, Darrell, Hanbury, and Sandy would push on south toward the spruce forests.

With the three of them on their own again, they began making a long cross-country trek on foot to find the headwaters of the Dease River. This waterway, Hanbury knew from his imperfect maps, eventually flows into Great Bear Lake, a body of water even more immense than Great Slave. But portaging to the headwaters was slow work, in part because they couldn't be sure of which way to head. Frequently they had to split up in order to scout things out. The fact they were also lugging nearly two hundred pounds' worth of geological samples, fossils, and other specimens Hanbury wanted likely didn't help matters. This included a complete set of arctic butterfly species that Hanbury had tasked Darrell with collecting. Fortunately, butterflies don't generally weigh too much (in my experience). All of this necessitated three separate loads on each of what proved to be many portages. But eventually they made it to a sandy creek, which Hanbury, in departure from his normal policy, and with a bit of wry humour, named Sandy Creek. It led them into the Dease River, which they followed down into the vast immensity of Great Bear Lake. With the Inuit gone, the party relied on fishing with nets and on Darrell's hunting to keep them provisioned.

This majestic lake, with its bewitchingly clear waters and wide-open horizons, supplied them with plenty of lake trout to eat. But their route back to civilization meant that they had to cross it. This entailed a very risky open-water crossing of more than twenty-two kilometres—a long way in a little canoe carrying three men. High winds and waves foiled their first several attempts, until finally they decided to chance crossing overnight in the dark, hoping to take advantage of the relative calm. Late in the season as it was, they had to rely on the stars to guide them as they paddled far out of sight of land. Only when they could hear the surf beating on the opposite shoreline did they realize they had safely made it.

From there they gradually worked their way south to the lake's outlet at the Great Bear River, which they then followed into the Mackenzie River. Although still deep in the wilderness, they were now on familiar ground for Darrell, at least, as he had navigated the Mackenzie before. It took them another month to canoe their way up it and arrive back at their starting point, Fort Resolution on Great Slave Lake. They made it there on September 28, 1902, having completed an extraordinary fourteen-month journey spanning some seven thousand kilometres. In doing so, they had quietly pulled off a feat of exploration seldom equalled anywhere in the world. Although parts of their route were of course known to Uttungerlah and Amer-or-yauk, or later along the arctic coast to Hun-il-yak and Pun-uk-tuk, it can be said with a high degree of certainty that in its seven-thousand-kilometre entirety, no one before, or for that matter since, had ever undertaken such an improbable journey.

8

LONE EXPLORER

By December 1902 Hanbury had returned triumphant from his expedition, going first to Ottawa and from there on to England. But curiously, Darrell, who could have taken this opportunity to leave the North with Hanbury and return to the farm in Manitoba, or even visit his family in England, whom he hadn't seen since he was sixteen, did neither. From their expedition, he might have expected a modest measure of accolades, but Darrell seems to have cared little for that either. Instead, Darrell stayed in the North. Without a companion, or even a dogsled, he went back to hauling his own toboggan, breaking his own trails, and living by his wits and rifle in the subarctic wilderness.

Darrell's family meanwhile were growing anxious that they hadn't heard from him even longer than normal. While he'd been gone with Hanbury, they had sent letters to the trading posts in the Northwest Territories under the mistaken impression that it might be possible to get word to him. But of course, it wasn't: they didn't realize just how spectacularly isolated and empty Canada's barren lands really were. When Darrell finally arrived back at a trading post, he took the time to answer their accumulated letters. He explained that over an immense area there weren't any posts at all: "You seem to think that the Hudson Bay Company have posts even out on the barren lands but it is not so. . . . On Hudson's Bay their furthest N[orth] post is Churchill. Draw a line W[est] to Athabasca Lake, they have no post N[orth] of that line . . . They have no post E[ast] of Great Slave Lake River or Lake, no post E[ast] of Mackenzie River." This vast area that Darrell described even today remains a place of incredible solitudes, as I knew from my own experiences retracing his routes.

Darrell's family, probably like many people, couldn't understand the appeal of such an inhospitable place. They wondered why Darrell didn't return to help Charles on the farm, which had continued to struggle. But Darrell explained that in his eyes, the arctic barrens were that "most interesting and utterly unknown region," and to explore it he now regarded as his life's true calling. This likely wouldn't ever make him rich or famous, but to him that meant little. The mere thrill of such wild places was its own reward: "I saw the midnight sun for two months. It is a most lovely country—the barren land of Canada. It's true one does not always get a meal in a day nor even two days, but what of that, it is nothing."

Clearly, Darrell came away from the expedition more under the magic spell of the wilderness than ever. He spent the winter and most of 1903 on his own in the Northwest Territories, resuming the life he had lived prior to the expedition. But he'd been deeply impressed by Hanbury's methods, and he wished that Hanbury might hire him again for a second venture. Failing that, he hoped he might find work on one of the official mapping expeditions that had earlier snubbed him. To this end, he tried to make himself more attractive to prospective employers by devoting himself with his characteristic discipline to mastering every skill that could be of possible use on an expedition. He kept up with his study of Indigenous languages—he could now speak at least some Cree, Athabascan, and Inuktitut—and tried to learn more about canoeing, including navigating rapids, sailing, packing, and lining. Besides these things, he even learned how to make his own waterproof moccasins.

But surprisingly enough, employment offers for a would-be explorer few people had ever heard of who lived alone in the middle of nowhere were somewhat slow. During this time, Darrell apparently did receive through the grapevine of the fur trading posts a couple of offers to be hired as a guide by sportsmen—but he turned these down as paying too little or otherwise beneath him. What he really longed for were the funds to carry out his own expeditions, or for his old "boss" Hanbury to launch a second journey—but Hanbury still showed no indications of doing so. In fact, neither Hanbury nor for that matter Sandy Turner would ever undertake another expedition. But Darrell, incredible as it sounds, was just getting warmed up. Impressive as the journey with Hanbury had been, it was minor in comparison with what Darrell would eventually do—feats that would make even world-famous Antarctic explorers, notably Roald Amundsen, sit up and take notice.

But as yet, Darrell didn't quite know how to make that happen. So, desperate for funds, he cast about aimlessly for options, indifferently prospecting in the hopes of finding gold or some other mineral worth something, taking fur trade work, and even at one point sinking so low as to contemplate the dreadful expedient of writing about his expeditions in the hope it might help pay for them. Fortunately, it didn't come to that.

But as Darrell sat brooding in his lonely cabin near Great Slave Lake, or trudging along through icy woods pulling his sled, his views crystalized on certain matters. With respect to exploring, he came to regard Sir John Franklin—still venerated as a national hero in Britain—as a blundering idiot. Apparently, those who thought highly of Franklin included Darrell's own family. In one of his letters, he mentioned he knew they had "read Franklin's travels and think him a great hero." But, as Darrell saw it, Franklin, in fact most English explorers in the Arctic for that matter, had been foolhardy. He didn't express these views very diplomatically, stating bluntly, "The English are notoriously stupid and old-fashioned in everything they do and they have to learn by experience, that is why so many succumb in their explorations to cold or starvation." It also seems that, having lived in Canada since he was sixteen, Darrell increasingly saw himself as a Canadian.

Darrell's earlier negative view of the monopolistic Hudson's Bay Company had also hardened. To his family, he wrote, "Personally I have no use for the Company. You may think they have been good to me, but I never got one ounce weight of help from them in anyway whatever." He acknowledged that within the company there were good individuals, but that this was in a strictly personal capacity. But if he held the company in low esteem, by comparison his views of missionaries in the North were positively scathing. He accused the missionaries he had seen as being dishonest and hypocritical. He felt that trying to impose their religion on Indigenous peoples was morally wrong. In a December 1902 letter to his parents, he seethed: "You speak a little about Missionaries. What good do they do? Absolutely none. . . . Did you ever see a missionary? I have seen lot's, they are all rolling in fat and say what a fine time they are having." He accused missionaries of attempting to turn Indigenous people—whom he had learned from his experiences to admire as courageous, resourceful, kind, and intelligent—into "sheep." Nor did Darrell confine his criticisms to missionaries alone; he further singled out what he saw as self-righteous busybodies who founded "societies" for the assimilation of Indigenous peoples, declaring that if it were up to him, such practices would be made illegal. For the time, his opinions were highly unusual to say the least, but then so were his experiences. Later, his views would somewhat soften on missionaries, though he'd continue to maintain that Indigenous people should be free to keep their own culture.

Darrell's views likely shocked his family back in England, and perhaps prompted them to wonder what they had done in sending their son off at such a young age to Canada's backwoods. Still, they loved him and often worried about him living alone in the wilderness. Darrell chided them for worrying so much, mentioning that even his aunt had written him a letter expressing her concern about his wanderings.

His responses likely didn't offer much comfort: "I am sorry you trouble yourself so much about me. All you England people are too conservative, you think a man must never go one inch out of the line of the golden rule set down by old grandmothers i.e.

to slave and grind everyday of the year all your life; to stick to one job, to go to church twice on Sundays and three times on special thanksgiving days; never to go away and enjoy yourself; to marry as a finale some sedate, sanctimonious old saint." Living in the wilderness, it seems, had changed Darrell not only physically, but in his worldview as well. Still, he wasn't the hardhearted sort, and in a later letter he expressed regret that his northern wanderings had caused his family anxiety. Nor could he turn his back on his brother Charles, particularly when he learned just how badly his farm was struggling.

It turned out that several young horses on the farm had died, the rains had caused crop failures, and then when a good harvest finally arrived in 1901, poor Manitoban farmers were unable to profit from it due to what they saw as a monopolistic "blockade" by the Montreal-based Canadian Pacific Railway, which wouldn't transport any additional grain to market. In Darrell's absence, the farm had only sunk deeper into debt, and even if Charles had tried to sell out, for such poor farms there were few buyers. With things in such a sad state, and the thought of a brother suffering who'd once been his only companion through many hardships, Darrell at last resolved to return. After another northern summer where he'd wandered as far as the Arctic Circle again, that autumn of 1903 Darrell headed south, paying his way by taking work on a riverboat transporting furs. After six years of adventures, the full scope of which he could once have hardly imagined, Darrell was back in Manitoba helping to bring in the harvest. While there, something totally shocking and unexpected would happen—he would fall in love.

9

ATTEMPTING A SETTLED LIFE

I t was a glorious October day as I drove west across Manitoba. Golden splashes of colour were everywhere in the fields and aspen-clad hills, and I thought to myself that the prairie was really rather beautiful, at least on a sunshiny fall day, with eagles soaring overhead and deer bounding across harvested fields. But that wasn't why I had come—I had come to find Darrell's old farm and to learn more about his time here.

Until now, I had mainly focused my investigation into Darrell on his wilderness wanderings. This had been simple enough, as it had merely entailed paddling a canoe alone in the Arctic for months on lonely lakes and remote rivers, with his journals to guide me. But clearly something momentous must have happened to Darrell over the roughly eighteen months he spent back in Birtle, Manitoba, in 1903 to 1905. Ever the lone wanderer, suddenly he'd fallen in love with a schoolteacher, Agnes Dudley, and even become engaged to her. Yet Darrell and Agnes—deeply in love as they seem to have been—were destined never to marry. In fact, shocking as it sounds, Agnes ended up instead marrying his older brother Charles, though that was years after Darrell's disappearance.

It seemed clear that there must have been more to this apparent love story—but whatever it was, I knew I wouldn't find the answer in the wilderness. On the other hand, since Darrell had vanished in 1910, it was obvious even the oldest person alive today was still too young to have known him. Darrell didn't have any children, and neither did Charles nor Agnes, so there seemed to be no trail I could follow in that direction either. But Charles and Agnes had both lived into their eighties, right up until the 1950s. So I figured there must be people still living who'd known them, and I hoped they might be able to shed light on these delicate questions.

I had supposed that in a place as tiny as Birtle—the population today numbers only six hundred people—that an explorer of Darrell's calibre must be well-known. But scrolling through the local museum's website, I found no mention of Darrell at all. Even a page devoted to notable people in Birtle's past didn't include him. I already knew that the world at large had forgotten Darrell, but it was a surprise to find that even in the place he'd once called home, he'd apparently also been entirely forgotten.

Nevertheless, I started drafting emails and making phone calls. I first tried the municipal offices (that led nowhere), then the public library (also no luck), and finally the museum, although it hadn't been open in years (first due to COVID restrictions, then renovations). Eventually persistence paid off, and I got in touch with the right people: two very kind and generous members of the local historical society, Brenda Evans and

Lorraine Snow. I was delighted when they said they could intro-
duce me to someone who'd once known both Charles Darrell
and Agnes Dudley. This individual, Margaret Ashcroft, was now
ninety years old, and they said she could also show me the location of Darrell's farm.

And that is how one pleasant October afternoon I found
myself sitting at the kitchen table of Mrs. Ashcroft in her nice
farmhouse in Birtle, Manitoba.

✳

Upon his return to Manitoba in the fall of 1903, Darrell seems
to have hurled himself into the hard labours of his brother's farm
with the same boundless energy and prodigious strength that
characterized his arctic wanderings. One can readily picture the
two brothers seated round the farm table or by the hearth, getting caught up on the past six years after long days spent toiling
in the fields. Hubert could tell of his northern adventures, while
Charles of the comings and goings in Birtle and how the deck
seemed to be stacked more than ever against poor farmers. At
the time, western farmers were deeply dismayed with the government in Ottawa, accusing corrupt politicians of conspiring
with the monopolistic Canadian Pacific Railway (CPR) on grain-
shipping policies. (Some things never change.)

Darrell respected his older brother's capabilities and sympa-
thized with his plight. He remarked in one 1903 letter to his
parents that "Charlie has slaved year after year and he is really a
good farmer. His advice is often asked by men double his age.
But what can you do when the weather & the CPR break against

you?" In the same letter, he commented with scorn: "You can hunt the world over and you cannot find a more . . . swindling lot of officials than those of the Canadian Government. You cannot find six honest men in all departments of the country." It seems that Darrell had added the Canadian government to the Hudson's Bay Company, missionaries, and official British arctic expeditions on the list of things he held in low regard.

But Darrell was not all bitterness. On the contrary, those who knew him described him as possessing a kind of stoic cheerfulness, which he must have had in order to have pulled off the arduous journeys that he did. During Darrell's stint back on the farm, he also took the time to reconnect with his old friends and even pitch in a hand on their farms too. But it seems the greater part of whatever free time he had was taken up over at the local schoolhouse.

As much as he remained consumed by wanderlust for the North, the immediate object of Darrell's desires ran in a different direction entirely—Agnes Dudley. Three years younger than him, Agnes lived with her family on a farm close to the Darrells'. Agnes's father, Joseph Dudley, also happened to run the local post office out of his farm (the rural population being too small and scattered to justify the establishment of a separate post office). He later also helped found and manage the first bank in Birtle, and—clearly an enterprising and ambitious man—he'd saved up enough to send Agnes for two years to a boarding school in England. Agnes had returned from her schooling while Darrell was still wandering about the North. She worked as a teacher in a one-room schoolhouse just southwest of Birtle. Years later, one of Agnes's former students recalled liking her very much, describing her as "strict but pleasant."

How exactly their romance first blossomed is not quite clear, but certainly, in their staid little world, both would have stood out in any crowd. Darrell because of his singular adventures exploring the Arctic while living in igloos (always a great conversation starter on first dates), and Agnes because of her polish and education. It was not long before they were engaged.

But Agnes, or more likely her parents, insisted that before any marriage could take place, Darrell would need to find some regular employment, or at least a less nomadic existence. One suspects that perhaps Mr. Dudley, ambitious postmaster, farmer, and banker that he was, maybe didn't think a penniless northern wanderer was exactly prime marriage material. Darrell, for his part, seems to have wanted Agnes to elope with him to the North, but she couldn't quite bring herself to embrace the hardships and deprivations such a life would inevitably entail—apparently a decision that she came to deeply regret.

None of Darrell's journals from this time survive, that is, if he ever kept any at all. As for the letters between him and Agnes, they were all burned after his disappearance. The only real source that I could dig up on their romance was an indirect one, made by Agnes's little sister, Margaret Dudley. In 1964, she'd written a response to a British archivist's inquiry asking if any local material had survived belonging to Darrell. In reply to this, Margaret Dudley explained:

> I am the sister of Agnes Dudley, who for many years was engaged to Hubert Darrell; and who in 1921 married his brother Charles. My sister died in 1959 . . . so I cannot give much information except what I remember as a small girl.

I know that they [Hubert and Charles Darrell] and my brother and sister were very good friends when they were young. My father kept the post office at our farm . . . so all the young bachelors came over for the mail; and many of them for dinner on Sundays, after church . . .

Hubert came back once [from the North], and wanted my sister to go back with him; but she was teaching school at the time, and thought they should wait until he had a home, and much less precarious mode of existence. I know that she afterwards regretted this decision. She heard from him as regularly as conditions permitted, and his untimely death was a great shock to her. She was ill for some time before her death, and so as to save me the trouble of doing it, destroyed all Hubert's letters, pictures etc. My brother had some pictures, but those were destroyed at his death. His brother Charles may have had some letters, etc. but nothing was found after his death.

✳

It turned out that my gracious host, Margaret Ashcroft, had actually grown up on the farm adjacent to the Darrells'. She'd been born at the height of the Great Depression in 1934, long after Hubert Darrell had already vanished. But she'd known his brother Charles, and also Agnes. To me, it felt a little odd and even surreal—having spent years reading Darrell's journals and retracing his steps through the wilderness—to be sitting across a small kitchen table from someone who'd actually known his brother and fiancée. Margaret then was only one degree of separation from knowing Hubert Darrell, and since I'd met her, strange as it seemed, that now made me only two degrees of separation removed from knowing Darrell—despite the passage of nearly a century between us.

As I sat at her kitchen table that October afternoon, Margaret kindly explained to me that although Charles and Agnes had married in 1921, their relationship had existed only on paper. Or, as she put it, "they parted ways on the steps of the church," with Charles returning alone to the farm and Agnes back into Birtle, where she'd been living. Their marriage had only happened because Agnes had wanted the Darrell name for her own, so that one day it could be etched into her gravestone. It turned out that she really did pine for her lost lover until the day she died.

That Agnes had once truly loved Hubert Darrell I never doubted, as the fragmentary paper trail that I had found already indicated as much. It was only the mystery of her later marriage to Charles I was unsure about, which Margaret had now cleared up. That she'd loved Hubert Darrell had been plain from the fact that she, more than anyone else, kept up hope of his return long after his disappearance. Agnes had taken the lead in corresponding with some of the world's foremost arctic explorers, in the hopes they might be able to find out what had happened to him. For his part, Charles, too, was clearly grieved and alarmed by his brother's vanishing and wrote to the Mounties asking if he could personally accompany any search effort.

I asked Margaret—who seemed sharp as a tack and certainly didn't look a day past eighty—if she could remember anything else about them. She remarked that Agnes was a strange woman, but then cautioned me that this was merely the impression of a young girl, and that her own parents had always told her that Agnes was very nice. (I suppose, having lost her intended in the Arctic and pining ever after for him, might make anyone seem a bit strange.)

As for Charles, or Charlie, as he was universally called, Margaret remembered him as a robust, active old man who was often to be seen riding the farm roads on his bicycle. She recalled that he was well-dressed, and that her parents had often said Charlie was a kind man. But by the later part of his life, the old farmhouse, where he still lived, had fallen into complete ruin. Charlie died in it, poor and alone, and was buried in an unmarked grave. Not long afterwards the dilapidated farmhouse burned down, destroying any pictures, letters, or journals of Darrell's that might have remained in it. Agnes, meanwhile, passed away at age eighty-two in 1959 and was laid to rest in the local Birtle and District Cemetery. Her headstone reads simply: "Agnes Clarissa Darrell" with no mention of who was her actual husband.

After our educational discussion in her kitchen, Margaret, myself, and Brenda and Lorraine from the historical society all drove out of town together to see where the old Darrell farmstead once stood. Today it's just a deserted field, one among many stretching to the horizon. All traces of the old farmhouse where Darrell had come of age are long since gone. But Margaret remembered exactly where it'd stood: it'd been situated well back from the quiet road, almost half a kilometre, on a slight ridge—a secluded, wild little place. Together we walked the field and over the silent grounds.

One hundred and nineteen years earlier, Hubert Darrell had walked these same prairie fields, torn by conflicting emotions.

As much as he may have loved Agnes, the spell of the North is not an easy thing to break away from—much less so in 1905 when Darrell happened to receive the very offer he'd longed for: a paid position on an expedition seeking to venture where few had ever dared, into the uncharted High Arctic. Such an expedition might be the making of any man. It seemed impossible to refuse, so Darrell promised he'd be back within a few years, well positioned by then to acquire a farm of his own. By summer 1905, Darrell was already headed north.

This time though, he'd never return.

10

UNDER NORTHERN SKIES

Darrell's hard fist connected with the aristocrat's soft face. If he'd once had the distinction of camping in an igloo with a British aristocrat, he now had the privilege of knocking another one out cold.

How Darrell came to fight an aristocrat in the Arctic takes some explaining.

In 1904, while still helping on the farm, Darrell had corresponded with a man named Alfred H. Harrison. Harrison was a well-connected British aristocrat who had pretensions of becoming an arctic explorer. He'd already done some hunting and travelling in Canada, and was a member of Britain's prestigious Royal Geographical Society. In this sense, he was similar to Hanbury, but as events would later make plain, he had none of Hanbury's brains or ability. Harrison had studied surveying, but he lacked practical experience and had never set foot in the Arctic. This didn't stop him from concluding he ought to lead an expedition there.

How exactly Harrison and Darrell first became aware of each other isn't clear. Harrison had done some sport hunting on Great Slave Lake in 1902–03 (while Darrell was off exploring with Hanbury) and he might easily have heard of Darrell through the trading posts there. If not, Harrison likely knew of Darrell through Hanbury's writings. Hanbury had already published several articles about his expedition. In any case, one way or another Darrell came to Harrison's attention. To fulfill his ambition of launching an arctic expedition of his own, Harrison needed reliable men. He explained in a letter to Darrell what he had in mind: a journey down the Mackenzie River, then by dogsled over the frozen Arctic Ocean, where with any luck he'd discover new lands or even an unknown continent, which would nicely round out the world's other seven.

Although today the notion of an eighth continent waiting to be discovered in the Arctic sounds absurd, at that time it was not quite as ridiculous. At the dawn of the twentieth century, most of the Arctic, and northern Canada for that matter, remained blank on maps. Unbroken sea ice that lasted year-round prevented any voyages into these mystery regions, and airplanes still hadn't been invented. Even after the Wright brothers made history with their first flight in 1903, it'd take another two decades before any aircraft was actually capable of flying over the Arctic. Beyond a certain latitude, months of continuous darkness and extreme cold made conditions uninhabitable, and even Inuit avoided these regions. As a result, much of the far North beyond the continental land mass remained utterly unknown and uncharted. Geographers speculated that within the Arctic Ocean significant land masses awaited discovery, possibly an entire continent. It turned out there was actually some truth to this: while there was certainly no continent, several arctic islands weren't found until well into the twentieth century. Borden Island in the High Arctic, for instance, didn't appear on any map until as late as 1947, when it was spotted by a Royal Canadian Air Force pilot flying overhead, making it arguably the last significant land on Earth to be truly discovered.

Harrison offered to pay Darrell a 110 pound salary, if he agreed to join the expedition and pilot their boat down the Mackenzie River—decent enough pay for a frequently penniless trapper and prospector. Naturally Darrell accepted: it was certainly more money than he'd make on the farm. So, in the spring of 1905, Harrison arrived in Canada accompanied by his brother-in-law. From Quebec City they headed west by train, meeting Darrell on route. At the time, Darrell was thirty-one years old, while Harrison was forty.

But before they'd even reached the wilderness, Darrell had doubts about Harrison's suitability. His first impression of him was that he didn't have the physical vigour needed for a punishing arctic trek. In a letter dashed off from Edmonton to his parents, Darrell confessed, "I must say I feel rather uneasy as to prospects and chance of success as the man is not Hanbury, he has not the resources of my former boss." He added, "If the [journey] North does not kill him the winter will."

Still, the money Harrison was offering wasn't easy to refuse, especially to someone under the spell of the North. From Edmonton, the three of them travelled north by horse-drawn wagon to Athabasca Landing, a small trading post on the Athabasca River. For Darrell the trip was completely pedestrian, but Harrison and his brother-in-law acted as if they were already roughing it. In fact, when they arrived at the river, Harrison's brother-in-law announced he'd enjoyed quite enough exploring for his tastes and promptly turned back for Edmonton.

This left Harrison and Darrell on their own. From the local traders Harrison purchased a scow, a type of flat-bottomed rowboat, of the sort Darrell was familiar with from his years in the North. On large bodies of water, these boats had certain advantages compared to canoes. Their size made them safer in rough conditions, and unlike a canoe, it was possible to sleep in them while drifting overnight with the current. They could be further equipped with a sail. But they generally required at least two or three people to handle, so to replace his brother-in-law, Harrison hired a local fur trapper, Felix Dumont.

Harrison would later explain in his published account a bit more about their method of travel: "We had a small stove in our scow, and cooked everything on board, which enabled us to drift night and day." He then claimed, "In order to let the men have their rest, I always took the night work myself." Somehow the notion that a novice took the lead piloting a riverboat in the dark while two river veterans slept seems unlikely. In fact, Darrell and the newly hired Dumont quickly formed a rather different assessment of Harrison's abilities. Despite his boasting, they both regarded him as out of his depth. Harrison, it seems, had exaggerated his background: he'd bragged to Darrell beforehand that he had fifteen years' experience of wilderness travel. The reality was he'd spent no more than eighteen months sport hunting in the company of paid guides.

Not only that, it turned out that Harrison had a habit of talking non-stop, which Darrell, used to solitude and long periods of silence, found irksome. Darrell recounted later in one of his letters that Harrison, "knowing nothing apparently in a practical way," would nonetheless "talk your head off about his theories. He nearly drove me crazy talking about it every day." As for Dumont, he found Harrison so incompetent that in spite of the wages offered, he quit as soon as he could at the next fur trading post, leaving Darrell on his own with Harrison.

On their first night on the river with just the two of them, when it was Darrell's turn to sleep, Harrison promptly ran the scow into a sandbar. To free themselves they had to lighten the boat, forcing both men to get into the water, but Harrison complained about having to get his feet wet. It took nearly two hours of heaving, hoisting, and shoving to get the boat free. Meanwhile, during the day, while Darrell rowed and navigated, Harrison amused himself by shooting at any black bears he spotted along the banks.

When he wasn't blasting away at the local wildlife, Harrison stood in the boat pontificating on the Arctic (which he'd never been to) and criticizing Darrell's abilities. In his account, Harrison recalled: "We had not drifted far from Fort Smith when Darrell, who was looking after the boat while I was working out some observations, took us down a cul-de-sac: this annoyed me very much; and I made him tow the boat back again into the main current, not a little to his discomfort."

In fact, without any sense of irony, near the very spot where he now was forcing Darrell to wade through water and haul him in a boat, Harrison recalled how two years earlier his guide on his sport hunting trip had abruptly abandoned him here. As Harrison explained it, "I had trouble . . . with this Indian, who was but a poor-spirited fellow, and he left me by myself at the mouth of a small river." Still, lest anyone fear for Harrison's safety, he asserted that he personally had little need for guides, as he was an expert hunter and had never once been lost. Or as Harrison put it himself in his published book, "I have never been lost, but I have often been left by the Indians: they are really contemptible savages, who delight in doing these things." Such views clashed sharply with Darrell's and further estranged the two. Harrison, meanwhile, given the wages he offered, regarded it as a great mystery why his guides constantly deserted him. (One begins to suspect that his own brother-in-law may have had other reasons for turning back.)

Three weeks into their boat journey, when they stopped at another little trading post, Darrell scribbled a letter to his parents, explaining his situation: "Harrison is as green as you can make them, although he should not be, having been engaged in this kind of thing the past 15 years. That just shows the difference between a man who has had to work and one who has someone to do it for him. I have to tell him every little thing. He will pull the oar the wrong way and cut wood on a stone with the axe just as cheerfully as you please. I can't understand a man of his experience being so green. I am very sorry I've gone with him." Darrell further expressed his regret at having to leave the farm and his hope that things would soon improve for Charles. He noted, "I never enjoyed anything so much as putting the crop in this year," but in spite of this, he felt there was no choice but to leave, since their harvest had failed again to turn a profit. So it seemed Darrell was stuck with Harrison.

When in August they finally reached Fort Resolution on Great Slave Lake, a fierce storm with huge waves pinned them down. They were to wait at the fort for the Hudson's Bay Company steamer, which would tow them across the lake's wide expanse to the Mackenzie River and down it as far as Fort Simpson. During this interlude at the trading post, Harrison, flashy as always with his money, offered fifty dollars to any man who could bring him a lake trout weighing more than fifty pounds. (None did.) But instead of trophy fish, what Harrison ought to have been worrying about was the lateness of the season. It was already well into September by the time the steamer cut them loose on the Mackenzie River.

Ahead of them still lay more than 1,400 kilometres of river before they could even reach the Beaufort Sea. And from here on out, they'd have to cover that distance by rowing, drifting with the current, or, if the wind chanced to be with them, sailing. But the bitter autumn winds howling out of the north stayed relentlessly against them, and in the little scow, even with the strong current, their progress was painfully slow. Soon, in addition to the wind, they were battling snowstorms. Further downstream the river was already freezing up: Harrison's plan of reaching the sea before winter appeared increasingly unrealistic. However, if Harrison is to be believed, he heroically exerted himself to get them there, claiming that he did most of the rowing himself and took all the night watches.

Meanwhile, Harrison described Darrell as practically incompetent: "During broad daylight one day Darrell ran the scow on to a sand-bar, which I thought we should never get clear of again. I had to get into the water and put my back underneath the boat, working it inch by inch for three hours, till it was once more adrift." But the sentence betrays Harrison as the novice he was:

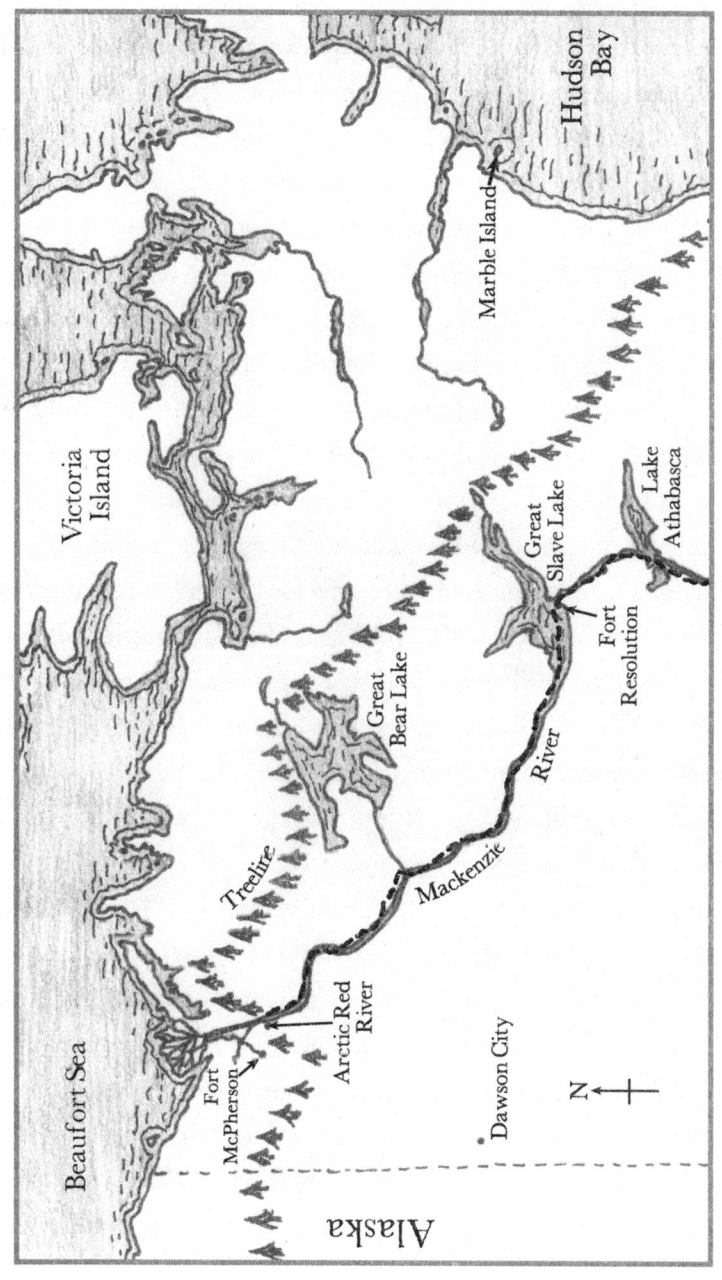

DARRELL'S JOURNEY WITH HARRISON IN 1905

sandbars are so common on the Mackenzie that anyone, at any time, can run aground on them even in a canoe, as I learned myself when I paddled it. Darrell, of course, had already successfully navigated the Mackenzie many times by scow, canoe, and steamer.

By October 4, with snow on the ground and winter upon them, but still stuck on the Mackenzie River, Darrell and Harrison limped into the tiny trading post of Arctic Red River, some two hundred kilometres north of the Arctic Circle. This was the last trading post on the river proper, before the Beaufort Sea. Here they were informed they'd never reach the Arctic Ocean by boat, as just a few miles further downstream the river had already iced over. It wouldn't be ice-free again until June. This news, however, had little effect on Harrison: he decided they'd just buy a team of huskies and then continue by dogsled. Harrison ordered Darrell to oversee their supplies while he set off with a North-West Mounted Police patrol to Fort McPherson, where he could purchase sled dogs.

The time alone gave Darrell a chance to reflect. It'd taken them nearly four months just to get as far as they had, a journey that Darrell normally did in only half that time. In a new letter to his family, Darrell labelled Harrison "utterly incompetent." As much as he yearned to explore, and as badly as he needed money, Darrell had made up his mind to quit.

But despite the fact that he'd forfeited four months already to Harrison and now found himself on the banks of the Mackenzie River with winter fast approaching, Darrell drafted out a bank note returning in full the half of his wages he'd been advanced, all fifty-five pounds of it—not even subtracting anything for his time and effort to get Harrison as far as he did. He then tore out a precious page from his notebook to compose a letter to him explaining his decision.

That should have been the end of the matter, but Harrison, on his return with the dogs, after finding the note, angrily confronted Darrell. He insulted him, calling him a coward for refusing to go on. Darrell, who, unlike Harrison, had ample experience of arctic travel, responded by challenging Harrison to a fight. Harrison foolishly accepted and, to the surprise of no one (but himself), was quickly and easily beaten by Darrell.

Harrison then ran off to the same Mounties he'd just spent the last week with, demanding they arrest Darrell. But the Mounties instead summoned both Darrell and Harrison to an inquiry to get to the bottom of things. (It seems they might have already formed their own assessment of Harrison's temperament.) After listening to both men, the police declined to press any charges against Darrell. Furious, Harrison demanded that they at least charge him for breaking his contract. But Harrison was forced to admit that the agreement between them was verbal only and that Darrell had already returned everything paid to him. Yet Harrison was still not satisfied and demanded that the Mounties somehow compel Darrell to remain in his service (thereby undermining his own claim that Darrell wasn't qualified). But this, too, the Mounties declined to do.

In his later published account, Harrison claimed that he had "treated this man with every consideration. I paid him half his money in advance, because he told me a very sad story about his brother who, he said, would probably be sold up . . . I was completely taken in by him . . . I said what I thought of him; and, thereupon, he challenged me to fight, and I was compelled to defend myself." Darrell, in a letter sent to his family, gave his side of the story, explaining that Harrison's habit of talking endlessly undid his own case in front of the Mounties. Darrell noted, "he told so many conflicting stories and showed so much spite and I told the simple facts and explained things, to the end that Harrison lost his case." But Harrison vowed this wouldn't be the end of the matter, threatening both Darrell and even Inspector Howard of the Mounties. Harrison boasted that back in civilization he had many powerful friends, including Sir Clements Markham, the esteemed head of the Royal Geographical Society, and that he would do everything to ensure that Darrell would never be hired on any expedition ever again.

Despite this setback, Harrison still remained determined to press on to the Arctic Ocean. To replace Darrell, he tried to hire any local natives he could find around the trading post, but they all refused to have anything to do with him. Enraged, Harrison fumed in his book: "The Louchaux Indians, who inhabit this country, could not be persuaded to accompany me to the Arctic Ocean . . . These were the sort of people I had to deal with. A more contemptible lot of natives I have never come across, and they are the same from one end of the country to the other." Having now made enemies of Darrell, the local Indigenous population, and the Mounties, Harrison was stuck where he was for the time being. Eventually, though, he managed to bribe a local trader to take him by dogsled north to the Arctic Ocean, where several whaling ships with their crews were frozen in for the winter.

Harrison figured that, with his natural gift for leadership, he could easily convince some of these whalers, and any Inuit who lived nearby, to follow him. As it happened, when Harrison arrived on the arctic coast, the anthropologist Vilhjalmur Steffansson was living in the area with some local Inuit. Stefansson explained what transpired when the British aristocrat showed up: "[Harrison] had been trying to buy an outfit from the whalers and to enlist the Eskimos to go with him. Everyone thought him crazy and refused to help." Stefansson, who spoke the local Inuit dialect fluently, further recorded that all the Inuit regarded Harrison as "hare-brained," an assessment that the whalers shared. To add insult to injury, in his published account Stefansson added, "Harrison had come North accompanied by Hubert Darrell . . . one of the best winter travelers that ever came to the North."

Harrison was at last made to see that his grandiose plans to discover a new continent weren't happening. But rather than return south humiliated, he came up with a new plan to salvage his reputation. On the mainland to the east of the Mackenzie River lay a vast unmapped area, which Harrison now proposed to explore and chart. He hoped that Stefansson, given his linguistic talents, might want to come with him. Stefansson declined, but helped persuade several of the local Inuit to accompany Harrison on his new journey.

Harrison ended up remaining in the Arctic for another year, mostly in misery it seems. Meanwhile, Stefansson, who'd been living with the Inuit much as Darrell had earlier done, speaking their language and sharing their hardships, was shocked when he later came across Harrison and saw in contrast how he'd been living:

Our arrival seemed both to surprise and delight Harrison who was having rather a lonesome time, for Kakotok, with whose family he was living, knew scarcely a word of English and Harrison had not mastered even the Eskimo jargon. It may have been because of his upbringing as an English country gentleman or because of a naturally aloof disposition that he was living in one house with his Eskimo servants in another, on terms about as intimate as if they were neighbours in a suburb. Getting someone to talk with was a relief to Harrison.

Of course, it could be that Stefansson had things backward: perhaps it was Kakotok and the other Inuit who couldn't put up with Harrison and therefore built him his own separate snow house. On his visit, Harrison invited Stefansson to play chess with him. (Naturally he'd packed a chess set as part of his expedition supplies.) Stefansson did report that he was at least good at chess, and that he was also a "good mathematician and enjoyed calculations and plottings."

When Harrison finally returned to civilization the next summer, having made it back up the Mackenzie River on a steamer, he made good on his threat to do whatever he could to hurt Darrell's chances of finding employment on any future expeditions. Back in England, Harrison published *In Search of a Polar Continent*, which laid out his theory that an undiscovered eighth continent lay north of Canada and slandered Darrell as both incompetent and dishonest. Incredible as it might seem, Harrison's book about a non-existent continent received positive reviews and he was praised as a bold and intrepid explorer.

Ironically, though, in seeking to ruin Darrell's reputation, Harrison would help turn him into a legend. Alone as he was in the Arctic, without even a dog for a companion or a cent to his name, but an aristocrat for an enemy—Darrell had become a desperate man, willing to risk anything and do anything. Such a combination opened the door for his greatest feats.

11

THE MAKINGS OF A LEGEND

With nothing to keep him at the tiny post on the Mackenzie River, Darrell decamped for Fort McPherson, a larger trading post farther west on the banks of the Peel River. This isolated outpost, situated above the Arctic Circle but still within the northern forest, had been established by the Hudson's Bay Company back in 1840. When Darrell showed up in 1905, it was merely a collection of log dwellings, one of which the Mounties had recently taken over as their first ever arctic post. Desperate for work as he was, he offered to perform any labour needed. The fur traders gave him a few odd jobs—helping transport goods by dogsled a hundred miles down the frozen river, and then overseeing a store for a month during another trader's absence. But such temporary jobs didn't last long, and with a fiancée waiting for him, and a brother badly in debt, Darrell needed something more substantial.

There was, as it happened, one job no one wanted—mail carrier. It paid next to nothing and came with an excellent chance of dying, but on the plus side, it provided plenty of fresh air and a chance to see more of the country. Darrell was desperate enough that he immediately accepted the position. The traders, who were in the charge of the mail, then explained what it entailed: travelling alone in the dead of winter for more than eight hundred kilometres across uncharted arctic mountains. Then they explained what was at stake: potentially the lives of up to five hundred whalers who were trapped by ice in the Beaufort Sea and running desperately low on supplies. They urgently needed to get word to the outside world of their plight, so that relief ships could be organized and sent north as soon as possible.

But the only way this could be done was to trek over trackless mountains into Alaska and from there on to Fort Yukon, where the letters could then be taken along an established trail south to the nearest telegraph station. Since no one else was willing, Darrell volunteered, even though he'd be travelling through lands he'd never seen before. He'd also be utterly alone, without even sled dogs. This wasn't just because Darrell didn't own a dog team and couldn't afford one. Even if he had huskies, it wouldn't have mattered: without trails, the mountain snows were too deep for dogs. If these things weren't daunting enough, the arctic winter promised limited daylight, the certainty of blinding blizzards, and a deadly windchill falling to sixty below. If he became lost or disoriented in the arctic darkness, or stumbled for even a moment in attempting to light a fire, the consequences would be fatal. Which is probably why no one else bothered to volunteer.

Yet in the depths of winter, on January 29, 1906, Darrell set off alone. (To wait any longer was impossible, news had to get south as quickly as possible if ships were to be outfitted and sailed north in time for the brief arctic summer.) With a rope tied around his chest to haul a hundred-pound sled that held all his meagre provisions, including some food, a fur sleeping bag, rifle, ammunition, and the all-important mail, on his snowshoes Darrell set off.

His eight-hundred-kilometre route took him across frozen rivers, through subarctic forests, and over the deep snows of the Richardson Mountains. He navigated intuitively, following the rivers and using the sun as his guide, stopping only at lunch to make a fire to warm his frozen body and consume rations. Travelling by night was too dangerous, so Darrell slept in his little sled in the open by a blazing fire. At times blizzards blinded him, and in the mountains avalanches were a constant danger. But with his iron resolve, cool head, and incredible strength and stamina, Darrell simply pushed on. The mountains reached heights of several thousand metres, and one can only imagine how Darrell ever managed to get his sled up and over them without trails in deep snow. The hardest part is actually going downhill: towing a toboggan uphill is straightforward, but downhill, with rocks and trees as obstacles, the heavy toboggan threatens to race ahead and careen wildly off course or spill over. So it must be painstakingly controlled with brute strength from behind with a rope. Nowadays, for those who enjoy this sort of thing, specially designed sleds, known as ski pulks, have harnesses that lace through stiff plastic piping, so that they can't race ahead of the puller. This makes things vastly easier, as the trekker can stay ahead of the sled even when descending. But Darrell never had such luxuries: he had only rope to haul his sled with. (When the time came for me to get a better sense of his extraordinary journeys by recreating part of his trek in the Yukon's wintry mountains, I hauled a sled with a rope, too, but just far enough to appreciate the enormity of Darrell's accomplishment.)

Once he'd crossed over the mountains, Darrell next followed the frozen Bell River down to where it joined the larger, ice-locked Porcupine River. Still trudging along over the river ice, he crossed the invisible boundary separating Canada from Alaska. On the hardest days, in the deepest snows or high in the mountains, Darrell barely managed to cover eight or nine kilometres. But when the terrain was flatter or the snow harder, with his iron resolve and superb stamina Darrell jogged ahead on snowshoes, his best day trekking a superhuman sixty-seven kilometres.

On March 1, after a journey that took a month, Darrell staggered into the little outpost of Fort Yukon, Alaska, on the banks of the Yukon River. The residents there were stunned by the arrival of this ice-encrusted phantom pulling a sled who'd come out of the mountains as if from thin air. But Darrell simply indicated he was the mailman, authorized by the Hudson's Bay Company to carry critical dispatches from ice-trapped whaling captains on the Beaufort Sea, and that there wasn't a moment to lose. At Fort Yukon, the letters could be loaded onto a dogsled, then taken south along established trails, which for safety had warming stations spaced a day apart, until they reached the most northern telegraph station then in existence: Eagle, Alaska. From there, the news could be relayed to the world and relief ships organized.

As extraordinary as Darrell's feat was, he himself made little of it. In a letter he wrote at Fort Yukon to his father just days after finishing his gruelling trek, he simply explained:

I offered to carry the mail for the "Baillie Island" and "Herschell Island" whalers to Fort Yukon as it was most important to get word out in time to send up relief ships to the fleet caught in the ice around the east side of the mouth of Mackenzie River. There are over 500 men and 12 ships wintering there not from choice but because the ice would not let them out. Some of the ships are only outfitted for 1 season and have been in 2 and some 3 years. Consequently, they are on rock-bottom and have to be supplied by ships which have more supplies. I agreed to carry it over and as the snow was so deep and there was no trail and the cold was great, I had to haul my own toboggan, and I had a very hard time of it as far as work went. The distance I came was 480 miles and it took 30 days . . . I passed right over the range of Rocky Mountains, which are low in these parts but for all that absolutely barren of vegetation near the summit. I forgot to mention above that the deep snow and cold would prevent dogs from making such a long journey for one would have to carry a big load of food for them, and dogs play out quickly when they have no trail.

This nonchalant account belies the extraordinary nature of what Darrell had done. Yet likely no one in the outside world would ever have learned of it, if not for the remarkable coincidence that two of the world's most famous polar explorers—Roald Amundsen and Vilhjalmur Stefansson—happened to be in the area at the time.

In the early twentieth century, the Norwegian Amundsen was widely regarded as one of the world's greatest and most

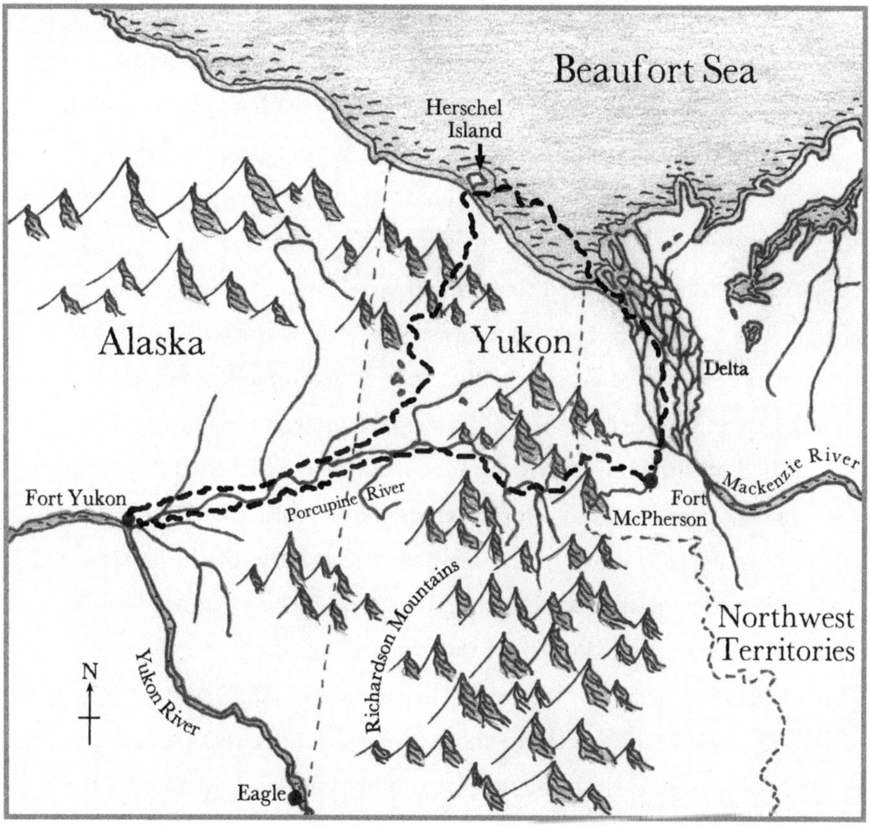

**DARRELL'S EPIC 1,800-KILOMETRE SOLO MAIL
DELIVERY JOURNEY ON FOOT IN 1906**

famous explorers, if not the greatest. To put it in Canadian terms, he was the Wayne Gretzky of exploration, with numerous awards and honours to his credit. A national hero in his native Norway, Amundsen had been part of the first ever expedition to overwinter in Antarctica, and he'd later make history by becoming the first person to reach the South Pole in 1911.

It just so happened that while Darrell was quietly making his solitary trek over the mountains, Amundsen was attempting to become the first person to successfully navigate the Northwest Passage. With a crew of six in his small ship *Gjøa*, Amundsen had sailed into the icy labyrinth in 1903, equipped with sled dogs and enough provisions to last more than three years if need be. After spending two years in the ice near the middle of the passage, Amundsen managed to sail through the rest in the brief arctic summer of 1906. But before the Norwegians could escape south, their route became blocked by drifting ice off the Yukon—trapping them in the Arctic for another year. Fortunately, Amundsen's small crew had enough provisions to hold out, unlike most of the whaling ships stuck elsewhere in the Beaufort Sea. Still, having been cut off from the world for a couple years already, Amundsen was overcome with impatience to get news out that he had successfully made it through the Northwest Passage.

To that end, he made up his mind to trek overland south to the nearest inhabited place, Fort Yukon, and from there another three hundred kilometres to the telegraph station at Eagle. Amundsen's past adventures in both Antarctica and the Arctic had well accustomed him to such arduous undertakings, but even he didn't think of attempting such a journey without dogsleds, let alone by himself. Luckily, the Norwegians had met a party of

Inuit passing over the ice on dogsled, and they knew the way south to Fort Yukon. From where Amundsen's ship had been frozen in, it was about an eight-hundred-kilometre journey. So, with three others and twelve dogs divided between two sleds, Amundsen left his ship and headed south, intending to return as soon as he had sent dispatches letting the world's newspapers know of their accomplishment. Even to the seasoned Amundsen, this overland journey was a serious undertaking. Passing through such remote arctic mountains, never in his wildest dreams did Amundsen expect to meet with anyone else, much less someone on his own without even a dogsled. Yet that is exactly what happened: Amundsen and his companions one day spotted a solitary figure moving over the distant snows.

At first, Amundsen's party could barely find words to express their surprise that in the middle of this frozen wilderness where temperatures plunged to sixty below and frostbite was only minutes away, they'd come across a lone wanderer who seemed as if he was just on a Sunday stroll. To let Amundsen tell what occurred in his own words:

One morning, soon after we had reached Porcupine River going north, Jim gave an exclamation of surprise and pointed to the distance ahead. His keen eyes had discovered a black spot moving on the snow. Soon I, too, could discern it. Another hour and we came up to a solitary man, his face black with smoke, accompanied not even by a dog, and dragging his toboggan behind him. This was Mr. Darrell, the mail carrier, taking mail from the mouth of the Mackenzie River over to the trading posts on the other side of the mountains. I could not believe my eyes. Here was a man, hundreds of miles from the nearest human being, with not a soul to aid him in case of illness or accident, cheerfully trudging through the Arctic winter across an unblazed wilderness, and thinking nothing at all of his exploit.

Amundsen, amazed by Darrell's fortitude and nonchalant approach, invited him half jokingly to come visit his frozen ship when he got a free moment. The ship lay hundreds of kilometres away over the mountains, which Amundsen was now journeying back to by dogsled.

Amundsen of course never imagined he'd ever actually see Darrell again. Yet, a few months later, back on board his ice-locked ship with the other Norwegians, Amundsen was stunned one day to discover Darrell casually standing beside it on the frozen sea. As if by magic he had appeared—alone and without any dogs. Darrell explained to the speechless Norwegian that he had come over a new route, traversing some eight hundred kilometres in the winter on foot across the mountains. That wasn't all: he'd hauled with him a sixty-pound sled loaded with bags of mail that he'd picked up while in Fort Yukon, which he now intended to deliver to the various ships trapped in the ice all along the Beaufort Sea.

Amundsen was, as he put it, "lost in admiration of this hearty and cheerful" wanderer. He insisted that Darrell remain on board the *Gjøa* as his guest for at least a few days. This furnished Amundsen with a chance to study Darrell's methods and character. He described him as "a most remarkable man, possessed of rare vigour, courage, and perseverance. He may have been about forty, short but powerfully built, and very fair." At the time, Darrell was actually just thirty-two years old. But with his face coated in soot from campfires, and doubtless also chapped from frostnip and windburn, and his beard probably long and untamed, he appeared older. Amundsen further reported: "He made us happy by remaining with us for a couple of days, and then left quietly and unassumingly to continue his journey as before. I stood looking after him as he disappeared from view, and I thought, if you got together a few more men of his stamp, you could get to the moon."

In Amundsen's autobiography, he added that he and Darrell became warm friends and later exchanged many letters. Among the things they discussed was Darrell joining Amundsen on his impending expedition to the South Pole, which was to include only the most elite handpicked crew. Amundsen recalled, "I was delighted at the opportunity to get him, and he would certainly have been a member of that expedition had not fate intervened." This was high praise indeed coming from the likes of Amundsen.

Nor was Amundsen alone in his assessment of Darrell. Not long after his solo trek across the mountains, Darrell crossed paths with the explorer and anthropologist Vilhjalmur Stefansson. Stefansson would later become, alongside Amundsen, one of the most famous polar explorers. And while he and Amundsen, as rivals, didn't often agree, on Darrell they saw eye to eye. Stefansson was astonished by what Darrell had quietly accomplished. As he put it, "To travel alone and without dogs, is an unheard-of thing even among Eskimos." Stefansson furnished some more context regarding Darrell's feat as well as his personality:

He was one that did not advertise, and although some of the most wonderful journeys ever performed in Arctic lands were done by him, the world would probably never have heard much of them even had he lived a longer time . . . It was the winter before I saw him that he made one of his most wonderful journeys . . . he had no dogs and only a small hand sledge which he pulled behind him; and on that sledge he carried sixty pounds of mail. He made his way from Fort Macpherson over the mountains by a more difficult route than that followed by Amundsen's party. Although he traveled alone he had no adventure and no mishaps (adventures and mishaps seldom happen to a competent man), and when he arrived on the Yukon the telegraph despatches recorded the simple fact that mail had arrived from the imprisoned whalers in the Beaufort Sea, and not a word of who had brought it or how it had been brought.

Stefansson, always eager himself for publicity, could hardly conceive how it was possible that Darrell remained anonymous and didn't even take credit for what he'd done. Even years later, after a long and varied polar career ironically full of many "adventures and mishaps," Stefansson still concluded that Darrell's mail trek was "one of the most remarkable things ever done in Arctic lands."

Both Amundsen and Stefansson sought to understand how Darrell managed it. To build up his muscles and stamina, Amundsen had famously followed a very strict physical regimen from a young age. Stefansson, on the other hand, came from a midwestern farming background not unlike Darrell's, but then he'd gone to university and wound up teaching at Harvard University. Amundsen had remarked on Darrell's powerful build, courage, and his quiet can-do optimism, while Stefansson, who came to know Darrell later, described him as possessing "energy and resourcefulness" to a rare degree. Stefansson further attributed Darrell's uncanny abilities to the fact that he was always calm and never panicky, able to cooly assess a situation and proceed accordingly. As an anthropologist, Stefansson was particularly impressed with how Darrell had managed to adopt and innovate from the techniques he'd learned while living with the Dene and Inuit. Yet Stefansson noted Darrell differed from them and everyone else in his predilection for travelling alone and without a dogsled.

That Darrell possessed unusual stamina, strength, directional sense, and survival instincts had been clear early in his life. But before his mail trek, such unusual abilities had remained in the background. Hanbury obviously thought highly of him, but he wasn't the type to go into much personal detail. As for Darrell's other early travel companion, Chief Yinto of the Dene, he didn't leave any written records. But indirectly it can be inferred that even at that early date, Darrell must have already shown signs of unusual qualities, or else Yinto would never have permitted him to accompany his small band on their critical hunting journey.

But clearly the Darrell who crossed the mountains to bring word to the outside world of the trapped whalers was a different man from what he had been up until then. The catalyst that had unleashed his true potential was ironically Harrison. In vowing to destroy his reputation and wrecking his hopes for the future that had been bound up with participating in a successful arctic expedition, Harrison had forced Darrell into a position to volunteer for an impossible task when no one else would. Harrison had also angered Darrell, and anger can be a powerful motivator. It's easy to imagine Harrison's arrogant voice calling him an incompetent coward echoing in Darrell's ears as he struggled alone through trackless mountains, giving him a little extra motivation, if he needed any, to succeed.

And succeed he did—with the critical letters Darrell delivered, relief ships loaded with provisions were organized, and hundreds of sailors saved. Few people at the time, or for that matter since, ever knew the part Darrell played. Stefansson and Amundsen didn't publish their stories until years later. But apparently none of this mattered to Darrell, as no sooner had he handed over the critical messages than he was off again.

12

DREAMS AND DISAPPOINTMENTS

The hardened whaling captain stood on the deck of his trapped ship, frozen as it was in the ice, and gazed out across the desolate expanse. Out there across the windswept snow and ice, nothing moved. In fact, nothing ever did seem to move across that snowbound, merciless ice except the occasional polar bear. Then the captain's keen eyes saw a speck materialize on the distant horizon. It appeared to be coming closer. The captain, John A. Cook of the American whaling ship *Bowhead*, later testified to what he saw that day:

> I saw something that looked like a man dragging a long sled. As sled-outfits included both a number of dogs and two or more men commonly, my curiosity was instantly aroused. Forthwith I fetched my binoculars and discovered a man without companions or dogs was approaching my ship, dragging a small sled. . . . That sled contained nothing apparently except sleeping equipment and rifle

and ammunition. The stranger came directly to the *Bowhead*—haltingly as if practically exhausted, halted on the ice below me and, in a weak voice, asked permission to come aboard to get something to eat and drink. He showed us letters of authorization given him by Firth at the trip's commencement [in Fort McPherson] and another one signed by the postmaster at Fort Yukon.

This mysterious wanderer was of course none other than Darrell. He'd rested barely more than a week in Fort Yukon, then, having been entrusted with the return mail for the whaling ships, he set off once more. Again, he travelled alone and on foot, heading this time northward through the mountains to the Beaufort Sea. Part of his route took him along frozen rivers that cut through deep mountain gorges. Even in extreme cold, some of these rivers, given their raging rapids, don't always freeze solid, leaving dangerous stretches of weak ice that Darrell had to guard against. To keep himself provisioned he hunted caribou, although before leaving he'd crammed as much food as he could onto his seven-foot sled. At times, too, he had no choice but to travel by night, even though this was inherently riskier. But it saved his eyes from the snow blindness that threatened him whenever it wasn't overcast.

When Darrell reached the bleak arctic coast, he crossed the sea ice to Herschel Island, lying about five kilometres offshore, where a half-dozen ships were trapped. After delivering their mail, Darrell pushed on east across the ice, following the coastline. Another seventy kilometres farther on, he came upon Amundsen's ship frozen in the ice. Here, he rested for several days at Amundsen's invitation, who also gifted him a pair of Norwegian snow goggles. Darrell then trekked on across the frozen sea until he'd found the other whaling ships and delivered the mail to them too. I can't claim much personal experience delivering mail, but what little trekking across sea ice on the Arctic Ocean I did once convinced me it's not something I'd want to make a habit of.

For Darrell to get back to Fort McPherson, he next had to find his way through the frozen labyrinth of the Mackenzie River's delta. The delta is an intricate maze comprising hundreds of twisting channels and low-lying willowy islands. Even today with satellite imagery, it's about as confusing a place as any to navigate. Darrell couldn't afford to get turned around in it, as the river ice was becoming soft as winter turned into spring. Luckily, he came upon a band of Inuit making their own way up the delta, though the dialect they spoke differed from the one Darrell had learned earlier. Still, with signs and a few words, it proved easy enough to determine that they were heading the same way. Darrell joined them, but the weakening ice slowed their progress.

Late spring is always the hardest time for travelling in Canada's North—the ice becomes too weak for safe passage, but the rivers and lakes are still too ice covered for canoes. These conditions render hunting and especially fishing difficult, since it's no longer safe to ice-fish, nor is it possible to fish from shore. As a result, historically famines often occurred in the early spring, which many northern Indigenous groups referred to as the lean months or the fasting time. Soon Darrell and the Inuit band he'd met were all reduced to living off roots and the occasional arctic hare.

By early June, the ice had started to buckle and break up on the Mackenzie River's mighty expanse. Darrell noted in one of his letters, "I had the chance of seeing the ice go out of the largest river emptying into the arctic and I can tell you it is a sight." It is indeed a spectacular sight: huge slabs of ice are split apart like the pieces of an enormous jigsaw puzzle, while the force of the river's current carries them along in steady procession, as more and more ice drifts downriver from farther up the Mackenzie's epic length. At times, when the ice suddenly jams together, it can lift pieces vertically into the air and create towering ice heaps along the shore. I once paddled and poled my canoe alongside these melting castles of ice on the Mackenzie River, soon after it had broken up in the spring, and the spectacle of them is not something I'll soon forget.

When Darrell finally strode back into Fort McPherson in early June 1906, the traders there could barely believe their eyes. None of them had ever expected to see him alive again. In total, he'd travelled on foot approximately 1,800 kilometres in a round trip that had taken roughly four months. The journey had been epic in every sense of the word. But at the time there was no celebration, no fanfare, and no accolades. Darrell had simply delivered the mail, as asked.

Still, it was understood by those in the North that Darrell had done something unprecedented. In a letter written shortly afterwards to his parents, Darrell himself acknowledged that his journey was one "that no one is likely to repeat and I believe it is thought a great deal of . . . but mind you I think nothing of it myself. I call it a pleasure trip for I consider I understand how to travel under great cold and privation with the least trouble." Darrell's definition of a "pleasure trip" probably differed somewhat from most people's. And while outwardly Darrell always appeared shy and reserved, inwardly he was proud of what he'd accomplished. This included not only his mail delivery journey, but all the things he'd learned on his own over the years he'd spent in the North. This pride shone through in his private letters to his family: "I should not boast, but I consider I know more about northern arctic Canada than any living white man and the modes of travel, for I have travelled from end to end of Canada in the arctic region and studied the habit of all the different tribes of natives, not only in theory, but in practice and experience."

In this, Darrell was certainly correct. Few people then, or for that matter today, had ever ranged over such a vast expanse, stretching thousands of kilometres from Hudson Bay to Alaska, north to the Arctic Ocean, and southward into the boreal forests. Notably, Darrell attributed his success to the knowledge he'd gained first-hand from Indigenous peoples, which included his old Métis neighbour he'd once shared a Christmas dinner with, Chief Yinto and his Dene band, and the Inuit hunters Amer-or-yauk and Uttungerlah. This approach, of course, was the direct opposite of explorers such as Harrison or Franklin.

But as extraordinary as his mail journey may have been, for the moment Darrell had to come back to the humdrum reality that he found himself once more penniless and unemployed. In such dreary circumstances he procrastinated over what to do next: the whole point of his coming north, after all, had been to earn enough money to secure his future. Yet after a year of hard efforts—first with Harrison, and now on his own carrying the mail—he'd managed to save up virtually nothing. So, for the time being, he found temporary work in the fur trade, sailing a small scow loaded with furs up the Mackenzie River.

Meanwhile Darrell's family were of the opinion, expressed in letters to him, that he should return once more to Charles's perennially struggling farm. But the trouble was Darrell's mail journey had only served to rekindle the other great romance of his life—the wilderness. Once more he was completely taken in by the spell of the North and, if anything, was now smitten more than ever by its wide-open spaces. In a letter to his family after his epic feat delivering the mail, Darrell wrote, "You must not think I am tired of wandering for I am not." He thirsted for another journey almost as soon the last had ended and hoped to join another expedition. As he put it, "if I could get with a man like Hanbury again, I fear very much that nothing will cure me of the northern travel."

Yet at the same time, Darrell remained conflicted. Often he must have thought of Agnes and the farm, and part of him yearned to go back. In fact, his letters expressed contradictory desires—a testament to the turmoil in his own soul. In one letter from that same year, 1906, he writes in reply to his parents' stated preference for him to rejoin Charles, "I quite agree with you, I think the sooner I quit the North the better." In another letter to his family, he adds that "it is too bad that the want of money is separating us all for it is only that in my case." His plan was still to return south, he explained, as soon as he'd saved up enough to marry and buy a farm of his own.

He even described his ideal farm that he hoped one day to settle down on. Not surprisingly, he stressed that it would have to be somewhere remote, where he'd have the freedom to wander. As he put it: "I don't care where it is as long as it is not in a crowded settlement. I want plenty of room, I want a place where I can get good hunting. . . ." But Darrell also mentioned without any sense of contradiction that "if I could travel all the time and see new lands I should never quit it."

To save up enough money, Darrell considered relocating to Alaska, where wages were higher and he could find full-time work with the American postal service. He'd rather enjoyed carrying the mail, since it let him wander and explore, and it even paid him something for it. But his enthusiasm for this idea seems to have cooled when he realized he'd most likely end up stuck with a regular route between established posts, travelling by dogsled. However, his parents again suggested in a letter to him that a better option than delivering mail was simply farming with Charles.

As much as he respected his older brother, Darrell had always had a strongly independent streak in him: leaving home at sixteen will have that effect, and years spent living on his own in the wilderness had only amplified it. While he'd enjoyed his brief interlude back on the farm, he hated not being his own master. As Darrell put it: "Charlie will be hurt at my leaving him, but he should not think for a moment that I don't like my independence . . . I'm a child no longer . . . we had good times together as boys 10 years ago, its different when a man is grown." And in any case, the farm never made any money, so as Darrell said: "What is the use of starving and worrying year after year and never make anything?" If he had to starve and be poor, he figured it should at least be while wandering the mountains. Later, though, he became convinced Charles would be all right based on what he'd heard from him in his letters, noting in one that "Charlie had a bumper crop; three years will set him on his feet."

His family still struggled to understand the appeal of the North, reading as they did letters that spoke of frostbite, snow blindness, temperatures down to sixty below, and months of little food. Certainly, not everyone loved it. With the long and bitter winter settling over the land, bringing months of isolation and darkness, some men snapped. Darrell mentioned two suicides among the traders over the winter of 1906 and two others who had died recently from illnesses, one of whom Darrell had cared for until he perished. He then had to bury him in the frozen ground. His remark in a letter about all this was simply "I wonder who will be next?"

In his relative idleness, Darrell continued to be vexed by Harrison's threats. At the time, Darrell didn't quite realize the impression he'd made on Amundsen, and he hadn't met Stefansson yet. So, Darrell believed that Harrison, given his connections, might really harm his ability to get recruited on another expedition. Several such expeditions in fact were already underway in the Arctic, and Darrell regretted that by the time he'd be able to get to the High Arctic, much of it would already be mapped and explored. He contemplated whether he should join Amundsen and head instead for Antarctica. Darrell prophesized that "Amundsen is going to reach the pole, of that I have not the slightest doubt." This, of course, proved correct: Amundsen, like Darrell, had studied and learned arctic survival from the Inuit and then adapted many of these techniques for the Antarctic. In contrast, Amundsen's British rivals, Robert Falcon Scott and

Ernest Shackleton, largely failed to do so, something Darrell had earlier criticized about British explorers.

Restless as ever and desperate for work, Darrell cast about aimlessly for a time, drifting in and out of Fort McPherson and the fur trade. His love of solitude and adventure led him to wander into the wild Richardson Mountains, where his curiosity had been aroused by reports of a different species of mountain sheep. He stalked and hunted these mysterious creatures, much like he'd done earlier with muskoxen. These were dall sheep, a northern cousin of the bighorn sheep found farther south. With their large horns, they're an impressive and majestic-looking animal, especially if you happen to see one perched on a mountain gazing out over the land like some monarch surveying its domain. These rare beasts are found only in a small area of northwestern Canada and Alaska. But hunting mountain sheep didn't pay anything. And it didn't seem like there were any other employment opportunities coming his way.

Just when it appeared that Darrell had no choice but to return south, an unexpected offer fell into his lap. Unknown to the world at large as he may have been, his extraordinary feat in carrying the mail had not gone unnoticed in the North. And now Darrell's peculiar skills and unusual abilities were suddenly called upon by a service that had a great need for them—the Mounties.

13

CANADA'S FINEST

The Mounties, they say, always get their man. And the man they wanted was Darrell. Darrell's feat delivering the mail had made quite an impression on the Mounties at Fort McPherson. Before that they'd already witnessed his honesty in the dispute with Harrison, when he'd returned on his own accord his wages in full. In fact, even though Darrell himself didn't quite seem to grasp it, his abilities were quietly becoming the stuff of legend among fur traders, hunters, and trappers across the North. So it's perhaps little surprise that the Mounties came to him with an offer: they wanted him to act as a special constable, in which capacity he would guide their patrols through the wilderness.

The North-West Mounted Police had been founded in 1873 with the aim of bringing law and order to the Canadian West, so that it didn't end up resembling the violence and vigilantism of the American West. But the eruption of the Klondike gold rush, which had caused a flood of American prospectors to come into the Yukon, had shifted the Mounties' attention northward.

To prevent violence and uphold Canadian sovereignty, they had established a string of detachment posts in the North, with Dawson City the main one. But these posts were focused almost entirely on the southern part of the Yukon and Northwest Territories. In the sparsely inhabited far North, there was effectively no formal law, courts, or police whatsoever.

Until now, much of these vast areas had been left to the domain of the fur traders and Hudson's Bay Company, which took a remarkably laissez-faire view of murders. But this state of affairs couldn't last indefinitely, especially with more prospectors, trappers, and traders slowly trickling northward—something had to be done. In 1903, a police patrol arrived for first time above the Arctic Circle at isolated Fort McPherson. It then became a tradition to dispatch a patrol by dogsled once a year from Dawson to Fort McPherson, which entailed a gruelling 1,500-kilometre round trip in winter through the Yukon's hazard-filled mountains. But Fort McPherson was a pinprick in the vastness of the North, a mere speck on the map.

Disturbing reports had come in of American whaling crews on the Beaufort Sea engaging in rowdy behaviour, such as shooting at each other to settle disputes or selling whisky to Inuit in exchange for valuable arctic fox furs, an activity that was illegal. So the Mounties had resolved to establish a patrol to Herschel Island, given that American whaling vessels were in the habit of overwintering there. It might seem incredible that the Mounties would even attempt to establish a police presence in such an isolated and harrowing location. But the rationale was actually twofold: since the whaling ships were American, there were concerns that their continued operations in the area would eventually undermine Canadian sovereignty, which was already shaky enough, existing as it did only on paper. This was especially the case given that much of the Arctic was still uncharted and subject to intensifying expeditions by American, Danish, and Norwegian explorers who hungered to claim whatever they found for their own nations. Less than forty years earlier, the United States had bought Alaska; Denmark already controlled Greenland, while Norway had a long tradition of northern exploration and was eager to claim more arctic islands of their own. It was therefore felt that an official Canadian presence of some kind needed to be established soon in the North, or else risking losing it, most likely to the expansionist United States.

The immediate concern for the Mounties, though, was the general state of lawlessness. In 1905, a Danish whaler, the roguish Christian Klengenberg, seized control of a whaling ship in the Beaufort Sea from its lawful owner and then sailed off beyond the map into unknown islands. His plan was to trade for fox furs with any Inuit he happened to find. But apparently not all the hijacked ship's crew were quite as enthusiastic about their new captain's plans. When Klengenberg rejoined the other whalers the next summer at Herschel Island, his original crew of nine now numbered only five. Klengenberg admitted to shooting one of them, but said it was in self-defence; two others he insisted had sadly perished after falling through some ice, and the fourth one had become sick and died. But when the five surviving crew members got free of their dreaded captain (who'd gone off again to plunder), they told a different version of events. They explained that Klengenberg had murdered the first man in cold blood, that the two who had supposedly fallen through the ice happened to be the only witnesses to the first murder, and that the one who'd died of illness was in fact chained up in the ship's hold, left there to starve or freeze to death. Klengenberg had forced the five of them to remain silent on their return to Herschel Island, by helpfully explaining that the penalty for murdering nine men was the same as murdering four, so that it would be advisable for the five of them to make sure their stories matched his own.

Given this anarchic state of affairs, one can appreciate why the Canadian authorities had decided it was necessary to establish a Mounted Police patrol to Herschel Island. In the brief ice-free summer, two officers made the journey there by boat from Fort McPherson. They were still effectively marooned on the island months later when their colleagues came to Darrell to request his services. With the Beaufort Sea now frozen, the Mounties asked Darrell to lead a patrol on an eight-hundred-kilometre round trip to the island by dogsled. There they'd meet up with the other Mounties, then all return together.

Darrell himself would have to cover the whole distance there and back on foot—going ahead of the sled to check the ice conditions and break a trail for the dogs. If this wasn't hazardous enough, since it was still December, there'd be almost no daylight, making travelling in the dark a necessity. Darrell consented to the plan: only one Mountie was to accompany him, young Corporal Haylow.

When the two of them reached the desolate frozen ocean, ferocious gales chilled them to the marrow, and navigating in such blizzards was impossible. They spent three days stormbound in a relentless arctic tempest, huddling with the dogs for warmth. The police had standard-issue canvas tents, more than what

Darrell had on his solo mail journey, but setting up a tent in howling winds was impossible. At one point, as they were struggling along the bleak sea ice in the arctic night, a sudden gale swept down on them. With no time to lose, Darrell dug a snow hole, threw the corporal in it, then jumped in himself with one of the dogs for warmth. Only when the gale abated could they push on again, mile after icy mile, Darrell always out ahead with his iron stamina, checking the ice for weak spots and breaking a trail through the snow for the dogs to follow, with the corporal riding on the back of the sled.

Crossing the frozen sea to Herschel Island proved the most dangerous part. Despite the intense cold, open cracks and weak spots remained in the sea ice. Darrell again went ahead, testing the ice every few steps by gentling tapping a pole on it. In one place when he tapped it, the pole plunged right through. (That's seldom an encouraging sign.) The ice was only a few inches thick. But they were already miles from the mainland, so Darrell gingerly pressed ahead, stepping lightly, testing the ice now with every step. Another step caused an ominous creaking sound beneath their feet—the ice was cracking up. Darrell jumped ahead just as a gap opened, but the lead dogs behind him plunged helplessly into the freezing water. Darrell and Haylow reacted at once, pulling with all their might on the harnesses and commanding the other dogs to pull for their lives. Fortunately, they quickly pulled them out, none the worse for the wear (arctic huskies are remarkably hardy), then not wanting to linger on the ice, pressed on. Soon more open cracks appeared, forcing them to detour around them, until at last they reached the island. Darrell later commented dryly in a letter, "Corporal Haylow does not know to this day how near he came to getting a ducking or worse."

At the island, it turned out there was only a single ship overwintering, as well as some Inuit who'd travelled there to trade. Unlike the year before, the whalers were well provisioned, so there wasn't much else to do. Darrell, however, had to now lead all three Mounties and himself back to safety across the ice and frozen wilderness, another four hundred kilometres to the outpost at McPherson. It proved a gruelling journey, especially for Darrell, who again went the whole way on foot ahead of the police dogsleds. Darrell described it as "the stormiest trip I ever had in my life." Although he felt the police were a bit green, he nonetheless praised Corporal Haylow's hardihood in making the initial journey in the teeth of terrible blizzards, calling him a "most excellent man." However, he conceded that the corporal had no idea how close he'd come to disaster several times.

It was on this return trek that Darrell for the first time encountered Stefansson, the anthropologist and later famed explorer, who was living at the time with some Inuit along the coast. Stefansson had already heard of Darrell's mail-delivery feat, and he later described the sight of this legendary wanderer leading the police over the deserted snows:

> He was on his way guiding a party of mounted police-
> men from Herschel Island to Fort Macpherson. That was
> always his way. He was about as new to that country as
> the policemen were, but still he was a competent guide,
> for he never lost his head, and after all, in most places in

the North it is not difficult to find your way if you keep your wits about you.

Stefansson's claim that it was easy to find one's way in the Arctic, like many of his boasts, has to be taken with a grain of salt. Although Stefansson made epic journeys of his own and was a talented linguist, he had a tendency to downplay the dangers of the Arctic, to the point that his cavalier attitude later ended up causing the deaths of several of his own expedition members. This occurred when he was leading the Canadian Arctic Expedition—tasked with exploring uncharted parts of the High Arctic and claiming any lands there for Canada. When his ship became caught in the ice, Stefansson abandoned most of his crew and trekked on his own to safety. While his trek was impressive, when several of the crew later perished from starvation and scurvy, Stefansson's reputation was seriously tarnished. Thus, his claim that it is easy to find one's way in the Arctic has to be read as partly deflective, shielding himself from the charge that he had deserted his own men.

The Mounties were impressed by Darrell and keen to make more use of his services, though Darrell himself was reluctant. Ever the lone wolf, he had little wish to enter into a longer contract and certainly had no wish to become a police officer. His soul instead was in the wilderness. In between stints guiding police dogsled patrols, he was often to be found on his own wandering among the mountains, crossing several times from Fort MacPherson back into Alaska and back again, covering well over two thousand kilometres on foot in just a single winter. Once he found himself pinned down in the mountains for five straight days "of terrible blizzards and snowstorms" that rendered all travel impossible. On most of these journeys, he trusted to his rifle to keep himself provisioned.

But the winter of 1907 proved an exceptionally harsh one, with the caribou herds migrating far beyond their normal range. To make matters worse, snowshoe hares, which undergo natural population cycles of booms and busts every nine years, happened to have one of their down cycles. Famines as a result broke out across the northern Yukon and Alaska among the Gwich'in people, a northern branch of the Dene. Darrell noted in a letter to his family, "There are no caribou in the country this year. No rabbits to speak of, consequently starvation prevails all over." During these periods of famine, Darrell lived off "a handful of roots" and "maggoty fish" and, as he put it, learned to be grateful for it.

During his solitary rambles, Darrell also developed a preference for travelling at night whenever there was moonlight to see by. This kept him from sweating, which can be dangerous in low temperatures, as sweat can quickly cause hypothermia when resting. Night travel also spared his eyes from the sun's blinding glare off the snow. And since it wasn't as cold during the day, sleeping then had the further advantage of requiring less firewood. Still, as much as Darrell enjoyed roaming to his heart's content in the wilderness, the other part of him knew he needed money if he were to secure a future back on the farm with Agnes. So, not without some wistful reluctance, in the summer Darrell took work on a small steamer sailing the Yukon River. This paid better wages than any other employment he could find, including with the Mounties.

The steamer took him all the way down the Yukon River's long, snaking course to the Bering Sea, directly across from Russia, then back to Dawson in time for the fall freeze-up. Dawson, by this point, was a mere skeleton of its former self, with the vast majority of its population having abandoned it after the bonanza faded. Gold mining still went on, but it was now mostly dominated by larger companies rather than independent prospectors.

Given Darrell's reputation, the raw recruits among the Mounties in Dawson looked upon him with something like awe. He was the lone wanderer who travelled by night and could seemingly appear anywhere, at any time. Darrell noted in a letter that he was "treated with great respect" whenever he chanced to visit the police barracks. The Mounties asked him to again serve as a special constable on their 1,500-kilometre-long dogsled patrol from Dawson to Fort McPherson that winter of 1907–08. But Darrell expressed reservations, as he felt when it came to wilderness travel the police were still a little "green."

But when they offered him four dollars a day pay, he accepted the assignment. In all there were to be four sleds, each pulled by a team of five dogs. Each sled was loaded with about six to seven hundred pounds of provisions, much of it dog food. But even with that much weight, it wasn't possible to carry enough food to last the whole journey, so Darrell carried his rifle to help keep them fed.

It promised to be exceptionally gruelling work: part of Darrell's responsibilities would be to snowshoe ahead to break trail for the dogs. Without a trail to follow, the huskies' short legs would soon be engulfed in deep snow. The only way to remedy this was to find the strongest, fittest person possible to plow ahead of them mile after mile, day after day. Anyone who has ever walked any considerable distance in deep snow without trails can testify how truly exhausting it is. But if there was one thing Darrell knew, it was how to toil onwards without quitting. To make things even harder, the large snowshoes normally favoured for northern travel—which by virtue of their size help distribute one's weight more evenly over the snow, and therefore not sink as deep into it—couldn't be used. Instead, only small snowshoes, about three feet in length and nine inches in width, could be worn by trail-breakers. This was so they could more effectively flatten down the snow for the dogs. Darrell wrote to his family before embarking, "I know of no harder work than breaking a trail for dogs in deep soft snow."

The most dangerous parts of the journey were crossing the many creeks on route. These swift mountain streams don't always freeze solid. Sometimes they would have a hidden layer of water sandwiched between ice underneath and the snow on the surface. One of Darrell's duties was to help figure out the safest crossing places—using his practised eye to judge the creeks and ice, and then often going ahead himself before signalling it was safe for the rest to cross. This he did without fail.

Though on occasion it was inevitable that someone's feet got wet. In temperatures that sometimes fell to minus fifty, wet feet could mean frostbite within minutes. So, another of Darrell's crucial tasks was to start fires quickly in any kind of condition, including howling winds or driving snow, ensuring that frostbite didn't happen. Although the word *frostbite* is often used nowadays to refer to what is actually only mild frostnip, true frostbite is about as horrific and as painful a thing as imaginable. It happens

Arctic Red River

Arctic Red River

NWT

Fort McPherson

Peel River

Arctic Circle

Wind River

Hart River

Yukon

Ogilvie River

N

Alaska

Yukon River

Dawson City

MOUNTED POLICE DOGSLED PATROL ROUTE FROM DAWSON TO FORT MCPHERSON

Darrell acted as a guide and trail-breaker on the patrols of 1907–08 and 1909–10.

when the blood inside the veins turns to ice, causing permanent tissue and nerve damage. In Darrell's day, whenever extremities got severe frostbite, amputation was the only solution.

Fortunately, the patrol reached Fort McPherson without any mishaps. After fulfilling their duties there, they turned around and repeated the entire epic trek back to Dawson, with Darrell again breaking the trail, while the police marvelled at this solitary, silent man of iron who seemed never to tire.

After this trail-breaking stint, Darrell drifted off again. He may have found temporary employment with the police, but he was still a prisoner of the North, as firmly under its spell as ever. Among the mountains, he hunted caribou and engaged in half-hearted prospecting, though his real aim seems to have been to simply satisfy his itch to explore. In the summer of 1908, he again took work on an Alaskan steamboat sailing the Yukon River. Come fall, he returned to Dawson once more to join the annual police patrol back to Fort McPherson. But he ended up missing it when he was laid up with illness at the Dawson hospital, which was run by the local church. In a letter to his parents, he assured them it wasn't anything serious and he'd soon be well: "I am all right and the only thing I kick about is the loss of my trip to McPherson. The Doctor thinks I am better away in the wilds." This may well have been the case: conditions in Dawson, like most northern mining towns, were notoriously cramped, so that illnesses spread easily, particularly in the winter. What exact illness afflicted Darrell isn't clear: typhoid fever, tuberculosis, dysentery, and scurvy were all rife in Dawson around that time. In any case, Darrell was soon back to his old restless adventuring.

The police again asked him to lead their annual patrol for 1909–10. There were to be four Mounties again, each with their own dogsled, and Darrell as usual travelling ahead on small snowshoes to break the trail. Darrell recounted afterwards: "I was the trail breaker all the way there and back . . . As three of them had never been on a trip of any account before and Dempster . . . was always with the dog teams, as it required his entire attention to get the green fellows along at all. However, they did their best and eventually did very well after they were used to the snow-shoes and dogs." This would be Corporal William Dempster, for whom the Dempster Highway, which links Dawson to Inuvik, was later named. It's a narrow gravel road winding through the Yukon's wilderness that follows nearly the same route that the Mounties took on their annual patrols. I've hiked it once on my own in springtime and driven it twice. The route passes through some of the grandest scenery I know. But to trek it in the winter I wouldn't dream of, at least not for four dollars a day.

When confronted with deep, soft snow, the dogs struggled to cover as little as ten miles a day. Other times, when the terrain wasn't as steep or the snow was harder, they could easily triple that distance. One of the route's major river crossings, the Windy River, proved particularly hazardous as it had significant open water on it. Darrell again was always the one in the lead, tasked with making the critical decisions of where to cross rivers and streams, and the best points to ascend and descend steep ravines and gullies. The most treacherous points that Darrell had to guard against were places where a swift stream, hidden under the snows, joined a larger river. This could mean weak ice or open water concealed under the thick snow. Darrell noted that he judged "everything by sound," tapping the ice with a stick and listening to the sound it made to reveal its strength. On return treks, too, his task was to find their old trail, which could have been obliterated by drifts or freshly fallen snow. But if they could find their exact trail they'd taken north, this made for a much easier return, since the underlying snow was already beaten down and hard-packed.

Under Darrell's guidance, they reached Fort McPherson in early February 1910, without mishap. Their trek this time had amounted to 845 kilometres, longer than usual because they'd detoured almost 150 kilometres to check in on a party of seven prospectors who'd come north looking for gold. By the time they reached McPherson, the four Mounties were understandably exhausted. But Darrell, never one to sit idle, added over three hundred kilometres of travelling just to visit some Inuit in the Mackenzie delta. By mid-March, the party had returned safely to Dawson, making the return trip in just twenty-four days without incident aside from enduring fierce blizzards.

It's another of the ironies of Darrell's forgotten life that he figured indirectly in one of the best-known and most tragic chapters in the long and storied history of the Mounted Police, although, as is typical, his name is almost never mentioned in connection with it. Soon after he vanished, the Mounties suf fered one of their greatest ever single-day losses of life. This was the doomed "Lost Patrol" of the winter of 1910–11, in which the entire Dawson-McPherson patrol, numbering four men, per- ished. Although this famous tragedy has been much written about over the years, what almost no one realizes about it is that the police had actually wanted Darrell to have guided it, as he'd done previously. But his unexplained disappearance had made that plan obsolete, and the Mounties had gone without him, only to find themselves hopelessly lost. As their food supply dwindled, the Mounties resorted to butchering their own dogs for food. This bought them more time, but they were reduced to travelling on foot, and still unsure of the way. Darrell had made it all seem so easy. At last, growing weaker as they were, the Mounties made the desperate decision to turn back. By this point, with merciless blizzards slowing them down and extreme cold further weakening them, starvation overtook them. Their frozen corpses, found later in the snow, told the tragic tale of their demise. There were no survivors.

✳

After successfully guiding the winter 1910 patrol, Darrell would make only one more trip with the Mounties. It was a most unusual one, in that it came about unexpectedly and entailed travel by boat rather than dogsled. In Dawson, the Mounties were all in a bit of a tizzy when they learned that the federal Minister of the Interior, at the time one of the most senior positions in government, was to visit Dawson City. But rather than take the expected route to Dawson, this was to happen on a roundabout and rather complex journey, with the minister, Frank Oliver, first travelling by steamer down the Mackenzie River, then to Fort McPherson, and from there following a rugged trail to the Porcupine River and descending it to the Yukon River, and then back up the river to Dawson. The Mounties were naturally expected to escort him from Fort McPherson onward. The only problem was that none of them had any experience of the proposed route. Darrell explained in a letter to his family:

> I was roused from bed by the police who were very
> [eager] and asked me to take a patrol of police over the
> Peel River to meet Frank Oliver, the Minister of the
> Interior who is coming to Dawson . . . There is no one
> here who knows the way right through and so they
> came for me. However, there is nothing much to know
> for they have nothing to do but ascend the Porcupine
> and Bell Rivers . . . I did not give them any definite
> answer. Except to say that I was going myself and
> wanted to be there by the 1st of July which is nearly the
> same date as they want to reach McPherson . . . The
> party to go are all police but myself. We shall no doubt
> be blessed with numerous mosquitoes and a great deal
> of waiting, but to counterbalance that is the healthy life
> in hunting we shall get.

There is something rather hilarious about Darrell suddenly getting woken out of bed to lead panicked Mounties on a trip to meet their boss, the Minister of the Interior. They might not have been quite so eager to bring Darrell along if they'd known his views on federal politicians. Darrell, in his signature fashion, told them he wasn't going to make any special trip merely to meet a cabinet minister, but that he happened to want to return to the far North on his own account around the same date they wanted, and so would show them the way. This he did, guiding them north along the rivers and then over the portages across the mountains. But when they arrived at Fort McPherson, Darrell kept his word that he'd only come to explore: he bid the Mounties goodbye, then struck off on his own.

The Mounties were sorry to see him go. The police would have been only too happy to have sworn him in as a regular officer, but this Darrell declined. He saw himself as an explorer at heart and had little wish to wear a uniform or stick to any kind of regular schedule or employment. Instead, Darrell yearned again for the freedom of wild places, where he could roam to his heart's content and not merely guide between established posts. Once more, he found himself overcome by an irresistible longing deep within his soul to seek out and explore the vast uncharted wilderness that lay just beyond the horizon.

14

YEARNINGS

D arrell had been growing more restless than ever. What particularly vexed him was the thought that while he was stuck guiding police patrols or working on river steamers, others were busy exploring the last truly blank spots on the map. He followed the news of explorers and expeditions as closely as he could, whenever some scrap of newspaper happened to come into his hands. In 1909, headlines were dominated by the competing claims of two rival American explorers, Frederick Cook and Robert Peary, each of whom claimed to have made history by reaching the North Pole first. Of the two, Peary had the more powerful backers, as he'd been sponsored by *National Geographic* and the *New York Times*, and they soon attacked and destroyed Cook's credibility. Meanwhile Peary was hailed as a true American hero and showered with honours, while these same sponsors ensured that Peary's expedition records would be withheld from scrutiny and kept under wraps. There were, in fact, some suspicions right from the start that the bombastic Peary might also be a fraud: the daily distances he'd claimed to have covered in order to have reached the Pole after his last support party had turned back (which included the only people other than himself who could verify distances) were dramatically more—double in fact—than his best recorded speed when others were there to witness it.

But not until the 1980s were Peary's records finally made available for examination. Sure enough, they were highly dubious, to put it mildly, and perhaps even more damning, his actual expedition journal made no mention of ever reaching the Pole. Instead, a loose sheet of folded paper had been inserted into the diary making this claim.

Yet while Peary's deception fooled most observers at the time and continued to do so long afterwards, there was at least one person he couldn't fool: a lone wanderer in the Arctic named Hubert Darrell. Darrell, it turned out, could easily spot Peary's fraud from a mile away (or, in his case, thousands of miles away). But then he was one of the rare few who'd actually experienced what it was like to travel over the ice of the Arctic Ocean. Darrell recognized immediately the preposterous nature of Peary's claims to have covered vast distances in such a short time, and in a straight line, something Darrell knew was impossible given the rugged, chaotic nature of sea ice with pressure ridges and piles of ice heaved up everywhere. (Peary was also fifty-three years old, out of shape, and missing seven toes from frostbite.) These details, and the distances reported in the newspapers at the time, were all Darrell needed to see through Peary's con:

> Cook has been denounced as a fraud. I was positive from
> the first account that he was . . . If they should denounce

Perry, it would complete things to my satisfaction. I want to know by what means he knocked off 120 geographical miles in a straight line in 4 days without Bartlett's work when he could not do that distance with Bartlett's aid and less loads and more men. I've had too much to do with the Yankee to have faith in his oaths or honour especially when such a prize as the North Pole is almost within reach with no one to prove otherwise.

Peary had abruptly ordered Bartlett, the navigator who'd accompanied the expedition and knew how to work out latitude and longitude, to remain behind when they were within a few hundred kilometres of the Pole. The immense fame and fortune that accrued to Peary after he returned from the Arctic as the man who'd first reached the North Pole brings into sharp relief the irony of Darrell's life: Peary's fraud led him to be feted by all and sundry, while Darrell's real accomplishments attracted little notice.

But while Peary was far removed from Darrell's immediate sphere, a bigger thorn in his side continued to be his old nemesis, Harrison. Harrison's book, *In Search of a Polar Continent*, appeared in 1908. In it, the aristocratic chess-player Harrison depicted the wanderer Darrell as lazy and incompetent. Such personal slights and attacks on his integrity don't seem to have annoyed Darrell nearly as much as the fact that Harrison's maps were wrong and his geography shoddy. This to Darrell was the real unforgivable sin. He commented in a letter: "Harrison's map of main channels of Mackenzie is of no value . . . his way of making a map showing the river of uniform width all through is absurd . . . I can draw a map which of course won't stand for a moment in the eyes of the R. G. S. which will show a man every quarter mile of the distance to Herschel Island." RGS stands for Royal Geographical Society, which Harrison belonged to and with whose powerful president, Sir Clements Markham, he was friends.

Darrell further dismissed many of Harrison's stories of arctic travel as "absurd" and a sure indication that he'd didn't know much about what he was describing, particularly with regard to dogsled travel over sea ice. Darrell noted that the rugged, uneven nature of sea ice meant that any team of dogs would soon get "hung up in a quarter mile without human aid. Except in places where the ice happens to be smooth, which it is not for any distance." Yet Darrell conceded that Harrison would be believed in England and elsewhere, since "it all goes down well with gullible old fogey's that are to be found in some places. But those who know him up in the North don't lay much attention to his stories. His so-called survey of Red River McPherson Portage, created great amusement. It was very much wrong at the time."

Darrell's family were much less sanguine about Harrison's book and even thought they should explore suing him for libel. But Darrell saw the futility of a costly lawsuit against a man as well-connected as Harrison, although he wished that there was some way he could debunk Harrison's geography. It frustrated him to think that Harrison's flawed maps were winning praise in official circles, while his own more accurate maps that he made himself, as he put it, "would be thrown in the fire by the Royal Geographical Society." But Darrell knew anything he might say publicly against Harrison's maps would be dismissed as stemming from personal animosity. Darrell had also never personally explored the remote region east of the Husky Lakes that Harrison claimed to have charted.

Harrison meanwhile had also been doing his best to make sure Darrell struggled to find employment. On his return journey up the Mackenzie River by steamer, he'd been telling anyone who'd listen his negative opinion of Darrell and advising the traders not to hire him again. Although this doesn't seem to have had the desired effect: Darrell's old friend and employer, the independent fur trader James Nagle, wrote a letter to Darrell telling him about Harrison's scheming. He mentioned that he'd told Harrison off to the point the two men were no longer on speaking terms.

Ironically for someone who was always such a lone wolf, Darrell was actually very popular throughout the North. Quiet and easygoing as he was, he could get along with pretty much anyone he encountered: Dene and Inuit hunters, Métis trappers and fur traders, whaling captains and their crews, prospectors, and Mounties. And although he wasn't necessarily close with many people, Darrell had a surprisingly large circle of friends. Besides Nagle, his fur trade friends included Dan Cadzow, another independent trader well regarded throughout the North for his honesty. Darrell was especially good friends with the Métis trapper Joseph Jacquot and his wife, Sarah, with whom he sometimes travelled on fur trapping expeditions. Among the Mounties, his closest friends included the veteran travellers A.E. Forrest and William Dempster, and even the raw recruits, whom he thought too green for such long winter journeys, he eventually warmed up to, calling them "excellent" once they got the hang of things. Darrell also had quite a few friends among the farmers back in Manitoba, including William North and Abe Nichol, and he further kept up a friendly correspondence with both Amundsen and Stefansson.

In fact, despite Harrison's best efforts, as far as explorers went, Darrell's reputation meant that he was in high demand. Besides the Mounties, a Danish-American expedition seeking to explore more of the Arctic Sea, known as the Mikkelsen expedition, tried to recruit Darrell in 1906. But he foresaw (correctly as it turned out) trouble with their plans to travel over the ice as far as they intended, and he declined to join them. (The expedition ended up running into the exact problems Darrell predicted.) Then in 1910, while he was still in Dawson, Darrell began to receive letters from an aspiring American explorer named Harry V. Radford. Radford was a wealthy sport hunter from New York City and only twenty-nine years old, but his fortune had allowed him to travel extensively. This had included some sport hunting in the Northwest Territories, where he'd first learned of Darrell's extraordinary reputation. The stories he'd heard had convinced him that Darrell was just the man he needed.

But it turned out that Radford was notoriously short-tempered, boastful, arrogant, and fame-obsessed. He informed Darrell in a telegram sent to Dawson that he wished to make an epic exploratory journey similar to Hanbury's, spanning thousands of kilometres and several years. Though this was normally exactly the kind of thing that would appeal to Darrell's tastes, his experiences with Harrison had made him wary of upper-class sportsmen big on ambition but low on experience. Darrell wrote a letter to his father in April of 1910 explaining his dilemma:

The explorer Radford is bothering me a great deal. He seems bound to get me and I received a telegram from him yesterday. But . . . from what I hear of him he is a bore and very green. That is why I don't care to go with him because I can see no end of work and bother ahead. Of course, I may be mistaken but the people at McPherson saw him last summer and they don't give me a very high opinion of him as a man who can stand hardship.

In a bid to impress Darrell, Radford bragged in another letter about how on a recent sporting trip to Canada he'd bagged a wood bison weighing 2,400 pounds. But rather than impress Darrell, this annoyed him. The government had belatedly banned bison hunting since they were endangered. Radford had only been able to shoot one by paying an exorbitant fee to obtain a special licence. Darrell felt strongly that the law shouldn't make any exceptions.

But restless as he was and desperate for money, it wasn't easy to turn down the chance Radford offered. Indeed, Radford was so determined to get Darrell as a guide that he promised him he could be in charge of everything, including any other members of their party and even the details of when and where they'd explore. Yet still Darrell hesitated: he didn't trust Radford, who uncomfortably reminded him of another arrogant, well-to-do greenhorn, Harrison. From his friends at Fort McPherson, Darrell learned more about Radford, who'd passed through there on one of his hunting trips. He'd apparently already boasted to everyone at McPherson that the legendary lone wanderer Darrell was to be his guide.

To assuage Darrell's doubts, Radford arranged to have a missionary send Darrell a letter testifying to his good character. But given Darrell's views of missionaries, this did little to dispel his concerns. Radford also reiterated his promise that Darrell would be the "boss." On paper it seemed like the chance of a lifetime, but Darrell still didn't trust Radford and so refused his offer. In a letter to his family dated May 28, 1910, Darrell explained:

Radford has been very determined to get me . . . but I yesterday gave a final decisive refusal . . . I think it was a splendid opportunity to go as he was so keen on getting me that he wanted me to be the boss and have all the say . . . and whenever he had other men, they were to be under my orders, but somehow I could not bring myself to go.

It turned out that Darrell was right to trust his instincts. Radford's arrogance and quick temper would later prove disastrous. Unable to secure Darrell's services, Radford settled for a young Canadian woodsman named George Street as his guide. Together, the two of them took the conventional route north to Great Slave Lake. Along the way, Radford managed with his ceaseless boasting to annoy anyone they encountered. From Great Slave, Radford essentially just tried to imitate Hanbury by copying his route. But the trouble was he was no Hanbury, and Street was no Darrell. After they'd reached the Inuit lands near Hudson Bay and managed to persuade several Inuit to act as guides, Radford acted excessively insulting and arrogant—issuing orders and making everyone else (including Street) do all the hard work.

Radford's fatal mistake proved using a dogsled whip on his Inuit guides; he tried striking one across the face with it. This didn't go over all that well. The other Inuit stabbed Radford with their knives, slit his throat, then left him for dead on an ice floe. The unfortunate Street, who by all accounts was even-tempered, was nonetheless also killed in the same fashion in fear that he might otherwise try to retaliate.

The whole story eventually came to light when one of the Inuit guides, Akulack, returned to Hudson Bay and told the traders there what had happened. When the Mounties were belatedly informed, they declined to any press charges. The American Radford, it was felt, had only got what was coming to him (Street's unfortunate death notwithstanding), and that it would be wrong to apply western legal standards to the arctic wilderness. As the official Mounted Police report put it, "Everyone who came into contact with Mr. Radford has stated that his manner in dealing with the natives was most overbearing and injudicious and that they are not surprised by his meeting his end in the way that he did." The Mounties took a rather culturally enlightened view of things and concluded that the Inuit had merely acted "in accordance with the custom of their tribe," which was "that all quarrels and disputes are generally settled by the death of one of the combatants." So no charges were ever filed and that was the end of the matter—and the end of Radford.

Darrell never learned of any of this though: by the time it had happened, he'd already vanished. Overcome by his wander-lust, Darrell had made up his mind that he'd simply launch an expedition of his own. "I have a great yearning for Arctic travel all the time, pretty nearly as bad as wanting to go home," wrote

Darrell to his parents, giving voice to the inner conflict tearing at his soul. "Both require a little money," he explained, but the Arctic required less, so, he wrote, "don't be the least bit surprised if you hear I have gone on some outlandish journey." The place that particularly haunted his imagination and spoke to his lonely soul was that wild landscape near the fabled Coppermine River that he had glimpsed and partially explored years earlier on Hanbury's expedition. Ever since, its rugged beauty and utter remoteness had haunted his dreams. As Darrell put it himself in one of his letters to his family, "All my life as far back as I can remember I used to study the map and wish I could go there and now that I have seen it, I am more restless than ever. Lack of funds is the only thing keeping me away."

But funds or no funds, Darrell at last made up his mind that nothing could stop him. That summer of 1910, now thirty-six years of age, Darrell resolved that he'd get back into the true wilderness—far from any trading posts, mail delivery routes, or dogsled patrols—with one of his closest friends, the Métis trapper Joseph Jacquot, and Jacquot's wife, Sarah. The plan was for the three of them to set off by canoe from Fort McPherson and head east into the Husky Lakes region. This was the heart of the area that Harrison claimed to have mapped. It would be extra satisfaction then to prove his nemesis's maps were fanciful. Darrell and the Jacquots intended to do some prospecting together, then split up, before meeting back up again in the winter for their return journey to Fort McPherson.

From the tiny post of Arctic Red River on the Mackenzie River, the very place where five years earlier he'd socked Harrison in the face, Darrell penned what turned out to be his final letter to his family. He assured them "don't get alarmed if you do not hear from me for a long while . . . I expect to go somewhere but I can't tell yet . . . I have no time to write more, but will write next opportunity, which may be long while. . . . Goodbye and best love and hoping you are all well. From your affectionate son Hubert Darrell."

15

DISAPPEARANCE

Reconstructing Darrell's movements after this point gets more challenging: I'd come to the end of his surviving letters and journals, so there were no more of these to guide me. Now the real detective work began: I had to roll up my sleeves and plunge down several rabbit holes to find what I needed. It was clear that Darrell and the Jacquots had canoed down the Mackenzie River and then headed east into the Husky Lakes, which are actually a saltwater chain of maze-like bays connected to the Beaufort Sea. While paddling through these often-stormy lakes, on September 21, 1910, the Jacquots and Darrell split up as planned. The Jacquots went off trapping, while Darrell intended to press on farther to explore the little-known Anderson River. The Jacquots and Darrell intended to meet back up again near the same spot they parted two and a half months later, that is, by December 10.

But Darrell never showed up. At the time, there wasn't much reason for alarm: Darrell was known to change his plans, and it was normal for him to disappear for months or more only to turn up later at some far-flung place. Not for many months afterwards would anyone even begin to suspect something might have happened to him. A contributing factor in all this was that the Mounties themselves were still reeling from the loss of their officers on the patrol that same winter Darrell vanished.

In fact, it wasn't until the following summer that Darrell's continued absence started to raise concerns. One of the new Mounties assigned to Fort McPherson, Corporal J. Somers, drafted a report noting that Darrell had not been seen or heard from for a considerable time. His report indicated that the Jacquots had returned to the trading post by Christmas and that they'd last seen Darrell on the Husky Lakes. From there, it was known that Darrell had continued eastward along the Beaufort Sea, and that sometime in late October, after the sea froze, he'd actually visited a whaling schooner, the *Rosie H*, which was wintering at Baillie Island off the arctic coast.

From this ship, Darrell had obtained a supply of provisions. This suggested that Darrell was possibly intending to stick around somewhere for a longer period, perhaps even building a cabin to overwinter, as he'd done elsewhere in the past. At the ship, Darrell had left a note for the explorer Stefansson, who was expected to visit the *Rosie H* sometime that winter. When Stefansson later got the note, he reported that it indicated Darrell had indeed established a "permanent camp" somewhere up the Anderson River, but that he still intended to return to Fort McPherson that winter with the Jacquots. After leaving the ship, Darrell was seen heading back in the direction he came, toward the Anderson River's mouth, more than a hundred kilometres away. Somers's report contained no further information.

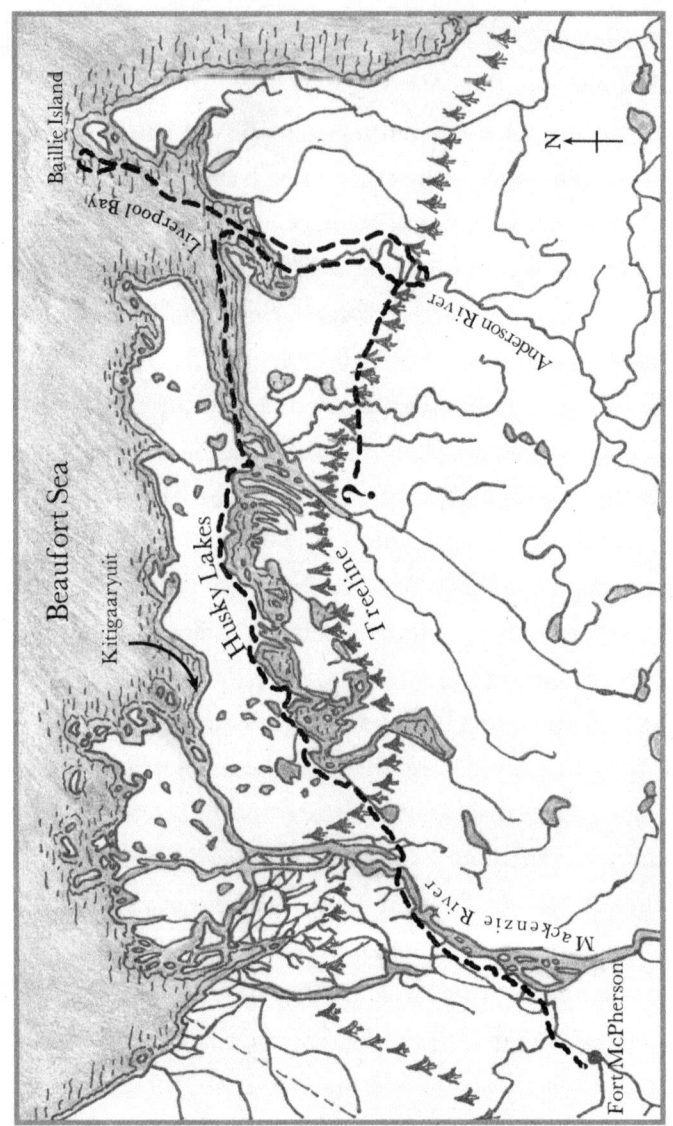

DARRELL'S LAST JOURNEY

Darrell left Fort McPherson in the summer of 1910, travelling by canoe east through the Husky Lakes, and eventually up the Anderson River. From there, he travelled to Baillie Island, back up the Anderson, and then overland west before vanishing.

When another month passed with no word of Darrell, some of his Fort McPherson friends, including the Jacquots, began to suspect the worse. If Darrell had chosen to overwinter in the interior to trap furs, naturally he'd be expected to return in summer to barter them at a trading post. But it'd now been nine months since anyone had seen or heard from him. At this time, coincidentally, a man who knew and respected Darrell happened to arrive at Fort McPherson: the famed gold rush poet Robert Service. It was Service who first brought the news of Darrell's disappearance to the outside world on his return to Dawson that same summer. The newspapers in Dawson and Alaska carried the story, with Alaska's *Fairbanks Daily Times* in their August 15, 1911, edition proclaiming "Hubert Darrell, Fearless Explorer in the Arctic Regions North of Alaska and Canada, Is Missing." The article reported:

> That Hubert Darrell, the famous Arctic explorer and musher, perished in the wilderness, is the belief of traders and prospectors in the region about the mouth of the Mackenzie River, where Darrell carried on his work last summer. He was last seen near Baillic island, east of the mouth of the Mackenzie, in October, and neither Indian nor white man has brought report of him since that time. News of the probable tragedy was brought here today by Robert Service, the Yukon author . . . Service stopped for a time at Fort MacPherson, where he secured what information he could in the matter.

Meanwhile the *Dawson Daily News* reported that "the disappearance of Hubert Darrell, the old time Klondiker . . . has caused the keenest regret among northerners." The paper praised Darrell as a "master explorer" famed throughout the North for his unmatched stamina and epic journeys. But despite Darrell's legendary abilities, the paper reported that it was now sadly the consensus among traders, trappers, and hunters that he must have perished, most likely from falling through a patch of weak ice—something that was an ever-present danger in travelling throughout the North.

These local stories were sent out over the telegram wire and soon picked up and carried by other newspapers across North America—each reprint, it seems, getting slightly less accurate. The *Montreal Star* carried it under the headline "Hubert Darrell, Explorer Missing: Arctic Investigator Has Not Been Heard from Since October Last." But the major papers treated Darrell's disappearance as relatively minor news, just one headline buried among many others. In contrast, given that he was a legend in the North, the Yukon and Alaskan papers reported on his disappearance at great length. Fortunately for my purposes of reconstructing Darrell's final journey, these local papers also had access to people who actually knew him.

Dawson's paper was able to obtain directly from Joseph Jacquot a detailed first-hand account of his last trip with Darrell. Jacquot, for his part, was reluctant to believe his good friend could really be gone, remarking, "if, as everybody seems inclined to believe, he is actually lost, it will be felt very keenly by his friends." Jacquot confirmed that Darrell's intention had been to "explore along the Anderson River on his own account." This sounds straightforward, but it actually speaks a great deal to Darrell's inner character: given that to do so, he'd rejected a well-paying offer from Radford to lead his expedition, all in favour of trying, for no pay, to disprove Harrison's claims to have mapped the Anderson River.

Jacquot recounted that they had travelled in two canoes, and that they also had with them four huskies in order to return by dog team in the winter. (Darrell of course would travel on foot.) Jacquot described his friend's great skills, including with a rifle, and also seemed to delight in telling the paper how fanciful they'd found Harrison's maps, which were missing major islands, bays, and rivers, while displaying others incorrectly. Darrell and the Jacquots had already covered well over three hundred kilometres together when they split up. Jacquot explained that he thought that it was getting too late in the season to push on, but that nothing would deter Darrell from venturing beyond Harrison's map. As Jacquot put it, "He had started on the trip with one object in view, and follow it out he would, in spite of all," which certainly sounds like Darrell, the man of indomitable spirit.

At the time they parted, Jacquot said Darrell was well equipped with both a rifle and a shotgun, plenty of ammunition, and enough provisions to last a month without resorting to hunting. Jacquot recalled, "My wife was the last to see Darrell as he went away; she walked across a point to watch him disappear into the distance on the farther side." When Darrell failed to show up later, the Jacquots had waited five additional days before starting their own return trek. But before they did so, at their camp they left a note for Darrell and a cache of frozen fish.

When word of Darrell's disappearance reached the bigger papers, his family were understandably alarmed. Until this point, it seems they hadn't been too worried by the long lapse of time since they'd last heard from him. Lengthy intervals between letters from Darrell was nothing new, and he'd mentioned in his last letter that they shouldn't be concerned if they didn't hear from him for a long while. With Hanbury, after all, he'd been gone over a year. But the headlines prompted Darrell's parents to write to the Mounties asking if they had more definite information on their son, or failing that, if the Fort McPherson patrol might be able to search for him.

This letter, with its sharp black ink written on faded yellow paper, was the first time I'd ever seen the handwriting of one of Darrell's parents. It had been written by his mother. The many letters that they'd sent over the years to their son in the wilderness, like the ones written by Agnes, haven't survived. Only some of Darrell's side of the correspondence partly survived, since it was sent to England and preserved there as a keepsake.

The letter from Darrell's mother to the Mounted Police I'd found in Ottawa in a box tucked away at Archives Canada. All of the historical records, case files, correspondence, and other material pertaining to the North-West Mounted Police, renamed in 1904 the Royal North-West Mounted Police (and later still the Royal Canadian Mounted Police), are kept at Archives Canada. The folder of material from the Hubert Darrell case file isn't very large—just a handful of papers. But it was a strange sensation to hold Mrs. Emily Darrell's actual letter in my hand: more than a century had elapsed since she'd written it, yet it was impossible not to feel the pathos in it. The shaky handwriting read: "Dear Sir, My husband and I are greatly disturbed at the reported loss of our son Hubert Darrell in the Mackenzie River district. And we should be most grateful if the R.N.W.M.P patrol in the region were directed to search for him or give us definite tidings. . . .

I hope I do not appear to dictate what should be done, but you can imagine our anxiety. We heard last from our son a year ago."

Separated as they may have been by circumstances, every indication is that the Darrell family nevertheless remained very close and affectionate. Darrell's many letters were always signed the same way, "from your affectionate son," and their contents clearly make plain his attachment to his parents and family. He often inquired after his sisters, and at one point even earnestly suggested that they should move to the farm in Manitoba and "become Canadians."

The Mounties replied promptly to Mrs. Darrell's letter. They forwarded her a copy of Corporal Somers's report and gently explained that it'd be impossible to launch any kind of search effort. But the Mounties also assured her that they didn't think Darrell was in any actual danger and that he'd likely soon turn up. Or as the officer put it in his response, an official copy of which was filed in the report I had wiped the dust off and read, "I think we shall hear from him later on, but it is quite impossible to account for the movements of the many who are penetrating the unexplored districts of the Canadian Northwest." Of course, it was true that the Mounties couldn't possibly mount an effective search operation. At that time they still had no aircraft of any description. They made only a single, hazardous patrol once a year from Dawson to Fort McPherson by dogsled—which Darrell himself had guided—and those officers didn't normally venture outside McPherson once they arrived there, though some did make the journey back and forth from Herschel Island. To venture far into uncharted regions as Darrell did was another matter entirely.

Meanwhile in Manitoba, Agnes was growing anxious, as was Charles. Charles wrote to the Mounties requesting permission to join any search for his brother, or at least to accompany the annual dogsled patrol to Fort McPherson where he could make further inquiries himself. There is something quietly heroic about Charles's plea: he had never so much as set foot in the North, but here he was volunteering to go thousands of kilometres into the frozen wilderness on a journey so hazardous the Mounties themselves had all perished on it just the year before, to assist in any way that he could in finding his brother.

The officer who received Charles's letter forwarded it to the RNWMP commissioner with the recommendation that permission be granted. The faded report that I pulled out of the old case file explained the officer's reasoning: "He will pay all his own expenses, and as he is a man accustomed to travel, I strongly recommend that permission be granted to him." It seems Charles, in his keenness to go, may have exaggerated his wilderness experience: he had certainly never been on a dogsled nor undertaken any arctic travel. On the other hand, he was a sturdy Manitoban farmer who'd done plenty of hunting around his homestead, so the Mounties granted his request.

Ultimately, though, Charles didn't end up leaving the farm. It may have been that on further reflection the thought of the long, daunting journey proved too much, or else the expense, for an indebted farmer, beyond reach. But most likely, when it was made clear to him that the Mounties couldn't undertake any kind of search, and would have their hands full with just the standard patrol, he at last realized the hopeless nature of the task. So Charles remained in Manitoba. In the meantime, with another long winter settling over the land, no further word would come from Fort McPherson until after the annual dogsled patrol reached there and then returned back to Dawson, which had a telegram station where news could be relayed to the outside world.

Darrell's family anxiously waited for the return of the patrol, hoping it'd bring good news. But it turned out that Darrell's old friend Jacquot, with two other trappers, completed the dogsled journey back to Dawson ahead of the Mounties in March 1912. So it fell to Jacquot to relay the sad news that nothing further had been heard of Darrell, and that all the fur traders in the North had given him up for lost. When this report went out from Dawson over the wire, it sparked more headlines. As before, the story was widely circulated, including as far afield as the *New York Times* and the *Los Angeles Times*. In Canada, a typical headline was the one that appeared in the *Kingston Whig-Standard*: "EXPLORER FEARED LOST. Hubert Darrell Not Heard From Since 1910." It added: "Hubert Darrell, the explorer, who went eastward in 1910, from the Mackenzie, has been given up for lost. No word has come from the explorer since his departure." After this, with no fresh clues to report, Darrell's disappearance dropped out of the news for a time.

✳

Back when I'd first started researching Darrell in earnest, I'd been a doctoral student at McMaster University. My actual Ph.D. research in history and archaeology had nothing to do with Darrell, as it dealt mainly with earlier time periods and the influence of Indigenous cultures on fur traders in the subarctic. But through the university I had access to all kinds of archival databases, including scans of old newspaper records. So many nights, when I probably should have been attending to my actual work, I was instead lost down digital gopher holes researching all the old news stories on Darrell's disappearance. What had completely absorbed my interest was the fact that, after months of no news, suddenly in September 1912 the papers were in a frenzy over Darrell again. Strange writing had been found on a tree in the remote area where Darrell had vanished. It was believed to be a message from him. The resulting story ran all over the North American papers:

TRACE OF MISSING ALASKAN EXPLORER
Indians Bring Probable Clue to Route Taken
by Hubert Darrell in 1910.
Sept. 5—Advices received at Dawson, Y.T., over the trail from the mouth of the McKenzie river, say that Indians brought in word to Fort McPherson that they had found strange writing on a tree east of the McKenzie delta, where Hubert Darrell, the Arctic explorer, was last seen. The Indians promised to bring in the writing on their next trading expedition.

The *Edmonton Journal* printed the news under a headline that proclaimed "Mysterious Writing Intimates Tragedy. Indians Tell of Marks on Tree Which May Indicate Explorer's Fate." Both the *New York Times* and the *New York Tribune* again carried the story as well, the latter under the headline "TRACES OF LOST EXPLORER, Writing on Trees Where Hubert Darrell Was Last Seen."

The report seemed almost too incredible to be true, more like something out of a pulp adventure novel or *Indiana Jones* than real life. But it turned out it was true, though given the glacial speed at which news trickled out of the far North, it'd take another year and a half for an Inuit trapper to reach the remote location, trace out the letters of the inscription, then make it back to an outpost for it to be read. Not until March 1914, with the return of the annual police patrol from Fort McPherson, did the details finally reach the outside world. The Mounties sadly reported that all hope for Darrell was definitely gone, and that he'd certainly perished alone in the wilderness. The inscription on the tree had apparently been his last words, and indicated that he'd been frozen in, or had his feet frozen. As usual, the newspaper stories were full of errors, making it difficult to disentangle what actually happened. The *Winnipeg Tribune* reported:

EXPLORER DARRELL GRIPPED BY DEADLY FROSTBITE
Dawson, Y.T. March 14—Joseph Jacquot, who has just arrived here, reports that the Rev. Harry Fry . . . found writing on a blaze of a tree on MacFarlane River by Herbert Darrell, the Englishman, formerly of Dawson, who was lost in that region while exploring. Darrell simply stated both his feet were frozen, and it is now conceded that he is dead. The last seen of Darrell was at Hutchison Bay.

This story, though, was obviously riddled with errors. Given the news needed to be relayed through so many different people from so far away, it was all a bit like a giant game of telephone. For one thing, Darrell's name was Hubert, not Herbert; there is no MacFarlane River in the Northwest Territories (he was in fact on the Anderson River); Reverend Fry wasn't the one who found the writing; and the last seen of Darrell wasn't on Hutchison Bay. The young reporter in Dawson who'd dashed off the story, apparently after interviewing the French-speaking Jacquot, had made numerous errors, which then got amplified and repeated by third-party editors after the story was sent out. Luckily, I found that an Alaskan newspaper, the *Juneau Empire*, had printed a more detailed version of this same report, which read:

> Joseph Jacquot, the old-time musher and trader of the Mackenzie country, who blew into town the other day from Fort McPherson . . . reports that Rev. Harry Fry, the Anglican missionary, has . . . found writing on a blaze on a tree on MacFarlane river bearing writing by Herbert Darrell . . . Darrell simply stated that he had frozen both his feet. Rev. Fry lost the copy he took, but I understand there was no other statement and no further trace of the man. It is conceded that he is dead.

While the story repeated many of the same mistakes as the *Winnipeg Tribune* article, it added the detail that the missionary, Reverend Fry, had apparently lost the copy he took of the tree inscription.

Given this much confusion, I'd hoped that the official report from the Mounties might clear things up. I found it in the same folder at the archives in Ottawa and blew the dust off it too. It was written by Corporal W. Hocking of the Fort McPherson detachment and dated March 6, 1914. Hocking's report stated:

Regarding Hubert Darrell, who perished near the Anderson River some three years ago. It was reported two years ago that some Eskimo had been in that district and had seen a stake blazed with some writing on it. They were asked by Mr. Stefansson [the explorer] to cut off the part with the writing on it on their next visit and bring it with them. I understand that the Eskimo have visited the district since then and have brought in a copy of what was written on the stake and gave it to the missionary at Kittegaryuit, an Eskimo village on the eastern branch of the Mackenzie River. Mr. Young of that mission says he had the paper but he left it down at the mission and he does not remember anything of what was written on it. Mr. Phillips of the H.B. co [Hudson's Bay Company], at that point says he read the paper and he thinks that Darrell mentions having been frozen twice and giving two dates, which Phillips does not remember. Mr. Darrell's signature was on the stake.

Although this report differed somewhat from the newspaper stories, the essential details seemed the same: the writing on the tree or stake had indeed been Darrell's, and it seemed to indicate that he'd been frozen twice, presumably from falling through the river ice attempting to cross it on his return trek to meet the Jacquots. In any case, there seemed little doubt that Darrell must have perished alone from hypothermia or frostbite. So that apparently ended the mystery. By the time the writing was transcribed, it'd already been three and half years since anyone had last seen Darrell. His friends in the North had long since accepted that the legendary lone wanderer had met his end.

Yet the mystery of Hubert Darrell is full of more twists than an arctic river, and fresh clues would soon emerge to complicate the picture.

16

MESSAGES FROM BEYOND

There was at least one person who still refused to believe Darrell was really gone: his fiancée, Agnes. In desperation, she'd written letters to Stefansson as well as Robert Service, asking if they could help mount a search for him. Service's reply isn't known, but Stefansson, writing back in the fall of 1912, tried to let Agnes down as gently as he could, telling her: "I think I shall be doing you the greatest kindness in my power by ending all suspense, so far as my opinion in the matter goes: I admired Darrell too much to concede any incompetence can have been the cause of his loss, which I fear is now only too certain: some serious accident or sudden illness must have come upon him." Stefansson added that if back in 1910 he'd had any reason to suspect Darrell had been in trouble, he gladly would have searched for him, but that by the time anyone realized the true nature of things, it was too late. He added: "I speak not only for myself and Dr. Anderson [another arctic explorer] but also Captain Wolki and Mr. Slate of the *Rosie H* when I say that had we realized the situation while yet there was any hope we should have made a search, not only for reasons of mere humanity but because of the admiration we all felt for his ability and character."

Stefansson, like the others, accepted that the discovery of the message on the tree had all but sealed the mystery of Darrell's disappearance. But not long afterwards, fresh reports emerged to muddy the waters. It turned out that the original vague reports of Darrell's inscription, which supposedly indicated that he'd fallen through the ice and frozen his feet, *were all wrong*. A new character had arrived on the Beaufort Sea, a strong-willed missionary named Isaac Stringer, who was an Anglican bishop appointed to the Yukon. Stringer was more diligent and meticulous than his predecessors, and he took the trouble to actually examine for himself the copy of the inscription found on the tree. Stringer interpreted some of the transcribed letters differently than had been done previously. This made Darrell's message differ substantially from what had been reported, though given years had passed since anyone had seen him, it was still assumed that Darrell must have suffered some fatal accident. The Alaskan newspaper the *Nome Daily Nugget* carried the story of Stringer's findings:

> What seems to be definite indication of the fate of Hubert Darrell, well-known Arctic explorer and former Klondike miner and prospector, was secured recently on the Arctic coast by Bishop Stringer. . . . Two or three years ago natives brought in word that they had found an inscription on a tree in that locality which they took to be his farewell message. Bishop Stringer this summer

met the natives who saw the inscription and had them show him a copy. They could not read English, but had made a copy of the letters as well as they could. The Bishop reports that . . . Darrell perished after the inscription was written and that at the time of the writing the man was in no danger . . . Bishop Stringer spent many hours with the natives who saw him alive. He had his camp on the Anderson river . . . In the following spring a visiting Eskimo found Darrell had left his camp, and on a tree he made a copy of the following inscription:

1910
Got frozen 112
October 4th
Leave here
today November 24
Westward
For Mackenzie
River

Bishop Stringer interpreted this to read "1910 Got frozen in Oct. 4th Leave here today November 24 westward for Mackenzie river." The story added: "Darrell left his camp and was never seen again."

This more careful transcription of Darrell's last note considerably changes things. It never quite seemed to make much sense how Darrell was supposed to have fallen in a river, frozen his feet twice, then taken the time to write out a note on a tree. But then the Mounties and others who'd relayed that information were getting it at best second- or even third-hand. Nor did any of their accounts inspire much confidence that they really knew what they were talking about. The official report by the Mounties noted that when their officer had asked Reverend Young, one of the missionaries who'd seen the transcription, about it, the reverend didn't even remember what it'd said. It was a fur trader, Phillips, who'd volunteered the information that the transcribed message had indicated Darrell had been frozen in. These vague, hazy reports were apparently accepted by the Mounties as more or less fact, and the matter was never followed up. After all, hunters, trappers, and prospectors disappeared regularly in the wilderness, so no one troubled themselves too much about the exact circumstances.

But Bishop Stringer, in the course of his own travels along the arctic coast, had found the whole mystery of the tree message quite curious. That errors might occur is only too easy to imagine: by the time the writing was found, it was already more than a year old and probably hard to make out. On top of that, the Inuit hunters who came upon it didn't themselves know how to read, but had tried their best to copy what they saw. Stringer interpreted the transcribed numbers "112" as actually having been two letters, *I* and *N* making the word *in*, so that it would in fact read "Got frozen in Oct. 4th Leave here today November 24 westward for Mackenzie river." This makes much more sense compared to the original supposition that Darrell had been referring to himself getting frozen twice, or somehow freezing his feet twice. Instead, it seems he was actually recording the date the Anderson River froze up (October 4, which would also make sense) and then the date of his departure westward to rendezvous with his friends, the Jacquots.

But if so, why did he wait so long between the date of the freeze-up, October 4, and the beginning of his overland trek through the woods and tundra back to meet his friends? Perhaps he'd been finishing his cabin? Another, bigger question was: if Darrell hadn't perished of hypothermia or frostbite, as the newspaper headlines had erroneously reported based on the flawed transcription of his note, what had happened to him? It never did seem all that likely that a man as capable and highly experienced as Darrell, who'd travelled alone across many thousands of kilometres of arctic and subarctic terrain, had fallen victim to such a novice mistake as freezing his feet. But even with Stringer's more accurate transcription, the general assumption remained unchanged among both the Mounties and the press that Darrell must have succumbed to falling through ice or hypothermia. As one December 1917 headline put it, "Explorer Believed to Have Perished in Arctic Region: Hubert Darrell, Former Klondyke Miner and Trapper, Probably Succumbed to the Rigors of the Far Northern Climate."

That, as it happened, was one of the last times Darrell's disappearance would ever make the news. With no further clues turning up, the whole mystery dropped out of the headlines for good. The Mounties made no further inquiries, his family and friends accepted he was gone, and even Agnes at last gave Darrell up for lost.

But as I studied the faded records and musty documents, I kept thinking of all the lingering questions that remained. For one thing, it occurred to me that, oddly enough, no one had ever actually gone and searched for Darrell. This was unlike Franklin, whose disappearance in the Arctic had launched a great many expeditions, or Colonel Percy Fawcett in the Amazon jungle, another lost explorer whose disappearance triggered numerous searches. Of course, the circumstances were different: Franklin had two whole crews of Royal Navy sailors with him when he vanished, and even Fawcett had been part of a party of three. Darrell, on the other hand, was a solitary explorer and therefore much less of a priority. The location where he'd vanished, too, was exceedingly remote, lying far from the nearest outpost of any kind. The passing Inuit trappers who'd later found the writing on the tree didn't even get back to the spot for another year or so.

What seemed especially intriguing to me was that Darrell had apparently built a cabin, and that no one had bothered to look for it. Stefansson had reported, based on the letter that he'd received, that Darrell had established a "permanent camp" somewhere up the Anderson River. For an experienced and hardy woodsman like Darrell to throw together a tiny, crude log cabin wasn't difficult, and could be done in little more than a week. Jacquot, for example, stated that he'd built a cabin for Sarah and himself near the Husky Lakes while they trapped there and waited for Darrell's return. In the past, Darrell had often built small cabins to overwinter in.

It'd been more than a century since Darrell's disappearance, but given the northern latitude and cold climate, the thought occurred to me that the ruins of his cabin might still be there, and perhaps even additional clues to his ultimate fate. Having pieced together the fragments of Darrell's life through his letters, journals, and whatever else I could dig up, I felt it was time for my investigation to move into a new and more active phase: locating his cabin. I liked nothing better than canoeing remote rivers already, so I resolved to set off into the wilderness to search for it.

PART II

17

FADED TRACES

Only once on any of my past adventures had I ever come across any tangible trace of Darrell. Having studied his diaries and letters, it often felt strange to me that I had almost no idea what he looked like. Forgotten by history as he was, there was no known photograph of him in any museum or published book. But in fact, Darrell did own a camera: he mentions it in his writings, and that he carried it with him on his sled or canoe. Agnes, of course, had photographs of him, but as her much younger sister, Margaret Dudley, later explained, Agnes destroyed all these shortly before her death. I had tried to find photographs of Darrell by ransacking various archival collections, but nothing ever turned up. I even once paid rather more than I would have liked for a copy of a collection of the explorer Amundsen's photographs, which included ones he'd taken on his Northwest Passage voyage. I'd hoped perhaps he might have snapped one of Darrell when he'd visited his frozen ship: alas, no such luck. Similar efforts I made with Hanbury's and Harrison's records of their travels likewise yielded nothing. (Darrell likely does appear in some of Hanbury's expedition photos, but only as an indistinguishable figure in the background.)

Then quite unexpectedly, when prepping for a new solo journey of my own, I happened to stumble upon an actual portrait of Darrell, which still remains the only clear photograph I've ever seen of him. At the time, May 2017, I was in the northern Yukon at a little place called Eagle Plains. This isolated outpost lies deep in the Yukon's wilderness, just off the narrow road styled the Dempster Highway. Established in 1978 to service the newly opened road, it consists of a single compound complete with gas station, motel, garage, saloon, and cafeteria. It's the only inhabited place between Dawson City (more than four hundred kilometres to the south) and Fort McPherson (almost two hundred kilometres to the north), that is, if a fluctuating population of eight or nine individuals counts. Outside the compound, a faded sign reads "Eagle Plains Hotel: An Oasis in the Wilderness." When I first strolled into it, it felt like I had passed through some magic portal back to 1978: this wonderful place looks (and smells) like it hasn't been remodelled or changed since the doors first opened. Along the wall stood a pay phone, vintage vending machines, and faded highway maps. Dimly lit corridors with worn carpets led to motel rooms and, most wondrous of all, to a grand saloon decked to the rafters with mounted animal heads and northern wildlife of all kinds: wolverines, grizzly bears, dall sheep, muskoxen, and others.

Interspersed with mounted animals, both in the saloon, adjacent lobby, and hallways, were black-and-white photographs showcasing the Yukon's past: the glory days of the gold rush, old-time prospectors and grizzled trappers, the death photo of the notorious Mad Trapper (shot and killed not far from Eagle Plains in the 1930s), and the men of the "Lost Patrol." As I examined all these relics, the musty, dimly lit atmosphere of the deserted place seemed to almost lull me into a trance, and I soon lost myself wandering from dusty wall to dusty wall squinting at old photographs. Tucked away in a corner, where it'd be missed by nine out of ten people who happened to walk by, hung a faded, grainy black and-white image of a seated, sharply dressed man with a striking faraway look in his eyes. I almost fell over when I read the caption: "Hubert Darrell, disappeared, 1910, Anderson River."

Staring at the portrait sent a chill down my spine: it felt as if I were looking at a ghost that had been haunting me for years. *Could this really be Hubert Darrell?* How did such a photograph come to be here? And how was anyone to know if that even was Darrell? In the photograph's corner was a second faded caption on a yellowed square of paper. It read "Hubert Darrell was a trailbreaker on the patrols of 1907–08 and 1909–10. He accompanied a police patrol across the Richardson Mountains in the summer of 1910. (Photo courtesy of Stephen North.)"

I recognized that name, but couldn't immediately place it. At the time, I had to leave on a four-thousand-kilometre solo journey across the Arctic, so I couldn't attend to the matter at once. But four months later, after I'd completed my journey and got back home to northern Ontario, I realized where I'd seen that name before. Back when Darrell had lived on the farm in Manitoba, one of his closest farm friends had been William North. And William North later had a son named Stephen

North: the same name as the person credited with supplying the photograph.

The collection of photos and historical curios assembled in Eagle Plains, I already knew from what I had read there, had been put together by the noted Yukon historian Dick North (no relation to Stephen North) when it'd first opened. I was familiar with Dick North's work, as he'd written several books on Jack London's experience in the Klondike and also on the Mounties. His latter research on the Mounties undoubtedly would have led to him learning about Darrell. So it was clear that, diligent historian that Dick North was, somehow or other he must have gotten in contact with someone in Birtle who'd put him in touch with Stephen North, who'd evidently supplied him with the only known photograph of Darrell.

The intermediary between Dick North in the Yukon and Stephen North in Birtle, I felt certain, must have been Peter Lorenz Neufeld. It was Neufeld who'd written that brief biographic entry on Darrell that had first caught my eye back on that memorable Friday night in 2011. Neufeld was a teacher, bus driver, school board trustee, and amateur historian from southwestern Manitoba who'd authored many articles and several books on prairie history. As a Manitoban farm boy himself, Neufeld had looked on Darrell as something of an unsung local hero who never got the credit he deserved. Besides the entry on Darrell I'd first encountered, Neufeld had written several stories in the 1970s and early 1980s on Darrell as part of a weekly column he penned for the *Brandon Sun* and other local papers. I'd obtained copies of these articles, which, although full of admiration for Darrell, were not always accurate. More than once I got lost down a false trail based on mistakes made in Neufeld's well-meaning old articles. (He thought that Darrell had come to Canada in 1882, that Harrison was an American, that Darrell had discovered valuable gold or copper deposits only for others to get the credit, that he was Hanbury's guide instead of merely his assistant, et cetera.) But Neufeld had produced some first-rate work in his attempts to find any surviving trace of Darrell in Birtle. By that time, the old farmstead had already burned down, and Charles and Agnes were already dead.

Neufeld found that very few people even in the 1970s in Birtle had any idea at all who Hubert Darrell was. However, an exception was a man Neufeld mentioned in one of his newspaper columns: Stephen North, the son of Darrell's old Birtle friend William North. Neufeld corresponded with him, and Stephen related what he knew second-hand from his father about Darrell. Stephen had explained, "My father and Hubert hit it off very well from the start. He was an extraordinarily fine man. I've talked to many people who knew him well, and that was the general consensus. Physically rather short but strongly built—very like his brother—with a very direct gaze. He was an extremely quiet and retiring man, not given to making friends quickly, and possessed an almost Thoreauvian honesty."

It seemed clear then that the photograph in Eagle Plains could only have originated from this same Stephen North. The photo would almost certainly have been taken some time in 1904–05, when Darrell returned to help Charles on the farm and he was either thirty or thirty-one years old. There was in fact, as I learned from my subsequent research, a photography studio operating in Birtle in 1904–05, which by that time had grown from a dusty farmers' crossroads to a bustling little prairie village. The photograph certainly seems as if it was taken in a studio: Darrell appears dressed in his Sunday best, clean-shaven, hair cut short and combed, and seated. Most of the time, of course, Darrell never looked anything like that—in the North, he generally worn a caribou-skin coat and didn't have time for shaving or haircuts. Amundsen had described his face as blackened by soot from campfires, and undoubtedly it was blasted by arctic winds and frostnip. But the one feature that remains unchanged and suggests the explorer is his eyes: he has that faraway look of one under the spell of the beyond. Stephen North had alluded to Darrell's "very direct gaze."

Neufeld, for his part, also seems to have tried to unearth photographs of Darrell, but without any success, other than perhaps the portrait that ended up in Eagle Plains. He did, however, report that he got in touch with one of the only other people still alive in the 1970s who'd remembered Darrell from Birtle—Agnes's little sister, Margaret Dudley. Neufeld wrote to her asking if by chance she had any photographs or other material pertaining to Darrell. But she replied, "I have snaps of Charlie but was too young to have a camera when Hubert was home. As a child, I liked both the Darrells; and can vaguely recall what Hubert looked like—but very vaguely." She again explained that her sister Agnes had destroyed all Darrell's photographs and letters shortly before her own death, adding, "I recall that Hubert sent my sister maps from time to time— But she destroyed everything." Margaret Dudley passed away in 1980, Neufeld in 1992, and Stephen North in 1993. So by the time I arrived on the scene, it was far too late to have tracked any of these people down in the flesh—but I followed their paper trails as well as I could.

Despite much searching, at the time of writing, that grainy photograph in Eagle Plains is still the only one of Darrell that I've ever found. But I'm convinced that others still exist—likely forgotten, collecting dust in an old attic somewhere. Hopefully one day they'll come to light. On that same note, photographs both of Darrell and ones taken by him were probably at the old farmhouse in Birtle, yet when it burned down not long after Charles's death these would have been lost, too.

In any case, having accidentally stumbled upon that photograph of Darrell in Eagle Plains, and then traced its origin and satisfied myself that it was authentic, I had followed this up the next year, 2018, by attempting to rustle up any other traces of Darrell in the Yukon and the Northwest Territories. Slim as the chances were, I hoped there might perhaps be some oral tradition that had survived of him. What I had in mind specifically was to interview as many elderly folks as I could in areas Darrell once passed through. The resulting trip saw me with two friends visiting Eagle Plains again (still the same old unchanged place), then Fort McPherson, where I chatted with whomever I could find that looked at least over the age of eighty. I made similar inquiries in Tsiigehtchic, Inuvik, and Tuktoyaktuk. But nowhere did I find anyone who'd ever heard of him. This of course was to be expected, given that he'd been a lone wanderer who'd never stayed put anywhere for long. If even in Birtle he'd been forgotten, I didn't expect anyone to know of him in places he'd spent even less time, particularly since it'd been over a century ago. But the trip was by no means a failure: even if I hadn't learned anything new on Darrell, I ended up acquiring much valuable information on other topics, which I felt might indirectly be of use to making sense of Darrell's story.

I listened with fascination to many accounts told to me by Gwich'in and Inuvialuit elders, which included tales of both grizzly and polar bear attacks, plane crashes in the Canadian wilderness, travelling by dogsled across sea ice, trapping wolverines, the ancient feuds between the Inuit and the Dene, the murderous Mad Trapper, and how best to stalk a polar bear. The most fruitful conversations I had were in Tuktoyaktuk, an Inuvialuit community on the Beaufort Sea coast. (The Inuvialuit are a western branch of Inuit.) Here I met with eighty-three-year-old Billy Jacobson, an Inuvialuit elder with a lifetime of hunting and trapping experience and extensive knowledge of local flora and fauna. Seated at his kitchen table, I listened to his tales with great interest, for he was regarded as one of the best hunters in all of Tuktoyaktuk. He even showed me the gun he'd used to fell many a polar bear. Of even greater interest to me, though, was when he told me that he'd once spotted perhaps the rarest bird in the world: the critically endangered Eskimo curlew. This ultra-elusive species is generally believed to be extinct, with the last confirmed one found in the 1960s. These birds had once nested in a small, remote area of the western Canadian Arctic. Jacobson said back in 1990 he'd seen a pair of them while on the Anderson River—the same isolated river, coincidentally, Darrell vanished on.

I asked Jacobson about any old cabins on the Anderson River, or anything else he could tell me about it. The lower section of the river he knew well, though not the inaccessible upper part where its course is lost among rapids and canyons. He'd once trapped and hunted on the lower part: accessing this part of the river was possible by motorboat or snowmobile from the Arctic Ocean. I had earlier met another local couple, James and Maureen Pokiak, who'd once actually had a cabin on the Anderson River's lower section. They told me they hadn't been back to it in almost two decades, but they were able to show me on a map precisely where we might find its ruins. But whether Darrell's cabin was to be found there or not, no one could say.

To round out our fact-finding mission, I also spoke with bush pilots, outfitters, and anyone else I could about the Anderson River. Most knew nothing about it, other than that it was a very dangerous waterway with a bad reputation for some past drownings on it. Fortified with this knowledge, we set off for it.

18

INTO THE UNKNOWN

B ased on what threadbare information I possessed, I figured that logically Darrell would not have made his cabin too close to the coast, where the river's tidal waters would be too salty for drinking. As well, close to the arctic coast there is no forest cover, just exposed, windswept tundra. So clearly building a cabin somewhere without trees would be a non-starter. On the other hand, I was certain that Darrell would not have paddled a canoe too far up the river's swift current, and certainly not beyond any of the rapids or treacherous canyons. That meant his cabin had to be somewhere after the river's last rapid but before the end of the treeline and salty water—leaving a search area of approximately 160 kilometres. This was substantial, to say the least.

The question was how best to search for it. The river's isolated location north of the Arctic Circle means there are no roads within hundreds of miles of it. If money were no object, the easiest method would be to charter a helicopter and fly over the river, keeping an eye out for any ruins poking out of the spruce

ANDERSON RIVER

forest. But if the cabin had collapsed and been grown over with willow bushes, it might not be visible from the air, and in any case, a helicopter charter was utterly beyond my budget. One alternative would be to try to hire a motorboat out of Tuktoyaktuk, and then make the lengthy and hazardous journey along the Beaufort Sea to the Anderson River's mouth, then go up it. But if there were shallows, rocks, or rapids, a motorboat might have difficulty getting beyond those points. A third option was to fly by bush plane somewhere in the Anderson River's upper watershed, get dropped on a lake there, then canoe the river, descending it to the Beaufort Sea. Bush planes are much less costly than helicopter charters, but they're limited in where they can safely land: only on deep water free of obstructions. As such, it wouldn't be possible to land on the Anderson River's meandering, rapid-filled upper course. But this I didn't mind, since I would be happy to make a longer journey and get the chance to explore more, simply as a bonus. So I went with this plan and set things in motion for the summer of 2019.

※

When I arrived in Yellowknife, I checked into the Day's Inn. It's true that it's a touch fancy, but such extravagances seemed warranted since I'd soon be roughing it. I waited there for my expedition partner to arrive, who was coming in on a different flight. Normally I do most of my expeditions alone, and while there would be a sort of poetic aptness in setting off solo after someone who was himself a solo explorer, my goal was to solve a mystery, not engage in romanticism. Two heads are better than one, and

Hauling a sled while trekking on snowshoes in the Yukon, retracing another of Darrell's old routes. PHOTO CREDIT: Adam Shoalts

Chuck Brill beside the floatplane in Norman Wells, preparing for our 2019 expedition to the Anderson River in the Northwest Territories. PHOTO CREDIT: Adam Shoalts

The ruins of a cabin built in 1911 by a trio of prospectors, including George Douglas, on the Dease River in the Northwest Territories. Finding and inspecting these ruins from just a year after Darrell vanished provided an ideal template for gauging the weathering and conditioning of any cabins associated with Darrell. PHOTO CREDIT: Adam Shoalts

One of our camps along the upper tributaries of the Anderson River. PHOTO CREDIT: Chuck Brill

Paddling on another wet, snowy day across lakes in the Anderson River's upper watershed. PHOTO CREDIT: Adam Shoalts

Chuck exploring a cave along a tributary of the Anderson River.
PHOTO CREDIT: Adam Shoalts

Scouting ahead in one of the Anderson River's many canyons.
PHOTO CREDIT: Chuck Brill

Paddling rapids on a cold, wet day. PHOTO CREDIT: Adam Shoalts

Chuck with the so-called "unknown" fish, the inconnu.

PHOTO CREDIT: Adam Shoalts

Guiding our canoe with rope down a shallow stretch of rocky rapids.

PHOTO CREDIT: Chuck Brill

"Chuck and I stared in wonder at a great bull moose standing on a willowy shore, looking for all the world like the king of the forest." PHOTO CREDIT: Adam Shoalts

A muskox staring at Chuck along the Anderson River. "Shaggy horned muskoxen roamed the banks browsing on willows. All of these animals would pause and stare at us curiously . . ." PHOTO CREDIT: Adam Shoalts

The ruins of an old cabin Chuck and I found on the Anderson River, near where Darrell disappeared in 1910. PHOTO CREDIT: Adam Shoalts

"The river had widened out to about half a kilometre, while enclosing it were rugged hills ablaze with fall colours: scarlet-red bushes of dwarf birch, bearberry, and arctic blueberries, mixed up with golden streaks from the aspens and willows and the more sombre hues of the spruces."
PHOTO CREDIT: Chuck Brill

Part of the enormous landslide that buried the Smoke River, which we spotted from the floatplane. PHOTO CREDIT: Chuck Brill

Hauling our canoe up and over a beaver dam on the Smoke River. PHOTO CREDIT: Chuck Brill

two sets of eyes can see twice as much. But when searching for a lost explorer's cabin in the middle of nowhere, it's crucial to choose the right partner. I needed someone who was steady, cool under pressure, and blessed with a sharp eye. We would be heading directly into polar bear territory, too, so it was also vital that it was someone I could easily outrun, if need be.

Three hours later the man himself appeared: Chuck Brill. Some years earlier he'd sent me an email inquiring about joining me on an expedition. I deferred at the time, but then a few years later, in June 2015, I happened to be embarking on a fresh expedition into the blackfly-infested swamps of the Hudson Bay Lowlands, and I needed a partner to help split the costs of a bush plane charter. So out of the blue I emailed Chuck, explaining that it promised to be a miserable time bushwhacking upstream through bug-filled alder swamps and logjams in the middle of nowhere. He responded enthusiastically, and a week later I picked him up at the Timmins airport in northern Ontario. From there, a short drive took us to the waiting bush plane, which we promptly boarded for Hudson Bay. For the next two weeks, we didn't see another soul other than each other, and by the end of it, I knew I'd found a perfect wilderness companion.

Chuck had grown up in Pennsylvania, where he'd hunted, fished, and camped from childhood on. He'd then gone off to college in the Adirondacks, studying ecology and in his free time competing in whitewater canoe races. After graduation, he'd travelled widely across the United States, including Alaska, and eventually he settled down in California. There he'd gone into real estate, married, and raised two children. When his son was growing up, he'd been a scout master of their troop, leading their camping trips. Chuck was twenty-seven years older than me, but despite this age gap, as the saying goes, we got along like two peas in a pod, and before our first adventure together had even finished, we were already planning more. The next year we went upriver in the Northwest Territories.

Among the traits that made Chuck a great adventure companion was his love of fishing, which meant fresh fish to roast over our campfire practically every night. He was also a great technical paddler, a legacy of his whitewater racing days. But more than these skills, what I really prized in Chuck was his level-headedness, rock-like reliability, unwavering grit and good nature, and, above all, a shared appreciation for the magic of wild places. When I'd been getting ready to embark on my solo journey across Canada's Arctic, Chuck had helped me out again by assisting in delivering my canoe to the northern Yukon, where he'd been with me when I'd stumbled upon Darrell's photograph. He'd also come with me, as well as his friend Mark, on my research trip to Tuktoyaktuk and other communities, and it was at that time the two of us had begun planning for our anticipated Anderson River expedition.

At the motel in Yellowknife, we went over our supplies. Each of us had our own tent, sleeping bag, rain gear and warm clothing, two pairs of footwear, camera, spare batteries, compass, maps, knives, first aid kit, and miscellaneous other survival gear. We stored these items in waterproof liners inside our backpacks. We also had two large plastic barrels that held our food rations: mainly oatmeal, freeze-dried meals, granola bars, jerky, and trail mix. Our other gear consisted of three paddles, two life jackets, bear spray, and a twelve-gauge shotgun. Usually, I never carried any firearms on my expeditions, but Chuck had a somewhat more American take on these matters, so I deferred to him.

Early the next morning, we flew three hundred kilometres north to Norman Wells, a small community on the banks of the Mackenzie River, where we were to meet our bush pilot and obtain a canoe. At the airline company's base, adorning one wall was a huge aviation map, which showcased the almost inconceivable vastness of the northern wilderness, spreading as it does across thousands of kilometres from Alaska to Hudson Bay. Within this massive district are more lakes than people. It's a land of primeval forests, windswept tundra, wild mountains, raging rivers, and trackless subarctic swamps—all once the wandering grounds of Hubert Darrell. Staring at the sprawling map on the wall really impressed upon one the awesome immensity of those vast solitudes. Even today, as I well knew, one can wander for months and months in these lonely places without so much as seeing another soul.

It was into the heart of this wilderness that Chuck and I were heading, far from any other people, roads, or cell reception. The plan was to fly by bush plane another 230 kilometres north, which would take us beyond the Arctic Circle, and then have the pilot drop us on a remote lake. From there, we'd canoe six hundred kilometres, through lakes and rivers, all the way out to the Beaufort Sea. The last half of our route would take us down the mysterious Anderson River, of which even today little is known. The imperfect maps and satellite imagery we'd obtained of it suggested that its upper course was filled with potentially dangerous canyons, falls, and rapids. Once we got through these obstacles, we'd search for any ruins of a cabin, then after reaching the sea, get picked up by bush plane.

After we filled out some information at the office on our height, weight, eye colour, et cetera, in case we disappeared ourselves, we headed out. Our enterprising pilot was a young man of about my age named Simon. Originally from Quebec, he'd been flying bush planes here for the past four years. But he'd never flown to where we were headed. The eighteen-foot canoe we secured to the single-engine plane's aluminum pontoon. Then, having weighed all our gear and stashed it and extra fuel aboard the plane, we took off from the small lake on the outskirts of town that functioned as the runway.

Bush plane flights are never particularly comfortable unless you like the roar and rattle of an engine that mostly rules out any conversation or quiet reflection. I kept my gaze fixed out the window at the seemingly limitless wild landscape passing beneath us: rugged spruce-clad hills, trackless muskeg, meandering rivers, and dark lakes. On a map, this whole vast area of the Northwest Territories appears like someone dripped blue paint all over the place: there are tens of thousands of lakes, most nameless. When we reached the north end of a large lake, Simon circled round, repeating his circling three more times to ensure himself that the water below was deep enough for a safe landing. Then he brought the plane down on it: we bounced off the water once, then skidded to a stop right near a willow-lined island. Chuck and I climbed out onto the bobbing pontoon and unstrapped the canoe from it. While one of us held the canoe fast, the other carefully loaded our gear into it.

Once we'd paddled a short distance away, we heard the plane's engine roar back to life and turned to see Simon waving through his window. The plane rapidly built up speed across the open water, lifted into the air, then disappeared into the clouds. With the drone of its engine fading away, silence took over. It was August 12 already, and we had hundreds of kilometres ahead of us. Some might think that it was already too late in the year to be setting off on such a journey, but given how intense July clouds of blackflies and mosquitoes are in the subarctic, both Chuck and I considered it a happy trade-off to have fewer bugs but colder conditions. Darrell, I figured, would have agreed.

What made us think that it might be possible to find Darrell's cabin ruins—despite the passage of more than a century—was the fact that Chuck and I had actually already found a crumbling cabin from Darrell's era deep in the wilderness of the Northwest Territories. Three years earlier, the two of us had made a canoe journey retracing the steps of an old-time prospector, George Douglas. Douglas had ventured up the isolated Dease River with two companions back in 1911. There they'd built themselves a log cabin to overwinter in, before returning the next spring. Armed with Douglas's account of his travels and his maps, when Chuck and I reached the spot in the river that seemed to correspond to the site of their cabin, we'd landed our canoe and pushed into the spruce forest. We didn't have to go very far before we beheld the decaying remnants of Douglas's cabin from more than a hundred years ago.

The roof had collapsed completely, doubtless from the heavy snowfalls. But the walls were still partly standing. In more southern latitudes, a cabin like this would never last: the greater humidity would cause the logs to rot entirely away, or at best become little more than an unrecognizable mouldering pile. But north of the Arctic Circle, the colder conditions mean preservation is much better. Inspecting this abandoned cabin, built only a year after Darrell's disappearance, provided us with an excellent template for gauging the approximate age of any other historical cabins we might stumble upon. On the other hand, in searching for Darrell's cabin we didn't have journals or maps to guide us, so it was bound to be a little like looking for a needle in a haystack. We'd simply have to do our best to scan both riverbanks for any hint of something made by human hands.

But that was a problem for another day. For the moment, we beached our canoe on a willowy shore and in the twilight of an arctic night made camp on a slight ridge. The wild laughter of a loon echoed from somewhere across the lake as I stretched out in my sleeping bag.

19

PATHLESS PLACES

To reach the Anderson River, we had to paddle first through more than a dozen lakes, ranging from weedy ponds to vast whitecapped expanses that tested our abilities, while also following interconnecting creeks. Most of these waterways weren't labelled on any of the maps we were carrying, but navigating was simple enough: in principle all we had to do was keep heading in a northerly direction, finding the outlets from each lake where it flowed into a creek connecting to the next one. Eventually they would all drain into the Anderson River's main stem. On a satellite image, the Anderson River appears like a crooked tree, with countless smaller branches joining it. We were now on those upper branches, working our way down to the main trunk.

The weather was rather dreary, with frequent rain and sleet and temperatures hovering only a few degrees above freezing. But Chuck and I were too enthralled with the splendour of these wild landscapes to much mind the weather, and besides, bad weather just makes a blazing campfire all the more enjoyable. The pristine lakes were ringed with ancient spruce forests, and in a land where few people ever set foot, the woods and waters were as rich with wildlife as any place I'd ever seen. Bald eagles perched in the tallest spruces overlooking the lakes, while in the waters below swam mergansers, buffleheads, wigeons, green-winged teals, mallards, tundra swans, and many other species. We frequently saw moose and caribou along the shore, many of which stood frozen, staring at us in apparent amazement, as if they'd never seen humans before. Beavers, muskrats, and river otters all passed curiously alongside our canoe. Grey wolves stalked through the dark woods: I caught a glimpse of one before it vanished into the undergrowth. Its size seemed incredible, no doubt from feeding on a diet of moose, caribou, and muskox. In my journal I further noted plovers, sandpipers, and arctic terns, yellow warblers and grey jays flitting through the trees, as well as ospreys and falcons soaring overhead. We spotted also a rough-legged hawk, which reminded me of a passage in Darrell's diary. On one of his rambles, he mentioned that he saw a hawk flying overhead with a rabbit (in actuality probably an arctic hare), which it then dropped. Darrell ran over to it before the hawk could get to it, and finding that it was still fresh, took it home and ate it.

Fortunately, I didn't have to resort to eating any rabbits dropped out of the sky. I'd brought along Chuck, and he kept us well fed with arctic graylings, a colourful fish with a big dorsal fin, often found lurking at the foot of small rapids, as well as northern pike and, best of all, lake trout, which we roasted on green sticks over our fire. Meanwhile we found an abundance of wild berries to snack on: lingonberries, crowberries, arctic blueberries, currants, and juicy orange cloudberries. Once I even came upon some tiny arctic raspberries on the exposed beachy shore of a big lake, which grew close to the ground to escape the harsh winds. These delicious little gems were among the finest-tasting berries I could ever recall eating.

Our fourth day brought a fresh challenge: a large, strangely shaped lake sprawled out before us, which we had to cross. In snow and freezing rain, we battled headwinds and waves working our way up to the point where we planned to cross. On the lake's opposite shore we expected to find a small river flowing out of it, another tributary of the Anderson River. But the howling winds and whitecaps defeated our best efforts to make the crossing; two waves had splashed over the gunwales already, forcing us to land and wait for better weather. Under the welcome shelter of a big spruce, we kindled up a cheerful fire to warm ourselves and make tea. Several hours passed, but the wind remained as fierce as ever, so Chuck and I resigned ourselves to staying put for the remainder of the day. Fortunately, Chuck had caught a large lake trout that morning, which he now occupied himself with filleting and cooking.

I meanwhile wandered off to explore the sodden, moss-draped forest surrounding our camp. Not far into the woods I came across a skull lying amid the fragrant Labrador tea bushes. It looked like a bear skull, but was hard to say definitely, as it was quite old and missing the teeth. Grizzlies were obviously common in the area, judging from the number of tracks we'd seen and the bountiful berry patches. Again I was reminded of a passage in one of Darrell's journals. In 1906, he'd been trapping with one of his fur trade friends near the Richardson Mountains. Darrell had, in his usual style, simply noted the weather in his diary, then added, "Big William got here at 11 with the news that Albert Ross had nearly been killed by a bear, having his leg broken and the flesh torn off from the thigh." Darrell didn't jot down any other details: such things were simply a part of life.

Before turning in for the night, we made sure to burn off any lingering fish scent from around our camp as best we could. We didn't want to end up like Albert Ross, after all.

✳

The next frosty morning, we were up before five, and though it remained cold, wet, and windy, we managed to complete our crossing of the lake. On the far shore we found the small, swift-flowing river we were seeking and followed it. It again had no name on our maps, but we knew it'd take us to the Anderson, which we were excited to be getting closer to—and closer, so we hoped, to Darrell's cabin.

We paddled along this winding river down frequent but minor rapids, until we reached the entrance to a small limestone canyon. The canyon looked risky, so we stopped on the right bank to scout things out. Pushing ashore through some willow bushes, we emerged in an open area of knee-high wet grasses. Here we noticed an area that had been flattened down where some large animal had slept: either a muskox or grizzly it seemed. But our immediate attention was absorbed by the river. At the entrance to the canyon, we could see that the river forked in two around a rock outcrop rising midstream, and not long after that it plunged over a ledge, generating rapids. Our hopes of possibly squeezing down the right passageway were dashed when we pushed on a little farther and found that the river came to an abrupt dead end. I'd never seen anything like it: the rushing waters, swirling about in a furious vortex, vanished right under the canyon walls. The turbulent water had evidently cut a subterranean passageway under the rocks, with the river remerging on the other side.

With all these hazards and obstacles, it was clear that we'd have to make a detour on foot. The opposite bank looked more promising for a portage, so we paddled back upstream a safe distance, then crossed over to it. There were of course no paths to follow, other than ones made by bears, but Chuck and I strapped on our backpacks, then pushed ahead into the forest. At first, they seemed to be ordinary spruce woods with fresh bear tracks and droppings. But when we came down a steep slope into a sheltered gully, we found the landscape completely transformed. It felt as if we'd passed into some lost world: lush ferns flourished, while green moss smothered the rocks, making it look more like we were in a jungle than the subarctic. Interspersed throughout this maze of willows stood giant limestone outcrops, rising up above the green willows like Maya ruins. Caves led off in different directions, and Chuck and I soon dropped our packs in order to explore some of these caverns. We entered into them cautiously, as any of these larger caves would make a perfect home for a grizzly. Some were large enough to stand upright in, while others we crawled through on our hands and knees.

The excitement of exploring these unexpected caves made me think of what Darrell must have often felt: the thrill and mystery promised by uncharted regions that lured him time and again. Given his route at the time, there wasn't much reason to think that Darrell had ever set foot anywhere near where Chuck and I now were, yet it was actually exploring these areas that I felt gave me a much better insight into Darrell's psychology than simply retracing his steps could ever have done. I felt that strange stirring in the heart, that incurable wanderlust, that longing for what lay over the horizon that had so afflicted him—and that had eventually lured him to his doom.

＊

Many nights, sitting round a campfire and watching the flames flicker and dance, or gazing out across the encircling forests with their secrets and mysteries, I wondered what had happened to Darrell. The common supposition at the time, even after Bishop Stringer's more accurate transcription, was that he must have fallen through a weak patch of ice somewhere on his return journey and died of hypothermia. To a certain extent this made sense, given that Darrell's route entailed travelling on foot over several hundred kilometres of sea ice, which even in the coldest winters can still have weak spots. But it seemed important to consider all possibilities. There were times when I couldn't help but wonder if Darrell had simply decided to voluntarily disappear in order to turn his back on the world and embrace the life of a hermit. But that was mostly before I'd studied his letters and diaries. After getting to know him better, it became clear that although he often came across as a lone wolf, he was nonetheless a man with many friends, a devoted fiancée, and siblings and parents whom he cared for. Moreover, if he had wanted that lifestyle, he'd likely have just gone up into the mountains and built himself a cabin within relatively easy distance of a trading post, where he could still post letters and barter for supplies. So I was certain that wasn't what had happened to Darrell. On the same note, there was also no indication from his private journals or letters that Darrell would ever have taken his own life.

But was it possible that Darrell had fallen victim to something darker? There was a line he'd written in one of his last letters that had always stayed at the back of my mind. In it, he'd seemed to hint at the potential for violence among wandering prospectors deep in the wilderness. In a letter to his parents dated March 10, 1910, Darrell had written: "Considering the great richness of some of the places, I have no doubts about the country. It's the men I have doubts about. I hear so much wildcat scheming that it makes a man careful." Despite the Canadian stereotype of a peaceful North, the reality is a bit darker: murders weren't uncommon in a time and place far from any courts, police, or other witnesses.

A particularly vivid example of such violence actually occurred the same year Darrell vanished. On the Mackenzie River, a waterway Darrell often travelled, the bodies of two trappers were found inside a log cabin. One of the corpses showed clear indications of violence. A member of the party who'd found the bodies noted that the "head was a shapeless mass, blown out of all resemblance to anything human." A note left beside the other body told the tale. Shut up inside the cramped cabin for months in darkness and freezing cold, and increasingly paranoid, one trapper had murdered the other, apparently shooting him in the head while he slept. In the confession note found by the bodies, the murderer had justified his actions by claiming that the other man had been cheating him out of his half of their rations. After this confession, he'd scrawled on the paper, "I am not Crasey," and then ended his own life by drinking poison. As a rule, I always made sure to give Chuck an extra helping of trail mix.

A more famous example of a solitary trapper turning violent is Albert Johnson (not his real name), otherwise known as the Mad Trapper. He had a cabin deep in the wilds near the Rat River in the shadows of the Richardson Mountains, right near Darrell's own stomping grounds in fact. In the winter of 1931, Johnson had abruptly opened fire on a Mountie who'd knocked on his cabin door (he perhaps thought he was selling something). Johnson then ended up shooting two other men, before he was ultimately gunned down by a posse on a frozen river. Though never proven, it was commonly believed that he was responsible for earlier unexplained murders in places he'd drifted through elsewhere in the North.

Another strange case happened around that same time, but more than a thousand kilometres away, closer to the rivers Darrell had once explored with Hanbury. There in the fall of 1931, two trappers, Gene Olsen and Emil Bode, were found murdered inside their cabin. The killings had evidently happened quite some time earlier, but given the cabin's isolation, no one came across the place for another year. Both of the victims' skulls had been smashed in by an axe, while outside their cabin, still attached to their chains, were the skeletons of seven sled dogs. The murders were never solved, though the Mountie who investigated them, a Métis officer named Archie Laroque, was convinced they were the work of an Inuk man named Telaruk, who'd been spotted in the district before vanishing. The last entry in Olsen's diary, which had been found inside the cabin, read simply, "We found Telaruk today." Laroque speculated that Telaruk had encountered the men while they were out on their trapline, returned to the cabin with them, then killed them with an axe while they slept.

Hanbury had noted in his account of his expedition, which was full of praise for the Inuit, that there was nonetheless, among the Inuit along Hudson Bay, one man who'd murdered six other men. The reason, Hanbury was told, had been disputes involving women. Though Hanbury had added that it was his opinion that murders were less common among the Inuit than they were among his own countrymen back in England.

During the Klondike gold rush, a man named George O'Brien was found guilty of having ambushed and murdered three other prospectors in the wilderness, for no other reason than to rob them. Other similar examples during the gold rush are too numerous to name. Darrell himself had warned earlier, in one of his oldest surviving letters, that he'd overhead some rough American mining characters threatening violence on another man.

But while these cases serve as a reminder that it'd be naive to discount the possibility of violence in remote locations, there is no evidence to think Darrell fell victim to it. For one thing, although practically everyone in the North had a theory of Darrell's disappearance, no one at the time, it seems, ever suggested foul play. Darrell's mild disposition meant that he could get along with pretty much anyone. Plus, he was in a highly remote area when he vanished, not shut up in a cramped cabin with another prospector, nor did he have any valuables worth robbing. The nearest other people to his location were some Inuit hunters more than a hundred kilometres away, but they knew Darrell and were friendly with him. They had also tried to help figure out what had happened to him, first by reporting the tree inscription and then by making a copy of it and bringing it a considerable distance to a post where it could be read.

And although on occasion violence did happen in the northern wilderness, fortunately it tended to be the exception rather than the rule. Most of the time, the remoteness and harshness of the Arctic brought out the best sides of human nature—making people kind and generous, willing to lend a hand, share food, or accommodate a stranger. Such hospitality, much more than violence, was and is the distinguishing characteristic of the North. The anthropologist Stefansson, who'd received the letter from Darrell and later spoken with perhaps the last people to see him alive, a party of Inuit hunters, concluded that only some accident, like falling through the ice or a sudden illness, could have overtaken him.

✳

After five days, we reached the Anderson River: it was an impressive sight, with high limestone cliffs, spruce-covered islands lying mid-river, and a strong, swift current. Navigating it kept us on our toes: we were astonished at the size of the canyons along it; some went on for miles and had towering walls nearly eighty feet high. We were awed almost into silence at times paddling through these twisting canyons. But whenever we'd hear the roar of whitewater ahead, we'd snap to attention, drop to our knees, and prepare for rapids. We managed to run most of them, smashing through standing waves and zigzagging between jagged rocks. In a few places, though, when confronted by a ledge or low falls spanning the river, we'd have to land onshore, and with a rope carefully guide the canoe ahead; this spared us from portaging and was much safer than gambling on the treacherous currents. It was easy to believe that past canoeists had drowned here.

Large cave entrances yawned along the canyon walls, while elsewhere the eroded cliffs took on odd shapes. Pillars of weathered rock rose high above the river like medieval watchtowers. At one point, as we zoomed through yet another snaking canyon, Chuck pointed ahead at an eroded rock outcrop and exclaimed from his spot in the canoe's bow, "That one looks like a man's face!" Personally, I felt it looked more like the backside of a beaver, but on these sorts of geological questions, opinions may differ. Meanwhile high overhead peregrine falcons circled, nesting as they did along cliffs.

Paddling the rougher and bigger stretches of rapids compelled us to stop onshore afterwards in order to dump out all the water from the canoe. It was freezing cold, but we were so exhilarated by the river's mysterious air that we didn't mind—even when we later made camp on solid rocks in wet snow inside a canyon. Whenever we stopped to camp or scout ahead, Chuck and I found the shore littered with marine fossils. Once, eons ago, all this had evidently been at the bottom of a now vanished sea. The abundance of these strange fossils—some looked like sponges, others like horns—only added to the feeling that we were in some primordial place.

In between rapids, Chuck would drop his paddle and snatch up his fishing rod. We had noticed prowling in the river's clear depths enormous fish, some of which appeared nearly four feet long. These big mystery fish at first proved difficult to catch—they seemed to lurk on the bottom, then strike suddenly at Chuck's lure, although without letting the hook set. But after a bit of experimenting, Chuck mastered the secret and got them to take the bait. After a sharp battle that made his rod bend round like a horseshoe, he reeled into our canoe a big, strange-looking fish with a giant mouth. Chuck had no idea what he'd caught, but from what I'd read I recognized it as an inconnu, literally the "unknown" fish. It got that name from French-Canadian voyageurs who'd accompanied Alexander Mackenzie on his journey to the Arctic Ocean in 1789. Having never before seen such a fish, the voyageurs simply called it the "inconnu," French for *unknown*, and the name stuck. Even today these fish are a bit mysterious; scientists know little about them, but it's believed that they migrate to the saltwater of the Arctic Ocean. As for their taste: it's rather oily, and not my favourite.

It took several days, but eventually we made it through all the river's canyons and rapids, none the worse for wear. With the river's fury finally slackening, we found ourselves back in calmer waters. But there was still much to hold our interest. Coming round a bend on what was another grey, wet day, Chuck and I stared in wonder at a great bull moose standing on a willowy shore, looking for all the world like the king of the forest. In other places we watched as caribou swam across the river, and shaggy horned muskoxen roamed the banks browsing on willows. All of these animals would pause and stare at us curiously, some of the caribou even trotting right up to us. Among the wildlife, there was only one exception to this behaviour: that most elusive creature of all, the wolverine. Chuck and I spotted one loping along the bank, though it didn't seem in the least impressed with us. It didn't stop to pay us any attention, vanishing like a ghost into the forest before we could paddle any closer.

We were now far north of the Arctic Circle, which meant waking up in the mornings to find the water in our cooking pot frozen. After getting my tent down each morning, I'd have to lie on my back on the frosty ground in order to struggle to pull on my waders, which overnight would freeze stiff as a board. Chuck would engage in a similar acrobatic performance to get into his neoprene dry suit each morning. In the canoe, we'd stamp our feet just to get the blood flowing. The forests were steadily thinning out, but there was still a fair amount of timber—enough at least for cabin building.

The river had widened out to about half a kilometre, while enclosing it were rugged hills ablaze with fall colours: scarlet-red bushes of dwarf birch, bearberry, and arctic blueberries, mixed up with golden streaks from the aspens and willows and the more sombre hues of the spruces. In one of his journal entries, after noting some fresh grizzly tracks, Darrell had jotted down, "Country is looking very beautiful with the change of the leaf." It was a sentiment that Chuck and I entirely agreed with.

We'd been paddling for a good five hours already on what was yet another cold, misty day, now nearly two weeks since we'd been dropped by the plane. That morning alone, we'd already spotted six moose. But it wasn't moose that I was keeping an eye out for: we were nearing the zone where I figured Darrell's cabin was to be found. From what we'd seen, I felt certain of my earlier supposition that Darrell would not have paddled a canoe too far up the river's swift current, and certainly not beyond any of the rapids. On the other hand, with the spruces still quite thick along the banks, if Darrell had built his cabin even a short distance inland from the river, we'd never find it. But if it was close to the water's edge, we might, with luck and a sharp eye, catch a glimpse of whatever was left of it.

From my place in the stern, I kept intensely scanning the high forested hills enclosing the river. Just as I was thinking to myself that spotting a cabin through the trees wasn't going to be easy, above a sloped bank along the eastern shore I caught sight of what looked like weathered logs. As we drifted closer, the slope concealed them from view. But if I wasn't dreaming, I thought that the logs appeared to form a right angle and, if so, must be something placed by human hands.

"Chuck," I said with suppressed excitement, for I didn't wish to get our hopes up, "I saw something up there that looked like the ruins of a cabin. Let's land here and check it out."

"Okay," nodded my steady-minded friend from the canoe's bow.

We beached the canoe on the pebbly shore and then, excitement urging me on, I bounded up the slope to the willow bushes, Chuck following behind with the gun. When we reached the crest of the ridge, the spruces and willows partially concealed what lay ahead. But another couple steps and I felt a sudden chill, and not from the misty weather: it was the ruins of a small cabin. I could barely believe my eyes, but I checked my own excitement. We'd have to examine it carefully before we could be sure of anything.

The roof had fallen in, and the walls were very low, indicating that it had been partly dug out, a common technique when building a short-term cabin. The approximate dimensions were only six by ten feet. The cut marks showed it had been built with an axe and handsaw rather than a chainsaw. The weathering looked similar to Douglas's cabin, and the lichen growth over the axe marks further indicated its considerable age. There was no hearth or fireplace, only a makeshift stove in the centre that appeared to have been fashioned from several rusty metal cans being cut up and hammered out. There were also no windows. In short, just a bare-bones, quickly built shanty for a single occupant.

These small trapper's cabins were historically known as tilts, since they had tilted roofs, which made them faster and easier for one person to construct than a traditional A-frame roof. They usually only had a dirt floor and no chimney or fireplace, though they might be heated by a small portable stove. Examining the surrounding forest, we found no other artifacts or litter of any kind, just sparse subarctic woods with no hint of anything disturbed, nor indication that anyone had been here in a very long time.

I went over my mental checklist as I scrutinized the decaying remnants: in every respect that I could think of, these ruins seemed a perfect match for Darrell's cabin. It was in the right location, and the weathering, lichen growth, and general state of the ruins all suggested a date consistent with the same era of Douglas's 1911 cabin. While the complete lack of any other artifacts or a cleared area of stumps indicated that it must have been occupied for only a brief period of time. The makeshift stove also seemed to correspond with Darrell, as he didn't have a portable stove with him and would have likely tried to improvise something. Lastly, the tiny size of the cabin clearly showed it wasn't built for a trapper with a family or two prospecting partners.

Yet despite all these tantalizing indications, I wasn't prepared to swear just yet that we'd actually found Darrell's long-lost cabin. After all, it wasn't as if his name was carved into it. As for any inscription on a tree, that would have long since grown over. As promising as things seemed, when we got back to civilization I'd have to do further research to see if I could find anything that might shed more light on it. Darrell's own letters and diaries were of no help, since the only surviving ones were written before this point. Still, it was a surreal feeling to think that we were quite possibly standing beside the ruins of Darrell's cabin from over a century ago. If solitude was what Darrell had sought, he could hardly have chosen a better spot. Taking a moment to step back and reflect on the surroundings, I had the overwhelming impression of a place hidden away from the hustle and bustle of the world, that really gave a whole new meaning to the term social distancing.

But for the moment, Chuck and I still had to canoe another 150 kilometres to the Beaufort Sea, avoid getting eaten by any polar bears there, and then get picked up by a bush plane for the flight back to Norman Wells. Along the way, we'd keep our eyes out for any other ruins.

We spent the next week canoeing the remainder of the river and then exploring some of the arctic coast. At times, we found ourselves paddling in snow and took to wearing four layers to stay warm. When it wasn't snowing, it was usually raining, or else fierce winds were sweeping off the frigid sea. When our feet felt numb, which they generally did, we'd land onshore and do jumping jacks to warm up. But the weather could still do little to dampen our spirits, excited as we were by finding the cabin and perhaps even more so by the awe-inspiring magnificence of the land. Whenever there chanced to be a let-up in the weather, Chuck and I admired the incredible splendour of the hills that seemed to practically glow with purplish-red fireweed. The colours were so vivid that they really had to be seen to be believed. It reminded me of a line that Darrell had once written: "It is a most lovely country—the barren land of Canada."

Herds of caribou bounded over the crimson hills while more muskoxen and grizzlies wandered the muddy shores. From the bank, one big grizzly glared at us in our canoe, then made a sort of huffing noise, before abruptly running off. As we neared the sea, the river's crystal waters became siltier, and the spruces disappeared altogether. In places the once-colourful hills suddenly became as grey and barren as a moonscape, appearing more like small mountains. In the misty rain, it gave them a fantastic, otherworldly aspect, especially since the only wildlife to be seen roaming over them were eerie-looking muskoxen. It'd been the desire to see one of these unique creatures that had led Darrell to first drift away from prospecting in the subarctic forests, out onto the arctic barrens.

Once we reached the sea coast, instead of grizzlies it was polar bears that reigned, and knowing that they were around made us much more cautious. Since the river's mouth was too salty to drink from, we scoured the tundra for little rainwater puddles to fill our teapot. With no trees to speak of, we instead gathered driftwood for our fires, or when there was none to be found, clumps of arctic willow. There were still quite a few birds to keep us company, though many others by this point had already flown south.

We ventured some twenty kilometres along the coast, scanning the grey seas with binoculars for any signs of whales, seals, or bears. But all we saw were phantom-like islands half hidden in the mist and what looked like mirages: once a pair of dark ship's masts appeared on the horizon, but the binoculars merely revealed Canada geese flying low over the water, their size and shapes weirdly distorted by the light, distance, and reflection off the sea. At other times either Chuck or I would suddenly exclaim and point to a white object on a distant point—a polar bear. We were greatly relieved when the binoculars revealed only white tundra swans.

I often reflected how tough Darrell must have been to have voluntarily chosen to live in such an environment, here at the very end of the North American land mass, when if all he wanted was solitude and wilderness, he could have chosen a far less remote place, such as Manitoba's lake country. But of course, Darrell's restless soul craved something more: he hungered for the unknown, cursed by his own all-consuming wanderlust to always seek out farther, wilder places beyond the horizon. The novelist Jack London, based on his own experiences in the Klondike, once wrote of the "common dread of the unknown lands" that made voyageurs and prospectors turn back once they reached the edge of the map—except for the rarest ones who found such mysteries appealing. Darrell was one of these, attracted, rather than repelled, by the unknown and all the hardships it entailed.

Chuck and I had continued to keep our eyes out for other ruins. At one point, after the treeline but still on the river, we landed on the shore to investigate what looked like a heap of cut logs. But it turned out to be merely a pile of driftwood. The only other human-made structures we encountered at all were ones we could easily identify. Near the river's mouth on the arctic coast, there was a shabby old white cabin built of plywood and other modern materials by the Canadian Wildlife Service, an agency of the federal government. It had been abandoned sometime in the early 1990s, and we'd actually been asked by the Wildlife Service to verify its current condition. It had stood up well enough, fortified as it was with steel mesh to protect it from marauding polar bears. Along the coast, we saw only a couple other structures, and these were obviously modern hunting cabins with similar bear precautions. We had also earlier stopped at the abandoned cabin of James and Maureen Pokiak, which they'd told us about ahead of time. It was plywood with debris scattered around it. The absence of any other historical cabins only seemed to reinforce the singularity of the ruins we'd found and the likelihood they were Darrell's.

Finally, after three weeks of fruitful exploration, Chuck and I packed up our things, loaded our canoe, and waited on another cold, rainy day for the dim drone of an engine somewhere off in the clouds. Soon a small plane materialized in the grey sky. Our excellent pilot, Simon, executed a perfect landing on the river's mouth and came in as close as he could in the shallow tidal waters. We strapped the canoe again to one of the plane's pontoons, loaded our gear, refuelled the plane from a generous supply of jerry cans stowed inside it, and then set off on the five-hundred-kilometre flight back to Norman Wells.

20

THE FOG OF TIME

W hen I got home to Ontario, flushed with excitement as
I was at discovering what seemed to be quite likely the
ruins of Darrell's cabin, I nonetheless had to put that aside for a
time in order to devote myself to leading some guided nature
hikes, which I did on occasion to earn a living. But I turned my
attention back to Darrell as soon as I could. What I needed to find
was some clue to throw more light on things, such as which bank
of the river Darrell's cabin had been on or how far upstream—in
short, anything at all that would help me identify the ruins we'd
found with greater confidence as Darrell's. So far, all I really knew
about it was that Stefansson had said Darrell had made a "permanent camp" somewhere up the river, and that the writing on the
tree had been found somewhere near it. The trouble was the fog
of history could be as bewildering as the fog of an arctic river,
obscuring points and misleading the careless navigator.

I already knew that much of what had been written at the
time on Darrell had proven incorrect. The *Edmonton Journal*, for

example, described him as a "Scotchman and only about thirty years of age and a well-educated man." All three points were in reality wrong: Darrell was of English origin, thirty-six years of age, and had no formal education beyond his sixteenth birthday. Other stories described Darrell as an Alaskan, a dogsled driver, or that he'd been missing since the year 1900. Even more misleading were all the reports that claimed he'd frozen his feet twice. One individual, however, who seemed to have a clearer grasp of things was Bishop Stringer.

I figured if I could get my hands on his journals or private papers, they might possibly shed more light on Darrell's cabin. Stringer, a bishop with the Anglican Church, had spent most of his life in Canada's North. In his own day he became known as "The Bishop Who Ate His Boots," because of an incident on one of his journeys where, destitute of provisions, he'd resorted to the age-old Canadian practice of eating one's own leather footwear to survive. I soon learned that Stringer's private records were kept at the Anglican Church's Toronto archive. So I reached out to the archivist there and explained my interests. Fortunately, the archivist proved very helpful, and not long afterwards I had in my hands the very documents that I'd sought: a letter written by Stringer in 1917, describing everything he'd learned about Darrell's disappearance. This letter, written in Stringer's neat handwriting, shed more light on things than I could have hoped. But as I read its pages, it was with something of a bittersweet feeling, as before I'd reached the end it dawned on me that we'd been lost down a false trail. Stringer's letter recounted:

While at Cape Bathurst in August 1917, I learned particulars from the Eskimos and others regarding Hubert Darrell, who is supposed to have perished in the winter of 1910 and 11 somewhere between Anderson River and Kitigajuit. I spent many hours with the natives getting all information possible. So far as I was able to learn, the natives who last saw Darrell alive were Olay Niulumaluk and wife Olga Nivikana and the wife's parents, Ulapana and wife Niviaksina. About the latter part of September or the first of October 1910, the above Eskimos saw Darrell at a place called Sangoyak on Anderson River, thirty or thirty-five miles from the mouth. Darrell was then going up the river in a canvas covered canoe. After the ice formed on the river, Darrell came down [walking] on the ice, and visited the natives. He asked them if they thought the ocean would be frozen sufficiently for him to go to Cape Bathurst where the schooner "Rosie H" was wintering. On learning that the ice was not yet safe, he returned to his camp which was about fifteen miles up the river from the Eskimo camp. About a week after this he returned again, and went to the schooner "Rosie H," where he obtained some flour, rice, beans and tea. He also got a pair of skis, with which he made a sled lashing the skis together. Capt. Wolki of the "Rosie H" . . . told me that Darrell was not well clothed, though he himself did not see him as Wolki was away from the ship when Darrell visited the place. I learned from others that Darrell got a pair of native boots from an Eskimo called John Angochinaog and a deer-skin coat from Olay.

These details agreed with Stefansson's account. The other particulars, too, matched up with what I knew of Darrell: his preferences for travelling light and for adopting native clothing, preferring as he did Inuit-made coats and boots over European ones. Also his preference for travelling on foot, without any dogs, and for making a sled to tow his things on. And although Darrell often seemed ill-equipped, this was how he'd always appeared: Amundsen, the whaling captains, and others had thought the same too. Travelling light was partly the secret of how he managed to cover such extraordinary distances quickly on foot. Stringer's letter also seemed to indicate that Darrell had learned enough of the local Inuit dialect to make himself understood, which makes sense given his talent for mastering languages. The level of detail in Stringer's letter was impressive, and it was clear that he was much more meticulous than the newspapers, Stefansson, or even the Mounties in his attention to detail regarding Darrell's disappearance. His letter continued:

On Darrell's return from the ship, he stayed one day at Olay's camp. Olay states that he had a gun and ammunition and snowshoes. He [Darrell] remarked that his load was too heavy, and gave some of his flour and other provisions to the natives. At the time Olay bought Darrell's canvas covered canoe, paying him for it, four or five white fox skins. The canoe had been left up the river at Darrell's camp, and Olay planned to get it in the spring. He borrowed hammer and boring drill and nails from the natives to repair his sled. A few days afterwards he returned to the native camp with the borrowed hammer and drill, and said good-bye to them, stating that he was going back to the Mackenzie River. He stayed only a few hours with the Eskimos and then returned, walking on snowshoes back up the river towards his own camp. The natives described Darrell's camping place as being four or five hours walk from the Eskimo camp or say about ten or fifteen miles. The date of this last visit was sometime in November, probably after the middle of November, and so far as Olay knows, he says he does not think anyone saw Darrell after this.

This was to me very interesting information, pointing as it did to Darrell's warm relationship with his nearest Inuit neighbours. He'd always gotten along well with both the Dene and Inuit, defending them from those who advocated assimilation, studying their languages, and sometimes living and travelling with them. But for my immediate purposes, the more important point was the distance mentioned by Stringer between Darrell's camp and the Inuit one: it sounded promising with regard to where Chuck and I had found the cabin ruins. I kept on reading.

In the following spring 1911, after the ice broke, Olay went up the Anderson River in his whale boat, to Darrell's camp to get the canoe which he had bought, and found it in the place where Darrell said he would leave it. Olay told me he noticed where Darrell had made his camp. He apparently had a tent. He noticed the spruce boughs where he had slept, and the fire place outside where the tent had been. Apparently Darrell had no stove.

My heart sank like a rock as I read these lines and then reread them several more times in disbelief. The fog of history had struck again: Darrell, so it seemed, never had any cabin at all. If he did, he wouldn't have been sleeping in a tent on spruce boughs, nor cooking over a fire outside. The vague reports that said he had a cabin, or at least a permanent camp, were evidently wrong, as Stringer's letter was far too detailed to second-guess, especially when contrasted with any of the other, hazier accounts. I kicked myself at the implications: this meant that the ruins Chuck and I had so painstakingly sought out weren't Darrell's after all. The cabin we'd found must simply have belonged to some other lone trapper, probably sometime after Darrell in the 1910s or 1920s. Certainly, if there'd been any wiggle room to think Darrell might still have built some temporary cabin, or that Stringer may have been mistaken, it would have been tempting to seize upon it. But this I couldn't do; objectively, the evidence pointed the other direction entirely. Given Stringer's attention to detail, the letter left little room for doubt. Indeed, Stringer had continued:

Capt. Wolki told me that Darrell said he used a small tin with a candle in, to warm himself at nights. Olay saw a blazed tree close to the camp, and on a smooth surface he saw some writing which he copied into a note book. The writing was somewhat blurred on the right-hand side and it was difficult for him to make out everything. He did not understand English, but copied out the writing as best he could. The tree was about six inches in diameter, and was situated on the right limit on a high bank above the high water mark. The writing was about four feet from the ground. Olay had his own book with him and from it I copied out the writing as follows . . .

The inscription that Stringer gave in his letter was the same one reported in the later newspaper stories, which had simply indicated that Darrell had struck camp and headed west for the Mackenzie River on November 24, 1910. Stringer added that many people had misinterpreted the inscription when it was first brought back. He went on to add:

So far as I know, Olay and Bert Kemiksena and Kotokak were the only ones who saw this writing. Kotokak saw it a year afterwards, and it is probably there still, though it is probably now very dim. Bert was with Olay when he went with the canoe . . . In travelling throughout the North, most people make a practice of jotting down on a tree or some other place where it may be seen by other travellers the date of any event, such as the time of their visiting the place, or of the freezing up of a river etc. To me there seems nothing unusual about the inscription on the tree. Hubert Darrell did what many other people have done, simply jotting down the freezing up of the river together with the date of his leaving and the direction which he intended to travel.

Stringer, I felt, was correct about all this. Jacquot himself had left a note for Darrell at the spot where they were supposed to meet. But as I studied Stringer's letter and absorbed all this new information, I couldn't help but feel deflated and crestfallen. It seemed I really had been chasing a phantom, one who'd left not even a crumbling cabin to be found. Even if I may have succeeded in stitching together much of the details of Darrell's life, it appeared that I was no closer to unravelling the mystery of his disappearance. Darrell, it seemed, may as well have vanished into thin air.

Having reached such a demoralizing dead end, I contemplated whether I should simply shelve my focus on Darrell and abandon the whole project. There was much else to occupy my mind anyway: I had an interest in finding and photographing Canada's various snake species, retracing other explorers' routes, different historical research, and then, to cap it off, I soon saw a falcon and got distracted by it, and I ended up paddling a considerable way after it. Plus, I was busy at home: I'd gotten married, had two kids who were now very active little ones under age four, and was as a consequence busier than ever. After finding Stringer's letter, months passed, then years, all in a whirlwind, and my folder and maps of Darrell's routes, and the research I'd done, got buried in my desk drawer. I felt I'd probably never pick it up again, nor do anything further with it.

Yet when I was off on my own solitary wilderness journeys, there were times when I'd find myself in some circumstance that would jog my memory of something I'd read in Darrell's journal: often it was simply sitting beside a wild lake, a crackling campfire at my feet, gazing in wonder at the countless stars. In those moments, I'd reproach myself for having left things unfinished.

Eventually, I persuaded myself to take a second look at the matter. Stringer's letter, after all, while crushing the cabin theory, hadn't been entirely devoid of fresh clues. He'd mentioned that in March 1916, more than five years after Darrell vanished, a trapper had actually found a camera and some other gear belonging to Darrell. I'd partly known about this already from some of what I'd dug up in the Mounted Police records in Ottawa. A report filed by the police sergeant at Fort McPherson, dated January 1917, had stated:

> Sir, I have the honour to forward a camera supposed to be the property of Mr. Hubert Darrell. This was found by an Eskimo while hunting in the vicinity of the Husky Lakes. This case was reported upon [earlier] . . . and no more information has been received since then, with the exception of the finding of the camera and a bag of fur which was completely spoilt and not worth bringing in. These articles were found suspended on a tree . . . Mr H. Darrell was travelling between the Anderson River and the Husky Lakes and the supposition is that he either fell through the ice on the Huskie Lakes and was drowned or met with some other accident.

I had hoped to track down what became of this camera, but this was the final record in the Darrell case file, after which no other reports were ever made. Of course, the camera, having been left exposed to rain and snow for years, would have been badly damaged by the time it was found. It may have been sent to Darrell's family, but if it was, it has not turned up since.

But Stringer's letter had given considerably more details than the police report on where the camera and other gear belonging to Darrell had been found. Stringer specified that the spot where it'd all been found was approximately "fifty or sixty miles" from Darrell's camp on the Anderson River, and about equal distance as the crow flies from Kitiqajuit, the small trading post near the mouth of the Mackenzie River. Though still quite vague, this at least gave me a couple fixed points, and a somewhat better idea of the general area where Darrell vanished: somewhere in the vast trackless wilderness that lay between the Anderson River in the east and the shores of the maze-like Husky Lakes in the west.

I debated with myself the idea of going to search this enormous area for any trace of Darrell. The odds were probably no better than one in a million of finding anything, but I thought to myself, why not? The wilderness beckoned to me, as it had to Darrell, and often enough I could barely contain my own deep yearning for those mysterious places far from any roads. Even if, as seemed likely, I found no trace of Darrell, to simply wander once more across wild landscapes would be satisfying in itself.

So I resolved that I'd go back and make one last search for any trace of Darrell.

21

SMOKE RIVER

I stared at the map sprawled out before me. Dozens of snaking lines were shown threading across it, indicating rivers draining north to the Arctic Ocean. Interspersed with the rivers were thousands of lakes of all shapes and sizes. On the right side of the map was the Anderson River; on the left, the immense, salty Husky Lakes. Between the two, as the crow flies, is about a hundred kilometres of arctic and subarctic wilderness. Somewhere out there Darrell had vanished. My plan was to choose one of the smaller rivers running through the heart of this area, canoe it down to the coast, then head west through the Husky Lakes, partly retracing what would have been Darrell's route back to Fort McPherson in 1910. In the process, I could search for any trace of Darrell, slim as the chances were of finding anything.

In Darrell's day, none of these smaller rivers were mapped: he'd vanished, quite literally, beyond the map. But one could be forgiven for thinking that in the twenty-first century, they've all been precisely charted. They haven't. Although the maps are infinitely fuller than what they were in Darrell's day, they're still not complete. That's because the only existing maps of this area were actually made "remotely," which is to say by government cartographers behind desks squinting at grainy black-and-white aerial photos snapped by aircraft flying overhead in the 1960s. Given the limitations of the photographs, details such as waterfalls, rapids, and islands can be missed. And strange as it sounds, the resulting maps remain the most up-to-date ones for a considerable chunk of northern Canada. For this reason, for planning purposes I rely as much on satellite imagery as on maps. But even satellite imagery can have limitations: sometimes only low-resolution images are available for isolated regions, or else the images are obscured by clouds, or were taken in winter when snow and ice cover everything. But an even bigger obstacle to obtaining accurate maps is the fact that many rivers in Canada's western Arctic change their courses almost yearly.

While much of Canada's northern geography lies over the solid, seemingly permanent granite rocks of the Canadian Shield, in the far northwest many rivers run over softer sediments, such as silt, gravel, or sand. As a result, strong currents often cut new channels, form and reform islands, and even landslides happen regularly, which can erase entire sections of river and also create new ones. For these reasons, I knew it was wise not to put too much faith in any maps or satellite images that were at best already years out of date.

Eventually though I zeroed in on a meandering river smack in the middle of the map. It was labelled as the "Smoke River." I began researching everything I could on it, which didn't take very long, as there was nothing, in fact, to research. If the

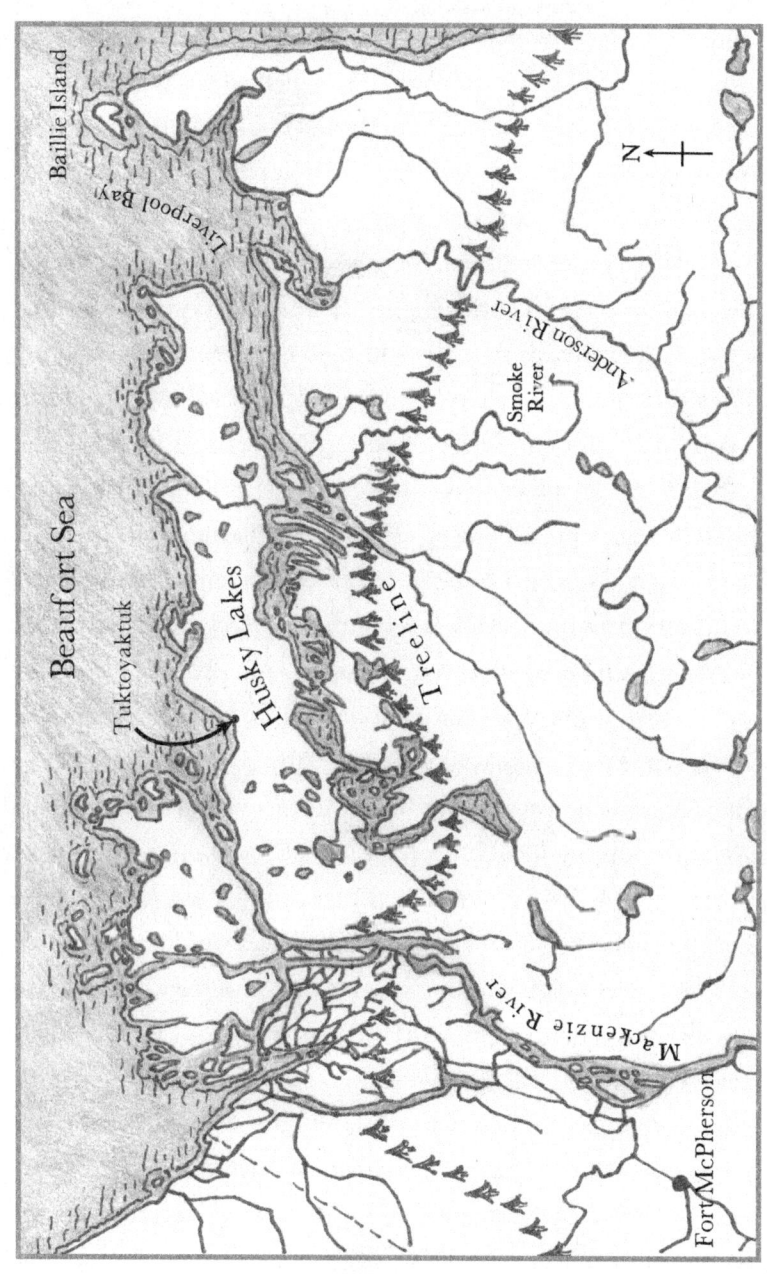

SMOKE RIVER

Anderson River had felt obscure, compared to the Smoke River, it now seemed like Central Park. I had tried all the usual sources: the internet, library records, canoe guidebooks, digital magazine archives, and wilderness canoe association records, and they'd all come back blank for anything on the Smoke River in the Northwest Territories. Even the government's Geological Survey files contained no mention of it. It'd been years since I'd come across any river with so little published data. But this suited my tastes just fine, all the better really, and I immediately made up my mind to canoe it. More importantly, the river emptied directly into the area I wanted to search for Darrell's final campsite, where his camera and other gear had been found.

I reached out to Chuck to see if he'd be enthusiastic about wandering around polar bear territory again. He responded that he was turning sixty-five that summer, hadn't paddled much in the last five years, and that he'd been suffering acutely from a sciatic nerve that made walking excruciatingly painful. Naturally then, he said he was in. Knowing him as well as I did, I had expected nothing less.

With Chuck on board, I next turned my attention to securing a bush plane. Getting to the Smoke River would be considerably more challenging than reaching the Anderson. It'd require a much longer (and more costly) flight, and from what I could glean from the satellite images, the river's tiny, snaking course would be too small for a plane to land on. I contacted the same company that we'd used previously, North-Wright Airways, which is based in Norman Wells in the Northwest Territories. They operate a fleet of about a dozen small planes, specializing in flying charters across the Northwest Territories and Yukon for hunters, fishermen, prospectors, mining camps, scientists, and canoeists. North-Wright informed me that they had never heard of the Smoke River, let alone flown anyone there. I had selected as a potential drop point a small nameless lake near the river's headwaters, approximately 415 kilometres as the crow flies north of their base in Norman Wells. This lake appeared just big enough for a float plane to land on.

To save money, I had decided that this time it'd be a one-way flight only. Instead of getting picked up by bush plane, we'd instead paddle all the way through the serpentine course of the Husky Lakes, searching the shores for any historical artifacts or other clues to Darrell's final camp, and then end our journey at the recently constructed road to Tuktoyaktuk. From there, I figured we could hitchhike south to Inuvik.

After a busy year of unrelated expeditions, I finally met up with Chuck again in Yellowknife on August 24, 2024 and from there we flew to Norman Wells. (The Day's Inn was now too great an extravagance, as the bush plane charter had used up all my funds. We skipped it in favour of the cheapest motel in town, which is probably best avoided if you'd been considering it.) In Norman Wells, we again obtained a canoe, this time a seventeen-foot one, a little banged up but serviceable. It was cheaper just to buy the canoe than rent it, due to the transport costs of trying to return it afterwards, and I figured we could probably barter it for a ride to Inuvik when hitchhiking. This done, we met up with our pilot, Simon, the same one who'd flown us five years earlier.

We had heard that he was now North-Wright's best and most experienced bush plane pilot, which was needed for where we were going. Not until noon the following day did the weather clear up enough for us to depart: unlike commercial aircraft, these small, antiquated single-engine bush planes can't safely fly in rainy weather, due to the lack of visibility. In the tiny, cramped plane, I took the co-pilot's seat beside Simon, while Chuck sat in the back with our barrels, backpacks, and paddles, though this time no gun. Normally, when we teamed up for expeditions, Chuck entrusted me to pack most of the gear, including any firearms, since it was a hassle for him to bring any of that stuff across the border. But this time I'd had my hands full (literally with all the gear at the airport), so to simplify things, I just skipped packing any gun altogether. I figured bear spray and bear bangers should be adequate, and if all else failed, we could have a foot race.

The flight north on the bush plane took three hours, twice as long as our flight five years earlier, as we were flying twice as far. Below us appeared nothing but endless wilderness that looked as if it hadn't changed since Darrell's day. The boreal forests steadily thinned out as we passed over the Arctic Circle, though along the rivers and lakes were still a respectable number of spruces. When the small lake I'd selected as our drop point swung into view on the horizon, Simon circled around to give us our first glimpse of the Smoke River, which drained out of the lake's north end. It appeared very small and meandering, really not much more than a big creek. But just down from where it left the lake was a vast morass of muddy debris extending more than a kilometre in length. It was apparently the remains of an enormous landslide that had utterly engulfed a section of the river, wiping out trees and everything spotted six moose. But it wasn't moose that I was keeping an eye out for: we were nearing the zone where I figured Darrell's cabin was to be found. From what we'd seen, I felt certain of my earlier supposition that Darrell would not have paddled a canoe too far up the river's swift current, and certainly not beyond any of the rapids. On the other hand, with the spruces still quite thick along the banks, if Darrell had built his cabin even a short distance inland from the river, we'd never find it. But if it was close to the water's edge, we might, with luck and a sharp eye, catch a glimpse of whatever was left of it.

From my place in the stern, I kept intensely scanning the high forested hills enclosing the river. Just as I was thinking to myself that spotting a cabin through the trees wasn't going to be easy, above a sloped bank along the eastern shore I caught sight of what looked like weathered logs. As we drifted closer, the slope concealed them from view. But if I wasn't dreaming, I thought that the logs appeared to form a right angle and, if so, must be something placed by human hands.

"Chuck," I said with suppressed excitement, for I didn't wish to get our hopes up, "I saw something up there that looked like the ruins of a cabin. Let's land here and check it out."

"Okay," nodded my steady-minded friend from the canoe's bow.

We beached the canoe on the pebbly shore and then, excitement urging me on, I bounded up the slope to the willow bushes, Chuck following behind with the gun. When we reached the crest of the ridge, the spruces and willows partially concealed what lay ahead. But another couple steps and I felt a sudden chill, and not from the misty weather: it was the ruins of a small cabin. I could shaggy horned muskoxen roamed the banks browsing on willows. All of these animals would pause and stare at us curiously, some of the caribou even trotting right up to us. Among the wildlife, there was only one exception to this behaviour: that most elusive creature of all, the wolverine. Chuck and I spotted one loping along the bank, though it didn't seem in the least impressed with us. It didn't stop to pay us any attention, vanishing like a ghost into the forest before we could paddle any closer.

We were now far north of the Arctic Circle, which meant waking up in the mornings to find the water in our cooking pot frozen. After getting my tent down each morning, I'd have to lie on my back on the frosty ground in order to struggle to pull on my waders, which overnight would freeze stiff as a board. Chuck would engage in a similar acrobatic performance to get into his neoprene dry suit each morning. In the canoe, we'd stamp our feet just to get the blood flowing. The forests were steadily thinning out, but there was still a fair amount of timber—enough at least for cabin building.

The river had widened out to about half a kilometre, while enclosing it were rugged hills ablaze with fall colours: scarlet-red bushes of dwarf birch, bearberry, and arctic blueberries, mixed up with golden streaks from the aspens and willows and the more sombre hues of the spruces. In one of his journal entries, after noting some fresh grizzly tracks, Darrell had jotted down, "Country is looking very beautiful with the change of the leaf." It was a sentiment that Chuck and I entirely agreed with.

We'd been paddling for a good five hours already on what was yet another cold, misty day, now nearly two weeks since we'd been dropped by the plane. That morning alone, we'd already else in its path. The course of the river here was not clear, and from what little we could make out from above, it appeared that the river had been buried underground. It wasn't possible for Simon to drop us anywhere beyond the landslide, as the tiny river was indeed too small for a landing. Given this massive obstacle, Simon asked through his headset if we wished to turn back. But we'd already come this far, and landslide or not, I felt we had to go on. Chuck didn't have a headset, but I knew he'd feel the same.

A more pressing problem was that the lake itself also appeared too shallow to land on. We circled the lake no less than seven times, carefully eyeing the water to try to gauge whether it was deep enough. The weedy surface looked somewhat alarming, but other lakes with similar surfaces do sometimes turn out to be surprisingly deep. On the eighth pass, Simon consented to attempt it. He brought the plane down and we soon skidded across the weedy water to a stop—it was deep enough after all.

Chuck and I helped Simon refuel the plane with the dozen jerry cans that were stowed inside, then loaded the canoe and set off. With the drone of the plane fading away, we were once more on our own, this time in a place more isolated than ever. We wasted little time paddling across the lake for the Smoke River's outlet, eager to find out what was in store for us. Whether it would be too shallow to paddle, clogged with innumerable logjams, or else filled with rapids, we had no real idea. From the air, we could only glimpse a few kilometres of its upper course.

But what we saw at first seemed promising: at the outlet from the lake, the Smoke River was clear, swift, and very shallow, less than knee-deep, but that was just deep enough for our canoe. Hemmed in by spruces and tamaracks, its narrow width measured only about thirty-five feet. Moose and wolf tracks were visible along the grassy shores, and before long we spotted mink, muskrats, beavers, red-throated loons, and about a dozen other bird species.

Soon, however, we reached our first obstacle: the massive landslide that we'd spotted when flying in from above. I'd seen landslides before on the Mackenzie River and in the Hudson Bay Lowlands. In those cases, the high, eroded banks of mud, gravel, and soft soil sometimes give way entirely due to the river's flow, heavy rain, or snow and ice melt in spring. But this landslide was far larger than any I had ever encountered: an enormous section of high bank had collapsed and wiped out the entire course of the river for as far as we could see. The force of the mud, gravel, rocks, and buried trees had completely filled in the river channel, diverting all the water into the adjacent bushes and spruce forest.

"This doesn't look good" was Chuck's accurate assessment from the canoe's bow. He had assured me that with the right combination of painkillers, he was still able to hike, but neither of us had counted on any landslides of this scope.

We attempted to canoe through the flooded alder and willow bushes, but they were too thick for us to get very far. We next attempted to wade and drag the canoe, but the water proved surprisingly deep. So, our third attempt was to hack our way back through the flooded alders to the landslide that had buried everything and try to portage over top of it. But we hadn't gone more than a few steps before we sank deep into the oozing mud.

Our only choice, it seemed, was to retreat back to the flooded forest and try to slowly and laboriously drag the canoe through it, jumping from little willow hummocks to try to avoid the deepest spots. It was a slog, but we were well rested from the flight and motivated to get through it. Eventually we bypassed the landslide, feeling much relieved to do so. Beyond it the river resumed its normal course, and we were able to get back into the canoe and paddle.

It turned out that there were many more landslides waiting for us along the Smoke River. They were obviously recent, as the trees half sticking out of them were still alive. Fortunately, none of these other landslides entirely blocked the river, so we didn't have to portage again. However, some nearly cut the waterway in two, leaving only the tiniest of channels for us to squeeze through, occasionally only a few feet wide. These slides also had the effect of acting as weirs, magnifying the river's already swift current.

Another effect of the landslides and the river's high, eroded banks was that soon after leaving the lake, we found the Smoke River's waters turned incredibly muddy. The river was even muddier than the Mackenzie River, which I had previously considered the muddiest river I'd ever seen. This meant that boiling tea or filling water bottles invariably resulted in drinking quite a bit of muddy sediment (what we in the business call extra protein). As for washing one's face or hands, they would only come out of the river muddier than when they went in. Fishing, too, proved of little use in such a waterway.

The river had dozens of smallish rapids all down its course, particularly the upper half. They were minor compared to what we'd found on the Anderson River, but they nonetheless kept us on our toes paddling, as many contained sweepers, that is, fallen spruces reaching across the water with their sharp, broken-off branches. If we weren't careful, the canoe might easily slam into one of these fallen trees, spin sideways, and flip over. But we both agreed that the river's dominant characteristic was its endless meanders. There were so many S-bends that we sometimes felt as if we merely paddling around in circles. The high banks, too, meant that in the canoe we often couldn't see much beyond the confines of the river. This was not necessarily a bad thing: the steep banks helped partially shelter us from the bitterly cold winds that were frequently blowing out of the North, coming as they did from the Arctic Ocean.

One thing we had both wondered about was the origin of the river's name. I had consulted the usual geographic databases in the hopes of learning it, but none provided any explanation. We each had different theories for how it had acquired it. Chuck felt the name reflected the murky, or "smoky," waters of the river, with all its mud and sediment washed in. But I felt that the name was more literal. It reminded me of a passage in the explorer Alexander Mackenzie's account of his 1793 expedition to the Pacific. He had mentioned coming upon a riverbank in the mountains that had, in his words, "chasms in the earth that emitted heat and smoke, which diffused a strong sulphureous stench." I had happened to be in northern British Columbia earlier in the year and had seen these steam vents myself, so they were fresh in my mind. I knew also of a passage in the explorer Sir John Franklin's book that described something similar more than a hundred kilometres east of here near the Beaufort Sea, where it was said that there were "smoking hills" that burned eternally from underground sulphur deposits. I wondered if something similar might exist on this river. If so, then perhaps at some point long ago some unknown hunter or trapper had wandered over the area and reported the smoke. Or if not that, maybe a bush pilot flying overhead might once have spotted smoke from above and thereby given the river its name.

On our third day paddling downriver, the landscape suddenly began to transform: high hills rose in the distance. Along the banks were dark red rocks and strange yellow ones. Then as we kept edging ahead, we saw steep cliffs of sandstone and sulphur. I pulled out my binoculars and scanned the horizon through a light rain; faint plumes of grey smoke were rising from the high, eroded bank ahead of us. We pushed on to investigate: sure enough, in various places, smoke was billowing straight out of crevices in sulphuric rocks. This was exciting, as it now seemed clear the name of the river must reflect this curious natural phenomenon.

Apparently, as far as we could figure out, the smoke comes from natural auto-ignition underground, which causes the sulfur-rich lignite deposits to burn continuously, as presumably they have for centuries. Besides smoking caverns, the entire landscape here looked like something from another planet: desolate grey hills devoid of vegetation and high cliffs of weathered red sandstone and yellowish sulphuric rock, mixed up with dark black soils from erosion. The rain and grey skies added to the odd, otherworldly effect. Given our extreme isolation and the fact that we hadn't been able to learn anything about this place beforehand, as we stood watching rocky cliffsides emit plumes of grey smoke, we felt almost like astronauts on another planet rather than merely canoeists. It again filled me with that feeling of irresistible wanderlust, the overpowering urge to explore mysterious landscapes, which had so driven Darrell.

Ahead of us, the river had more surprises in store. It plunged through a couple of canyons, where we zigzagged down through rapids, cautiously, as we didn't know if there were waterfalls or other hazards ahead, the maps being of no particular use. After these canyons, the banks remained high and steep, with more landslides nearly cutting the river in two. The grey skies and occasional drizzle added to a sort of hazy, dreamlike sense of this whole section where nothing looked like anything we'd ever seen before. Only gradually did the river regain a more normal appearance, with spruces growing again on either bank. It was by that point a welcome change to get back into something less alien-feeling.

Hopping about in the sparse spruce woods, we spotted dozens of plump ptarmigans, their plumage having half turned from brown to white already, an indication that winter was not far off. These birds at times seemed almost as tame as chickens and were easy to approach. Darrell had often mentioned making meals of them. Besides the ptarmigans, the Smoke River had a great number of birds of prey, including peregrine falcons. The falcons were nesting along the cliffs or high banks, while we also spotted a merlin, bald eagles, and a splendid-looking hawk owl perched atop a spruce. These northern owls are unique in being active during the day. In a lonely land, such feathered companions are always a welcome sight. Frequently, Darrell had noted in his diaries the birds he saw, and sometimes how, alone at his camps, he'd listen to the hooting of nearby owls as he drifted off to sleep. Just now, curled up in my sleeping bag, jacket on and hood up, I did the same, thinking of owls, vanished explorers, rocks that emitted smoke, and what tomorrow might hold.

22

HUSKY LAKES

By far the biggest grizzly I'd ever seen was staring right at us. We had continued downriver after breaking camp, passing low banks with willow bushes. Just as Chuck and I were remarking how odd it was that we hadn't seen any bigger animals, I looked up from my place in the canoe's stern to behold a massive grizzly glaring at us. It was only about forty feet away on the bank and just stood there motionless as if astounded by us, while we stared right back in equal wonder. It was really a beautiful bear, with a thick shaggy coat of dark undersides and an almost blond hue to the top, with a big oval face. At this time of the year, the bears are putting on as much weight as they can for the long winter, when they go into hibernation. When we drifted upwind of it, the bear took off into the willows.

The trees had continued to thin out as we went down the Smoke River, and soon the only ones to be found were right along the sheltered river valley, with nothing but windswept tundra lying beyond. Eventually even these last stunted trees faded away, and we found ourselves on the true arctic barrens. The river in total measured longer than I had anticipated, some 225 kilometres, as the countless snaking S-bends and meanders make it much longer than one would guess. Our progress down it had been considerably slowed by fierce winds, which chilled us to the marrow and made paddling at times painfully slow.

Nowhere on the entire river did we see any sign of past human activity, not even so much as a cut stump. But Darrell, at most, would only have briefly passed over this river when it was frozen, on his final trek from the Anderson River back to meet the Jacquots. As such, I hadn't expected to search for any trace of him here, as Stringer's letter suggested his last campsite, where his gear had been found, must have been somewhere near the shores of the Husky Lakes.

When after a week we reached the river's outlet on the Beaufort Sea, it was a sight to see: a vast and pitiless expanse of frigid ocean. At the river's mouth lay a bewildering maze of channels and islands covered in salt grass and driftwood. At high tide some of these islands disappear altogether. Chuck and I snaked our way through them, then formulated a plan of where to head next. Ahead of us lay Liverpool Bay, and on its eastern side the entrance to the Husky Lakes, which on a map resemble the gills of a giant fish: five long narrow bays, which then connect into a series of vast, peninsula-riven lakes. The whitecaps and fierce winds sweeping off the Arctic Sea made it too dangerous for us to cut straight across Liverpool Bay's expanse (it's more than fifteen kilometres wide), so our only choice was to trace out the shore the long way around. But this wasn't a bad thing, as I had wanted to do this anyway to keep an eye out for any relics or other indications of Darrell's last camp (and truth be told, even if conditions had been dead calm, the idea of canoeing miles from land across arctic waters home to whales and polar bears wasn't all that appealing).

We had filled our water bottles before leaving the Smoke River, as we knew it would be a long way before finding fresh-water again. Jacquot had mentioned in his account of his trip with Darrell that they'd had a hard time finding any drinking water along the salty Husky Lakes. To purify saltwater over a campfire is a cumbersome and difficult process: boiling doesn't do anything to eliminate salt, so you must instead painstakingly collect the condensation from the steam, which isn't very prac-tical when travelling daily. Nor do the standard water purifiers sold at outdoor stores work for saltwater. As a result, we had no choice but to carefully ration our supply.

A more immediate concern were polar bears. Soon after reaching the coast, I had scanned the horizon with my binocu-lars for any sign of them, and spotted in the distance what looked like a large white boulder. I was pretty sure it was only a rock, but it seemed prudent to paddle as far away as we could before making camp.

Meanwhile, my attention was absorbed by Darrell. The letter written by Stringer, the Anglican missionary, was dated October 1917. That was already seven years after Darrell was last seen, but Stringer had been meticulous in recording everything he could from his Inuit informants. He'd learned some additional crucial details, which I've transcribed from his handwritten note in full here:

In March 1916, an Eskimo, Robert Chokituk found a "cache" apparently belonging to Darrell, near the Husky Lakes, about fifty miles from Darrell's camp on [the] Anderson River. Chokituk was setting a wolverine trap when he came across the "cache." The bundle was under a tree covered with a piece of canvas, and may have been originally hung in the tree. He found in it a Kodak and some flour and tea, and some old clothing, and the remains of four white fox skins (probably the ones Olay gave him for the canoe)—also a Baking Powder tin containing a little baking powder was hanging on a willow nearby. He saw many trees and willows chopped, as if someone had camped here for a considerable time.

William Kwisitehya, an Indian, with whom I journeyed this last summer for a couple of weeks, gave me particulars of the matter. He was at Chokituk's camp when he brought back the Kodak, about half a days journey from where it was found. The Kodak was taken to Kitiqajuit and given to Mr. Phillips of the Hudson's Bay Company, who sent it to Fort MacPherson. Mr. Smith told me it was sent out by the Police last summer. The place where the "cache" was found was about fifty or sixty [miles] from Kitiqajuit, and almost the same distance from the Anderson River. The snow was on the ground when the natives visited the place, and nothing more was seen. If it were visited in summer possibly the remains of Darrell or other indications of his whereabouts might be discovered.

My hope was to locate the place described in this letter. But given how vast the Husky Lakes are, knowing that the camp was somewhere near them didn't narrow things down much at all. The crucial clues were the distances recorded by Stringer. He had noted that it lay about "fifty or sixty miles" from Kitiqajuit, and almost an equal distance from the Anderson River. Kitiqajuit, or as it is more commonly spelled Kitigaaryuit, was once a small trading post that had existed near the Mackenzie River's mouth, though it's abandoned today. I determined its coordinates, and then from there, measured a line on a map fifty to sixty miles east, and did the same thing with a line running from the approximate site of Darrell's camp on the Anderson River. Where the two lines met would be the rough location of where the "cache" was found. But the problem was the two measurements didn't precisely line up, leaving a grey zone between them. This appeared to be somewhere along the western end of the Husky Lakes. But given the vagueness of the estimates, it was impossible to be sure. We'd again just have to keep our eyes out, it seemed.

Our first day of saltwater paddling brought us southwest along Liverpool Bay's windy expanse. There are no trees here, only waist-high bushes of arctic willow and dwarf birch. Fortunately, though, we found plenty of driftwood for fires and wild berries to eat, as well as tasty bolete mushrooms, which we roasted like marshmallows over our fire. Even though we were now nearly four hundred kilometres north of the Arctic Circle, I hadn't packed any camp stove, as I trusted from past experience that we would be able to find enough arctic willow and driftwood to burn. That's what Darrell and the Jacquots had done, after all.

Most of the shoreline was dominated by steep, eroded

willow-clad hills. The tops of some of these made ideal vantage points from which to scan the horizon for anything out of the ordinary. But the only human thing we could see lay far away in the distance on a peninsula jutting into the Beaufort Sea: its vague outline, with domed structures, metal towers, and antennas, looked jarringly out of place on the arctic landscape, more like something from a science fiction movie. It was an old Cold War–era military radar station, known as a Distant Early Warning site. Some of these stations are apparently still in use, though reportedly they've been entirely automated for decades. In any case, it was far away and not where we were headed.

Rough weather made paddling along the big open water of the Husky Lakes a challenge. We had to carefully select our crossings between points and battle hard against wind and waves. The tidal nature of these "lakes" further complicates paddling. When the tide is going out in the narrow sections it creates swift currents. On the bright side, in the salty water there were plenty of purple jellyfish to look at, and we also spotted several seals. One of these seals surprised me by its large size when it surfaced amid whitecaps just as we were battling big waves in the canoe. The Jacquots and Darrell had also reported coming across many seals along these shores. But so far we hadn't found any human artifacts, just bear tracks, caribou, ducks, geese, loons, and nesting arctic terns, as well as various shorebirds.

✳

While pinned down for an entire day during stormy weather, I took the time in my tent to restudy the printed copies of Stringer's letter. It had begun to feel like a hopeless task, and I was starting to get a bit discouraged, thinking we would never find anything. But curled up in my tent in the rain, studying Stringer's letter for the umpteenth time in the hopes of gleaning some clue from it that I might have overlooked, something finally hit me like a sack of bricks. The letter had mentioned that the bundle of Darrell's things had been found "*under a tree covered with a piece of canvas, and may have been originally hung in the tree.*" This was it, the vital detail staring me in the face that I'd been over-looking: everywhere we had seen along the Husky Lakes had no trees, only open tundra.

That "trees" meant actual spruces, and not just willow shrubs, was also evident since Stringer had written that "he saw many trees and willows chopped, as if someone had camped here for a considerable time." The letter clearly distinguished then between "willows" and "trees." The report from the Mounties, too, writ-ten before the Stringer letter, had also stated that Darrell's camera and bag of furs had been found suspended in a tree. Evidently then, we had been looking too far north, as we were beyond the treeline. Wherever Darrell's final camp was, it must have been somewhere spruces grew.

I had packed with me a 1960s-era topographic map of the Husky Lakes, which included the approximate extent of the tree-line. It showed only a single location where the treeline overlapped with the Husky Lakes. But perhaps the position of the treeline had changed since Darrell's day. Fortunately, I had also packed a modern satellite image of the Husky Lakes. I compared this with the older map to see if there was any hint that the treeline had shifted north or otherwise changed over the decades. But it hadn't:

it aligned perfectly with the old map. Even today, the only area where the treeline overlapped at all with the Husky Lakes was in their southeastern extremity, near the end of a long tapering bay. To be certain, I again measured out the estimated distances given in Stringer's letter to see if this pocket of forest fell within their radius—*it did*. The thought gave me chills: this then, I felt, must be the place where Darrell's final camp was to be found.

There was just one problem. We had already passed well beyond that point, and it now lay nearly a hundred kilometres back the other direction. Given the lateness of the season and the rough, windy conditions, there was no way we could detour back there and still catch our return flights. Even if we could somehow change them, or just miss them, winter was near at hand. Once snow blanketed everything, we'd have no hope of finding anything. The thought vexed me as I lay in my sleeping bag, listening to the rain patter off my tent as I drifted off to sleep.

A couple of days later, still canoeing along the windy arctic shores of the Husky Lakes, Chuck and I heard the low drone of a distant engine. It was now the second week of September, and we had not seen another soul since the pilot had dropped us almost two weeks earlier. Soon we could see a small boat coming down the coast with a caribou lashed across the front. On board were five people. When they came alongside us, they expressed considerable shock at meeting anyone out here in a canoe. They were even more surprised when we said we'd come from the Smoke River. They told us that they'd never heard of anyone paddling that river. They were an Inuvialuit family from Tuktoyaktuk and invited us to have lunch with them (the fresh caribou). (Afterwards they told us they assumed we must be Germans, as they said no one else would be crazy enough to canoe here in September.)

The leader of the party was sixty-eight-year-old Chuck Gruben, a hunting guide from Tuktoyaktuk. It turned out that I had actually met and interviewed several of his elderly relatives, including his uncle, Billy Jacobson. With Gruben was his brother, cousin, son, and granddaughter (I shall call him Gruben, as it'd be otherwise quite confusing to refer to two Chucks). We enjoyed a lively lunch and northern hospitality at its finest, sipping tea and munching on crackers and fresh caribou. I explained my interest in Darrell and locating his final campsite. I was hoping they might by some chance know of some old camp matching the description in Stringer's letter, but alas, like everyone else, they had never heard of Darrell. But I immediately thought how we might be able to collaborate to search more ground, especially the spot with the apparent trees that I identified on the map as the most promising. This, however, wasn't possible right away. For one thing, their boat didn't have enough gas to get there—a trip back to Tuktoyaktuk to stock up on jerry cans would be necessary. Secondly, Gruben told us bad weather in the form of high winds and heavy rain was expected for the next week or so, which would rule out travelling anywhere.

In the meantime, Gruben gave us a ride in his motorboat the rest of the way back through the Husky Lakes. There is no road access directly to the Husky Lakes, but with the completion in 2018 of a road linking the Dempster Highway to Tuktoyaktuk, the lakes can be reached by ATVs. At the trailhead to Tuktoyaktuk, we split up, as they were heading north for Tuktoyaktuk and Chuck and I had to go the opposite direction to Inuvik. To get there, Chuck and I paddled and portaged our canoe through a chain of little lakes that took us directly to the road. Here we camped another night on the tundra, now a brilliant blaze of fall colours. The next day we caught a ride south, bartering my canoe for it (a fair trade it seemed to me, as I couldn't afford to ship it home anyway).

But I was consumed now more than ever by the mystery of Darrell's disappearance, and I felt almost beside myself with the thought that his final campsite might be within my grasp. Once the forecasted bad weather passed, it seemed there was time to squeeze in at least a week of searching before it snowed. Chuck couldn't stick around for that: he had a trip booked to Greece, and so he had a flight to catch back home to the United States. But I made arrangements to head out as soon as I could with Gruben in his motorboat. He'd said he'd be happy to take me wherever I wished to go, and where I wished to go was that spot on the map where the trees overlapped with the tip of one solitary finger-like bay.

23

CHASING GHOSTS

Luckily, I had no trouble hitching a second ride back to Tuktoyaktuk, a roughly four-hour drive north from Inuvik over a rough gravel road across the tundra hills. There I met Chuck Gruben at his house, and we soon loaded up all our provisions in his boat. His brother Ron and cousin Jonas were joining us for the trip, as they had planned to do some caribou hunting while Gruben and I searched for Darrell's last camp.

By this point, daytime temperatures were just a few degrees above freezing, and in the autumn sky, long lines of ducks and geese were to be seen flying south. On our passage through the shimmering blue expanse of the Husky Lakes, we stopped frequently to hunt the stately caribou that roamed the surrounding hills. They joked that since I was the youngest by several decades, it was my job to haul any caribou they shot back to the boat. I ended up hauling one large buck over willowy hills about a kilometre. But my efforts were more than repaid by being fed fresh caribou three times a day (breakfast, lunch, and dinner) and especially by the vast store of rich knowledge I gained from the three of them. Over the week we spent together hunting and exploring, I asked them to tell me everything they could about the history of the region, including any trapping, hunting, and other stories.

Even if they didn't know Darrell, I felt there was much to be gained from these stories. Moreover, I wanted to visit any historical sites that they knew of, whether or not they had any connection to Darrell. This resulted in Gruben showing me a gravesite from 1934, some remains of very old "houses" (actually semi-hovels dug into the ground more than a thousand years ago), a place where he once found a woolly mammoth tusk sticking out of an eroded bank, and several old encampments. Indirectly all of this was useful and raised my hopes that it might be possible to find the place described in Stringer's letter.

My reasons for cautious optimism were twofold: in the first case, the arctic climate means wood doesn't rot quickly. Stumps cut in the 1800s still remain. Even areas cleared of slow-growing arctic willow in some cases more than century ago, as Gruben showed me, remain notably denuded today, which might mean that some trace of the area Darrell had once cleared could still be visible. Stringer's letter had said "He saw many trees and willows chopped, as if someone had camped here for a considerable time." That was what I hoped to find.

My second reason for optimism was the fact it was fairly easy to distinguish traditional Inuit or Indigenous campsites from what would be expected of Darrell's. Since most of the Husky Lakes are ringed by steeply eroded shores that prevent any landing, possible campsites are few and far between. The best ones are naturally on low sandy shores with freshwater streams nearby, and for that reason, the same sites tend to have been used and reused for centuries. At any of these places, signs of past use are sure to be found—quartered caribou bones, rusty old cans, and other discarded items. But Darrell, travelling alone and cross-country from the Anderson River, would have simply hit the Husky Lakes wherever he did, and not at an opportune camping spot like a low shore or beach with a stream.

Rainy weather and winds were an impediment to travel, even in a motorboat, and our base during this time was Gruben's hunt cabin, a little one-room structure made of plywood on Liverpool Bay. From here I sometimes took long hikes over the tundra hills, turning over the pieces of the puzzle and digesting the things I'd learned. I had asked Gruben if he knew of any old spots where wolverines were traditionally trapped, since Stringer's letter had mentioned that the hunter who'd found Darrell's camera and other gear had been setting a wolverine trap at the time. But Gruben indicated they could be trapped in many places, so this didn't help narrow things down any further.

Finally, with calmer conditions but still another cold, wet fall day, the two of us at last headed to the area I felt was the most promising for Darrell's final camp. Since almost all the Husky Lake's shoreline is treeless tundra, it left only that extreme southeastern corner that overlapped with the treeline to search. In the boat we headed up a long narrowing bay in a light rain to where clumps of black spruces started to materialize on the otherwise barren hills. Gruben dropped me onshore, allowing me to climb up the steep cliff-like banks and hike along the top, while he piloted the boat down below. The ground was difficult to walk over because of all the mossy hummocks, lichens, and low shrubs. The area, given the difficulty of accessing it from the water, didn't seem like a place anyone would camp under normal circumstances. Everything I saw, including the weather-beaten spruce trees, looked undisturbed.

Just as I started to think that I should turn back and try somewhere else, I came upon a spot that looked like it may have once been cleared: the knee-high clumps of arctic willow that dominated everywhere else were sparse or absent here. Stringer's letter had said that where Darrell's gear had been found, the willows had been cleared away, as if someone had camped there for a while. Among the scattered spruces, I searched until I suddenly came upon a sight that gave me chills: a cluster of ancient, worn stumps, more than a dozen in all. The slash marks still visible in them showed that they had been felled by an axe. Someone had evidently once camped here for some time: the lichens encrusting the stumps were the crucial clues to figuring out just how long ago. In the Arctic, it takes approximately fifty to a hundred years for lichens to establish themselves on a surface, with an estimated growth rate of less than 0.1 millimetre per year. I bent down and carefully examined the profusion of lichens growing over the cut marks on the stumps. Their robust growth suggested that these weathered stumps had to be at least a century old. They were in the right location too— near the Husky Lakes, within equal distance of the Anderson River and Kitiqajuit, and on the approximate course Darrell would had to have taken to reach the point where he and the Jacquots had split up. I looked around at the deserted tundra and sparse forest: could this really be where the epic saga of

Hubert Darrell had come to an end? Was this lonely spot his final resting place?

His skeleton would probably have long since been scattered and gnawed away by wolverines and other scavengers—that is, if his remains hadn't first been dragged away by a bear. Traditionally, in the Arctic, human remains are piled over with rocks to prevent animals from scavenging them (permafrost makes digging graves difficult), but Darrell of course wouldn't have had anyone to do this for him. I searched among the lichen, moss, and bushes for any telltale artifacts, but saw none. This, however, was a clue in itself: suggesting as it did that the site was likely used only by a lone individual who had stopped there relatively briefly, since if it had been occupied by a larger party or for a longer time, then other traces would remain. (This was clear from the historical encampments Gruben had shown me, where dozens of rusty old tin cans and other discarded items were invariably to be found.) Gruben, who had landed the boat and come up to join me, felt this must be the place, as he knew that there was nowhere else trees could be found except in this bay. Nor did it seem at all likely that any Inuk hunter would have bothered to climb such a steep bluff to cut down straggly little spruces, when much larger driftwood logs could easily be found along the shore.

Then again, maybe this was just the remains of some other lone wanderer's camp from long ago. But somehow it didn't feel like that. Somehow, standing there on that windswept, lonely plain with its ancient, scattered spruces, looking out toward the red sun sinking below the horizon, I felt in my bones that this was where Darrell's journey had ended.

Sulphur and sandstone cliffs along the mysterious Smoke River. "Besides smoking caverns, the entire landscape here looked like something from another planet: desolate grey hills devoid of vegetation and high cliffs of weathered red sandstone and yellowish sulphuric rock, mixed up with dark black soils from erosion." PHOTO CREDIT: Chuck Brill

"Sure enough, in various places, smoke was billowing straight out of crevices in sulphuric rocks." PHOTO CREDIT: Adam Shoalts

"A splendid-looking hawk owl perched atop a spruce. These northern owls are unique in being active during the day. In a lonely land, such feathered companions are always a welcome sight." PHOTO CREDIT: Adam Shoalts

"We spotted dozens of plump ptarmigans, their plumage having half turned from brown to white already, an indication that winter was not far off." PHOTO CREDIT: Adam Shoalts

A big grizzly bear staring at us on the Smoke River in September. At this time of year, the bears are putting on weight for their long winter's sleep. PHOTO CREDIT: Adam Shoalts

One of our camps along the coast of the Beaufort Sea near Liverpool Bay. PHOTO CREDIT: Chuck Brill

Chuck Gruben, an Inuvialuit hunter from Tuktoyaktuk with a lifetime of hunting and trapping experience. PHOTO CREDIT: Adam Shoalts

A caribou herd on the tundra hills near the Husky Lakes.
PHOTO CREDIT: Adam Shoalts

A view of the windswept Husky Lakes and their steeply eroded shores. Note also the absence of trees: most of the Husky Lakes lie north of the treeline. PHOTO CREDIT: Adam Shoalts

A curious seal in the Husky Lakes. Seals are the main food of polar bears, and for that reason, the bears sometimes wander into the Husky Lakes. PHOTO CREDIT: Adam Shoalts

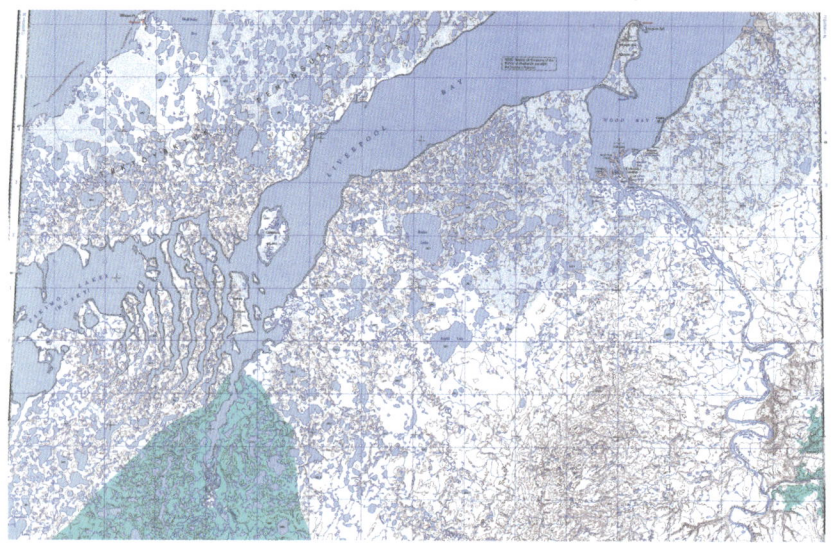

A topographic map showing the labyrinth of thousands of lakes, creeks, and rivers between the Anderson River (the big, squiggly blue line on the right side of the map) and the Husky Lakes (the peninsula-riven lakes on the left side of the map). Green shaded areas show the approximate position of the treeline and forest, a critical clue to deciphering the location of Darrell's last campsite. At the time he vanished, he was travelling overland from the Anderson River to the Husky Lakes. CREDIT: Natural Resources Canada

A photograph of a makeshift canvas tent on the arctic tundra in 1911. Note the small spruces placed around it for additional shelter. This set-up is probably very similar to what Darrell often used, including at his final camp. PHOTO CREDIT: George Douglas

The site of Darrell's presumed last camp in 1910. The arctic willows (the red bushes visible in the upper left of the photograph and background) had been cut away long ago. PHOTO CREDIT: Adam Shoalts

Ancient, weathered stumps chopped by an axe and encrusted with lichens. In the Arctic, it takes an estimated fifty to a hundred years for lichens to establish themselves on a surface. These stumps, part of a larger cluster of around a dozen, are consistent with Darrell's time and are in the exact location he would have had to cross on his final journey when he vanished. PHOTO CREDIT: Adam Shoalts

Polar bear tracks. With his friends the Jacquots, Darrell came across large polar bear tracks on the Husky Lakes in the fall of 1910.
PHOTO CREDIT: Adam Shoalts

A polar bear in the Arctic in 2024. PHOTO CREDIT: Adam Shoalts

There was something else, too, that had become clear to me: the standard explanation that Darrell had most likely perished after falling through the ice on his return trek is almost certainly incorrect. I'd been trying to fit the various pieces of the puzzle together in my mind, and I'd at last arrived at a conclusion about what had happened to Darrell. It wasn't what I had thought originally, but it was the horrifying explanation that all the evidence hinted at. As I stood there on the tundra, among the weathered stumps, I felt I could now visualize pretty fully how Darrell's last days had unfolded . . .

24

PIECING THE PUZZLE TOGETHER

*D*arrell had reached the tip of the Husky Lakes after a journey on snowshoes of five or six days from his camp on the Anderson River. He knew, from his earlier canoe trip with the Jacquots, that wood was scarce anywhere on the lakes. So he naturally decided to make camp here, in the last little clump of black spruces he'd see for a while. The trees would provide a bit of shelter from the bitter winds and wood for a much-needed fire. It was a comfortable spot for a camp, on a high cliff-like bank that commanded an excellent view of the surrounding territory and the route ahead. He then unpacked his things from his light sled, carefully slinging his prized camera in its bag up in a tree, so if the snow turned heavy it wouldn't be buried. After rigging up a small canvas tarp that served as his makeshift tent, Darrell set himself to gathering a supply of wood.

Later, however, the weather turned severe, with heavy snow and all the makings of a blizzard. Come the next morning conditions showed no signs of improving. Another man might have tried to push on, impatient to get back to his friends and the comforts of Fort McPherson.

But not Darrell: experience had taught him that it was foolhardy to travel in such weather and that it was better to stay put for several days, or longer if need be, before resuming his trek. He'd done the same when leading young Corporal Haylow of the Mounties to Herschel Island, hunkering down in a hastily built snow shelter for three days while they waited for an arctic gale to subside. He'd first learned not to risk travelling in such weather from Yinto, and with Hanbury he'd often been stormbound for days at a time. Ever since, he'd obeyed this wise rule.

Having left his Anderson River camp on November 24, 1910, it was now about the first of December. The Jacquots were expecting him by December 10, so there was no need to hurry, as many times before he'd covered a similar distance in less time. And in any case Darrell had plenty of food: besides the rations he had obtained from the whaling ship, he had his shotgun for hunting ptarmigan, now white as snow in their winter plumage, and his rifle for caribou. In fact, the country he'd passed through since he'd left his camp on the Anderson River had abounded with game. Caribou were to be found by the dozens, and he hunted them like he always did when travelling, quickly cutting up the meat and carrying it on his sled.

But with several days of bad weather, though he didn't lack for meat, his wood supply was running low. It'd been two or three days with no let-up in the blizzard, and Darrell now had more than a dozen stumps surrounding his camp; some he'd felled for his fire, others to make a windbreak to prevent the snow from drifting over his camp, and the green boughs he'd collected for his bedding, to insulate himself from the freezing ground. The surrounding arctic willow, too, he'd mostly used up. To secure more wood, it was necessary then to go a little farther, a hundred yards or so, where there was another cluster of lonely black spruces. In the bitter arctic cold, large quantities of wood were needed to stay comfortable.

So axe in hand, Darrell went a short distance outside his camp. The snow meanwhile was still coming down steadily, and given it was now December, there was no sunrise. Darkness had settled over the land, and it would remain for another month. In the faint gloom, he could just make out the outlines of the spruces ahead. The wind and the crunching of the snow under his snowshoes were the only sounds to disturb the dark silence. But something suddenly made the hair on the back of his neck rise. What was that on the wind? A slight odour, some pungent smell. Darrell turned quickly and tried to survey the desolate landscape around him as well as he could: endless miles of snowbound tundra, without a human footprint other than his own for at least a hundred miles. Across that white expanse of swirling snow, only a few scattered, straggly spruces punctuated the barren landscape. Darrell knew that the scent of meat would sometimes attract a grizzly into a camp: only four years earlier his fellow trapper Albert Ross had been badly mauled by one. But the grizzlies were now well into hibernation and would not emerge from their dens for another five months.

Polar bears were another matter. Unlike grizzlies, the great white bears don't hibernate, hunting and prowling all winter long. These giants, the largest land carnivores on Earth, mainly stay out on the sea ice, killing seals and the odd beluga. But Darrell knew that they came into the Husky Lakes too; with the Jacquots, he'd seen their enormous tracks just a few months earlier. Jacquot, being a trapper who normally stayed south of the treeline, had been staggered at the size of such monstrous tracks. It certainly seemed that any creature that had made them must never know fear.

Darrell regretted leaving his rifle at his camp. On his person he had only his axe and belt knife, as he needed his hands free to gather wood. The falling snow and eerie moan of the wind made it even harder to see or hear anything in the darkness. After standing motion-less for as long as he could bear in the frigid air, Darrell dismissed his doubts and turned back toward the wood he'd been gathering. Despite their formidable size, polars bears are patient, ambush hunters: relying on their white fur to camouflage them into the snowy landscape, wait-ing in silent invisibility for their prey to show themselves, and then suddenly striking with an explosion of speed and power.

In an instant, a white bear that had come in from the ice, attracted by the smell of meat and human flesh, was upon him. Darrell's startled shouts echoed across the empty land where none would ever hear them. He frantically jabbed with his knife at the enormous monster pinning him down, mercilessly tearing into him with its bone-crushing jaws and the razor-sharp claws that were adapted for gripping sea ice. Darrell, the fearless explorer who had crossed mountains in the dead of winter when no one else dared, who'd guided Mounties and saved the lives of others, who'd faced perils beyond count, was now in the fight of his life against an adversary as terrifying as any that walked the ice. Again and again Darrell stabbed at it, but the bear was impervious to his steel blade—protected by a two-inch-thick coat and a five-inch fat layer that his short knife couldn't get through. Even a well-placed rifle shot doesn't always bring down a polar bear, as many a hunter has learned too late. Brave and strong as Darrell was, against the monster of the ice he had little chance, and he knew it. It was all over soon, the bear dragging his body across the empty tundra, consuming nearly all trace of him, other than perhaps some bones to be scavenged by wolverines. Only the bloodstains briefly told of the strug-gle, which were quickly blotted out by the falling snow.

✳

For years, I had assumed that Darrell had most likely fallen through a patch of ice somewhere on his return journey. That, after all, seemed to have been the common opinion at the time, and I saw little reason to doubt it. But it'd finally dawned on me that this explanation didn't make any sense. If Darrell had fallen through the ice, then all of his supplies (which he towed behind him on a small sled) would have been lost with him, either directly when he plunged through the hole, or later when the ice broke up. But Stringer's letter showed that Darrell's possessions—his Kodak camera, the tin he used as a makeshift stove, flour and food rations, furs and other things—were all found still intact at his camp. Darrell wouldn't have left these things behind. That means he wasn't travelling at the time, and instead points to some sudden, unexpected disaster overtaking him while he was still at his camp.

What could that have been? It was obvious Darrell didn't starve, as he'd obtained more than enough provisions from the whaling ship, *Rosie H*, and in any case he could hunt. Nor was he lost: the route back through the Husky Lakes was known to him, and no more difficult than many past routes he'd taken. If a sudden illness had overtaken him, then presumably at least some of his remains might have been found near his tent or he would have left another note of some kind in a tree or elsewhere indicating that he was ill. Some Mounted Police reports had speculated that Darrell had perhaps perished in a snowstorm while he slept, the snow falling so quickly and packing so hard that he couldn't get out. But this was again before the remnants of his camp were found, and since Darrell had endured countless arctic blizzards before, including days-long gales on the frozen Arctic Ocean, it doesn't seem very likely. Stefansson, who was in a better position to judge, had ruled this out, concluding that, as far as Darrell's final trek went, "there was nothing to be feared from blizzards or cold, nor was there any danger of his missing his way and suffering starvation for that reason—some other men might have been in danger from these things, but not Darrell."

That doesn't leave many other possibilities for something suddenly killing Darrell at his camp—except, that is, a polar bear. To paraphrase Sherlock Holmes, when you have eliminated the impossible, whatever remains, however improbable, must be the truth. Except in this case, there is nothing at all improbable about a polar bear attack, especially on a lone person camped in the darkness of arctic winter without even a sled dog. Across the North, polar bears are universally regarded as very dangerous, aggressive apex predators with little fear of humans, and examples of fatal attacks on humans are easy to find. For this reason, both today and historically, Inuit usually travel in groups, seldom alone, and often with huskies to sound the alarm of an approaching bear. To camp alone in polar bear territory would be inherently risky indeed, particularly at the time of the year Darrell was travelling: late November or early December, when at those latitudes there is twenty-four hours of darkness. No matter how skilled or experienced Darrell may have been, in the darkness of an arctic night, he stood little chance against a polar bear.

Nor is this all: there are actual hints from the time that Darrell had indeed been killed by a polar bear. Stephen North, son of Darrell's Manitoban friend William North, recalled that "nothing official was ever learned of his disappearance, but Charlie did his very best, contacting whomsoever he could . . . Various rumours filtered out of the Arctic for years—Eskimos had discovered his remains, he'd been killed by polar bears etc., but absolutely nothing authentic."

At first, I had viewed this statement as only a vague rumour, as I had initially thought that the inland area near the treeline where Darrell was camped wasn't a particularly likely spot for a polar bear. Normally polar bears are found offshore on the sea ice where they stalk their main prey, seals. Gruben had also told me that nowadays polar bears were only occasionally seen in the Husky Lakes. However, when I later read up on historical fur trade reports, I learned that polar bears may once have been more common in the Husky Lakes region. But what really changed my perspective on the matter and sent a chill down my spine was finding Joseph Jacquot's first-hand account of his final trip with Darrell. Jacquot had stated that while travelling through the Husky Lakes, they had actually come across "a polar bear track, a very fresh and large one. It resembled more than anything else the bottom of a barrel." That description rings true: the enormous, unsettling tracks of a polar bear, if left in snow or sand, often appear rounded if the wind obscured the edges.

This direct testimony from Jacquot seemed to cast things in a new light, proving as it did that polar bears were around the Husky Lakes at the time Darrell proposed to travel through them—alone, on snowshoes, without even sled dogs. The Jacquots, notably, had four tough huskies with them at the time Darrell left them, and they'd also been staying in a log shack they'd quickly built, not in a canvas tent like Darrell. If Darrell had fresh meat in his camp, which he more than likely did, the scent might have further attracted a ravenous, stalking bear. And if Darrell did fall prey to a bear, then it could have only been a polar bear, as grizzlies at that time of year are hibernating, whereas polar bears are active year-round.

In fact, there is even some evidence that the Inuit hunters and trappers of the area had themselves believed a polar bear was behind Darrell's disappearance. The rumours that Stephen North recalled seem to have originated from Inuit hunters who would have visited the nearest trading posts—the same posts Charles sent letters to asking if anything had been heard of his brother's fate. The traders in charge had apparently written back indicating that it was believed Darrell had been killed by a polar bear. Further corroborating these vague reports is an account written by the spouse of a Mountie stationed in the Arctic about twenty years after Darrell's disappearance. Luta Munday and her husband, Walter, lived in the North for many years, becoming friends and neighbours with many Inuit families. In her memoir, Munday actually made a passing reference to Darrell, commenting that he'd perished "from an attack by a polar bear." She gave no further details, but it seems clear that she could only have learned this from Inuit sources, as Darrell had by that point faded completely from the news or other publications, none of which had ever mentioned a bear attack in connection with him. Taken with Stephen North's earlier recollection of such rumours, Jacquot's statement of finding polar bear tracks, the circumstances of Darrell's last camp, the fact he was alone on foot at the time, and that few other explanations hold up, the odds seem to strongly favour a polar bear as the cause of Darrell's disappearance. Of course, other possible explanations exist, and although we can never know for certain, at minimum it seems safe to say that whatever befell Darrell did so suddenly at his camp, and not while he was travelling across open ice as originally supposed. Whatever did happen to him, it was the opinion of his contemporaries that Darrell would have met it with the same courage that characterized his extraordinary journeys. As Darrell's fellow explorer Stefansson put it, "It is not likely we shall ever know what the ultimate end of Darrell was; but whatever it was, those who knew him feel sure that he met it bravely."

I felt I had now followed the mystery and the breadcrumb trail left by Darrell as far as humanly possible. Winter was coming any day, and so, with our exploration finished, the next morning we headed back the 160 kilometres by boat to the put-in spot at the end of the Husky Lakes. I spent another day in Tuktoyaktuk with Gruben and his family, enjoying some wonderful hospitality and fine cooking, before flying home.

25

LEGACY

As we had made our boat journey back through the Husky
Lakes, passing golden willow-clad hills, I found myself
reflecting on Darrell's legacy and the many ironies of his life. Just
four years after Darrell had vanished, the Yukon and Alaskan
newspapers were again running headlines about a noted traveller
disappearing in the wilderness: none other than Darrell's closest
friend, the Métis trapper Joseph Jacquot. Jacquot's body and
overturned canoe were later found washed up near the mouth
of the Mackenzie River. Jacquot, like Darrell, had originally
come north during the Klondike gold rush and had remained
ever since as a fur trapper, dogsled musher, wanderer, and adventurer. No wonder then that the two got along so well. (They'd
first met shortly after Darrell had punched out Harrison.)
Jacquot's own disappearance and death is a reminder that such
stories were not uncommon for the time, to the point one almost
wonders how the local newspapers could have stayed in business
without them.

To travel alone in a land where temperatures could fall to fifty below and inflict frostbite within minutes, where there were months of unbroken darkness, deadly avalanches in the mountains, sudden landslides along the rivers, immense distances between inhabited places, blinding blizzards, scarce food resources, vast storm-prone lakes, and icy rapids wasn't for the faint of heart. To survive in such a place required tenacity in spades, and life was often hard and usually short. Nowadays, as our society becomes ever more digital, there is a tendency to romanticize the receding past and what survival in such an environment was actually like. One eye-opening statistic, though, comes from archaeological studies of Inuit life expectancy in pre-contact times, which estimate it at less than thirty years. Hanbury, who greatly admired the Inuit, was nonetheless struck by how he'd encountered virtually no elderly individuals anywhere in all his long travels among them. The "old" grandfathers were often only in their mid-thirties, since it was commonplace for good hunters to have their first children while still teenagers. A nomadic lifestyle that demanded hard travel and constant hunting on dangerous, shifting sea ice was difficult to sustain beyond a certain age. Inuit and Dene oral histories are filled with stories of hunters who disappeared on the ice, perished in blizzards, drowned in fierce storms, starved in hard winters, became disoriented and lost their way, were killed hunting bears, or otherwise met with fatal accidents. One might wonder then, given how difficult and harsh conditions could be, what Darrell found so strangely appealing about it.

Like thousands of others, Darrell had first been drawn to the North by the lure of quick riches in the goldfields. But unlike most of those fortune-seekers who found the frozen isolation and other hardships too difficult to endure and soon left, he stuck around. Jack London, who became famous for his stories of life in the Yukon, lasted only nine months and was bedridden for much of it with scurvy. At the first opportunity, he quit, never to return, heading back to his home in sunny California. Yet ever afterwards he seemed to be haunted by the memory of it, writing more than eighty stories set in the North, including *White Fang* and *The Call of the Wild*. And while London liked to cultivate a public image of himself as a tough, hardscrabble adventurer of the wilds, he lived in a mansion with servants. Darrell, in contrast, really did live the life that London described in his stories, and aside from his brief summons to help on the farm, he would remain there ever after. In one of his letters, Darrell had remarked, "You have no idea how enjoyable it is in the North to those who know how to adapt themselves to the surroundings." Then he added, "To those who do not it is a life of misery."

Even Dawson was far too crowded for Darrell's tastes. His restless wanderlust seemed to drive him to seek ever more remote, wilder places far from the beaten track, at a time when most people were going the other direction: leaving the countryside for the booming cities of the industrial age and the new opportunities they offered. Darrell turned his back on all that in favour of the wilderness. And not just any wild, like the picturesque woods and lakes not far from Birtle, but the most distant places he could possibly find.

Hanbury, who understood Darrell better than most, provided a partial answer for what drove him. "Exploring the barren Northland," observed Hanbury, "has a wonderful fascination for those who have once penetrated its solitude." There is indeed something almost intoxicating about the awe-inspiring immensity of the arctic plains, where nature still seems utterly untamed. There are few landscapes on Earth where a person feels as alone as on the seemingly limitless arctic tundra. To wander in these vast places is to enter a kind of magical world where one can travel for months and months without coming across another soul or even trace of humanity. Only perhaps at sea could a similar feeling be found; but for most, to go to sea meant to sign onboard a ship under someone else's orders, and to submit to strict discipline. But the wilderness was a place where one could be their own master, to roam free. True, that freedom came at a steep price: often back-breaking labour, harsh conditions, and high risks. It was that, more than anything, that attracted Darrell, and why he found it so hard to return to farm life.

In the wilderness, life was lived in the open, stripped away of all mental clutter and distractions. All one's worldly possessions had to be pulled on a sled or loaded in a canoe. Every day was a fresh adventure where nature beckoned, and though conditions were often brutal, the simplicity of things granted a strangely liberating feeling. Each night promised somewhere new to call home: spread out under the stars beside some enchanted, nameless lake with its crystal waters and ancient rocks, or perhaps on a lonely hillside beside the murmur of a cascading stream, as far from the smog, sprawl, noise, and bustle of the hurried modern world as one could get. In his journal, Darrell had once scribbled a description of one of his remote campsites: "hills, valleys, and lakes galore, beautiful country, green and full of flowers and grasses." To experience such places at times could feel almost like drifting into a dream. Particularly after a hard day of wet, weary travel, to halt for the night in such a place created the feeling that to get warm and dry before a blazing fire, sip a cup of tea, eat something, and lay out on a dry bed was all one really needed to be perfectly content.

Hanbury had described it as a "spell" that seemed to hold Darrell and those like him with almost magical power to the northern wild. But none captured this strange dynamic better than the Yukon poet Robert Service. Service knew of Darrell and his reputation for incredible solo treks, and it seems plausible that Darrell inspired some of Service's famous poetry. Service wrote of "the lure of the timeless things" that bewitched adventurous souls: the wild life, free but dangerous, the age-old roaming existence that defined humanity for the vast majority of our species' history—and for that reason, I think, speaks to something deep inside all of us, even if it is often dormant. But as Service also put it, "yet the Wild must win in the end." It did with Darrell, and Jacquot, and so many others.

And while most of those Klondike prospectors who dreamed of riches thought of getting away somewhere warm—Jack London made his home a Californian mansion, Service retired to the French Riviera, and even Hanbury settled down on a San Francisco Bay estate—Darrell, tellingly, once penned a letter explaining what he'd do if he ever got rich: "If I could only get lot's of money I would devote my time to exploring the unknown land North of Canada."

Though riches were always to elude him, Darrell did succeed in wandering over a truly immense area stretching thousands of kilometres from Hudson Bay to Alaska, and north even onto the frozen Northwest Passage—places few outsiders had ever seen. In this, he was regarded as without equal: certainly, he saw more of the North than virtually any of his contemporaries. Even more remarkable was the fact Darrell did his wanderings mainly alone and on foot, something that, as Stefansson said, was an unheard-of thing in age when travel by dogsled was the norm.

While to the world Darrell remained largely unknown, to those who chanced to cross his wandering path, he seems to have left an outsized impression. Hardened whaling captains marvelled at this strange wanderer who would appear suddenly out of the arctic mists at their ships, Antarctic explorers like Amundsen could only express their awe for his nonchalant approach and iron stamina, Yinto and the Dene hunters uniquely invited him to join their crucial hunts, Mounties entrusted their lives to him, Inuit trappers such as Olay had wanted Darrell as a trapping partner, fur traders extolled him for his honesty and reliability, and even back on the farm the quiet young man of few words was universally regarded for his work ethic and honesty.

After Darrell's disappearance, Amundsen, in his autobiography, wrote that he couldn't "forbear taking this opportunity to pay tribute" to the memory of Darrell, whom he described as "one of the finest men of the Northern breed that it has ever been my good fortune to meet." Coming from someone who knew Shackleton, Scott, and every other leading polar explorer of the era, this was high praise indeed. Amundsen further stated that if fate had not intervened, he would certainly have selected Darrell to be one of his elite band to make the historic first ever journey to the South Pole. That would have made Darrell the only non-Norwegian member of the party, and had interesting international ramifications given the national rivalries involved between Britain and Norway to reach the South Pole first. But it was not to be: as with many other chapters in Darrell's life, the chance to go down in history slipped through his fingers.

Stefansson, for his part, admitted in his own autobiography that "Darrell had to his credit more real achievement than many who are famous for their work in the north." Privately, he went even farther. A handwritten note in pencil, scribbled on the back of his typed manuscript stored in an American archive, reveals Stefansson's inner thoughts on Darrell: "The few white men who were on the north coast of Canada between 1906 and 1912 agree that Hubert Darrell was its greatest arctic traveller." Stefansson then added: "He did not have the advertising to make him famous but he had the ability that made him great." Indeed, despite Darrell's extraordinary accomplishments—his 1,600-kilometre solo trek to bring word of the trapped whalers' plight to the outside world; his epic journey with Hanbury, including his scientific work collecting a complete set of arctic butterflies; his guiding of the Mounties in the teeth of blizzards and over endless miles of ice and snow he never received any accolades, honours, fame, or, in some cases, even credit for what he did.

But perhaps the most touching tribute to Darrell was the one made by his friend Jacquot, who had stated that he was certain the Mounties of the "Lost Patrol" would have lived if only Darrell had been there. Neufeld, the fellow Manitoban farm boy who'd earlier tried to rescue Darrell from historical obscurity, claimed that "had he lived longer, Hubert Darrell would undoubtedly have ranked . . . as a giant of polar exploration."

Despite Darrell's reticence and shyness, his letters and journals make it clear that in his private heart he did wish to become known as an explorer. The *Dawson Daily News* reported at the time of his disappearance that Darrell had hoped his new journey would lead to him joining the ranks of "all the big explorers." On top of that, the paper reported that Darrell's overriding ambition had been to "discover new lands to be added to Canada" among the uncharted High Arctic islands. The paper further reported that Darrell's hopes of distinguishing himself as an arctic explorer were disappointed when he was not selected as a member of Joseph-Elzéar Bernier's official expeditions. That same year Darrell vanished, Bernier had been appointed by the Canadian government to chart the arctic islands and claim them for Canada—before the Americans, Danes, or Norwegians could do so. This had long been a goal of Darrell's, and it was the hope of doing so that had in part enticed him to join Harrison's expedition. And with almost Shakespearean irony, it was ultimately Darrell's desire to disprove his nemesis Harrison's claims to have mapped the Anderson River that lured him there on his final, doomed quest. By that point, Harrison had long since decamped to his English mansion, never to set foot in the Arctic again.

In contrast, Darrell, at the time of his death, had only thirteen dollars and seventy-five cents to his name. Before embarking with the Jacquots, he'd left his meagre savings in the keeping of his old friend Nagle, the independent fur trader at Arctic Red River. After it became clear Darrell was lost, Nagle turned over his effects to the Mounties. A report by Corporal Somers itemized all of Darrell's worldly possessions that he'd left behind:

List of property: ten mink skins, eight white fox skins, five lynx skins, $13.75 in silver: one coat, one blanket, letters and papers. There is also one registered letter here for him. Darrell was well known in the Yukon . . . will you please inform me as to what disposal should be made of his property.

I have the honour to be, sir,

your obedient servant,

Sgd. J. Somers, Corp.

In charge of detachment.

Darrell had remained almost penniless then despite all his years of hard efforts, and his hopes of saving enough to buy a farm of his own and marry Agnes were as remote as ever. In 1913, Corporal Somers brought Darrell's furs and other effects south to Edmonton. From there, Darrell's property was sent to Charles in Manitoba. Agnes's little sister, Margaret, many decades later, recalled, "When Hubert disappeared his papers, etc. were all in a trunk . . . He also had some fine furs, destined for my sister—so she said—in his trunk. . . ."

Perhaps, if he had lived longer, Darrell's wanderlust might have eventually slackened and he might have settled down on a farm and married Agnes. His heart had long been torn between these things. As Darrell himself confessed in a 1907 letter, "What I hope to do is certainly to settle down but what I will do is another thing." What he really wanted was for Agnes to join him in the North, the way the Jacquots travelled the wild together. But for Agnes, a schoolteacher whose father had saved to send to her boarding school, such an unconventional path at the time seemed unthinkable. Though Agnes apparently was haunted ever afterwards by her decision not to go north.

Darrell soon vanished from the newspapers, public memory, and history, almost as surely as he had in the wild. In Birtle itself he'd been virtually entirely forgotten after Charles and Agnes's deaths, without any mention of him even in the local museum there. Neufeld's claim that Darrell deserved to be ranked among the greatest polar explorers in history is debatable, but at minimum, he had accomplished remarkable things and his countless journeys all added up to a record few could match. Stefansson was probably correct that Darrell was the greatest traveller of his kind in his day. His hand-drawn maps, too, were impressively accurate, and Darrell's penchant for adapting local clothing, learning native languages, and advocating for Indigenous cultures set him far apart from others, including more famous explorers such as Franklin, Peary, or Harrison.

Yet, ultimately, Darrell had his own weaknesses: though he was unflagging when given an impossible task—overcoming any measure of adversity or obstacles in pursuit of what had to be done—when left to his own devices, he often procrastinated and was unsure of what to do. That was the case with his endless vacillating over whether he should return to the farm, take work on a steamer, pan for gold, trade in furs, or enlist in someone else's expedition. Darrell never did quite succeed in figuring out his own exploration plans and how to put them into action. Instead, he was at his best when assigned a mission by others, notably guiding the Mounties, delivering the mail, or assisting Hanbury. Still, by any measure, Darrell deserves to rank highly in the records of arctic exploration, and in his relatively brief career, he managed to accomplish on his own more than many a more celebrated explorer ever did.

History can be notoriously capricious: some explorers, such as Franklin or Peary, end up famous, while others, like Darrell, remain utterly unknown. Stephen North, the son of Darrell's friend, once commented, "My father would want nothing more than his old friend to finally get the recognition he deserves." That, it seems, was also the wish of Darrell's family—who preserved his letters and journals in the hopes that they one day might be noticed. In stumbling upon those records, and following Darrell's old trails through the wilds, I was lucky to experience many wonderful things, ranging from wildlife encounters and natural splendour beyond any of my imaginings to meeting many kind individuals who generously shared with me their knowledge and stories. These things in themselves made my quest after Darrell worthwhile. But if in a small way this book also helps to pull Darrell out of the shadows and give him his proper place in history, then I shall have achieved more than I could have hoped.

EPILOGUE

To enter into Darrell's world is to journey to a land of lonely lakes, snaking rivers, and mist-shrouded mountains, wide-open vistas and moonlit forests, where lynx stalk silently in the shadows and caribou roam free. It's a place of ancient trees home to far-seeing owls, sparkling streams and roaring falls, deep canyons with crystal waters that harbour monstrous fish, pathless valleys, wandering wolf packs and wild goose flights, and the "magnificent aurora which lit up the whole country," as Darrell put it. A land of impossible horizons where nature remains raw and untamed.

Yet today, more and more it seems we are determined to squander all that as if it was nothing special, and push back the wild, in favour of development that entails less forests, less wetlands, and less nature, but more roads, highways, and sprawling cities with their associated infrastructure reaching like tentacles ever deeper into the diminishing wild—hydro corridors, pipelines, and mines. If Darrell were here today, I'm certain he'd tell us we are making a mistake. I think he'd say that in the end, the precious thing he sought wasn't gold, but the wild itself. That is the real irreplaceable treasure, one that is becoming rarer than ever. And yet we have more need of it than ever.

If we can find the will to preserve vast natural spaces—and I mean truly preserve them, not just tiny parcels that become managed parks full of asphalt parking lots, well-trodden trails, wifi hotspots, and other infrastructure—we will not only save a part of our shared human heritage, but make it possible to go on experiencing the spell of the wild. In an ever more urban, digital landscape, that, to my mind, is something well worth saving.

ACKNOWLEDGEMENTS

I n researching Darrell's story and writing this book, I bene-fited from the help of many individuals. I must thank for their assistance the staff at the Scott Polar Research Institute at the University of Cambridge in England, where Darrell's letters and journals are kept. The staff at Archives Canada (home to the North-West Mounted Police archive), the Anglican Church of Canada's archive in Toronto (where Bishop Stringer's papers can be found), and the Rauner Special Collections Library at Dartmouth College in the United States, (which houses Stefansson's papers), were likewise all very helpful to me. Truly, if you ever find yourself seized by a sudden urge to go squint over half-legible, faded old documents, I know of no friendlier and enthusiastic a bunch than professional archivists.

In Birtle, Manitoba, I was fortunate to experience the kind hospitality of Brenda Evans, Lorraine Snow, and Margaret Ashcroft. Their expertise was also very helpful and much appreciated. Birtle is a wonderful place, and I highly recommend a visit to it, particularly the revamped local museum.

In the North, I met with kindness from many people. James and Maureen Pokiak and Billy and Eileen Jacobson in Tuktoyaktuk were generous enough to share with me their knowledge and stories. I want to especially thank Chuck and Veryl Gruben for all of their help and hospitality. Chuck Gruben's expertise and assistance, as I hope this book has already made clear, proved essential. But more than that, he was an excellent guide and host, whose stories could fill a book of their own. Veryl too, when I stayed at their place afterwards, treated me like family, with cooking that on its own would have made my trip more than worthwhile. Jonas Lucas and Ronald Gruben were also very generous hosts, excellent guides, and shared many fascinating insights and stories with me. For all their help, I must express my sincere thanks.

My good friend Chuck Brill, of course, played a major role in helping me retrace Darrell's journeys. Having now done seven expeditions and counting together, I can happily say that Chuck's outdoor knowledge, fishing and paddling prowess, uncanny ability to make a fire in any kind of weather, and unfailing good humour in the face of any challenge, no matter how daunting, make him the perfect wilderness companion. Chuck further introduced me to his friend Mark Richard, who twice joined us on northern trips not detailed here. With Mark along, things were always a blast, and his worldly knowledge and experience were an added bonus. I thank both these gentleman for their assistance.

I must also thank the Royal Canadian Geographical Society for their support. The Society's backing has helped enable me to mount many of my expeditions, including several of my Darrell-focused ones. In particular, I extend my gratitude to Peter and Brigitte Westaway for all their encouragement and support, including of my research on Darrell. Since 2020, I have been thrilled to hold the title of Westaway Explorer-in-Residence at the Royal Canadian Geographical Society, a position named in their honour.

On the book side of things, I have once again benefited greatly from the outstanding team at Penguin Random House Canada. My editor, Nick Garrison, as always brought his sharp eye to bear on the manuscript, and offered much needed encouragement and words of wisdom to actually see this book through to completion. I must thank also Kristin Cochrane, CEO of Penguin Random House Canada, and Marion Garner, Publisher of Penguin Canada, for their support and encouragement of this book and the story behind it. Not every publisher would take on a story about a lost explorer virtually no one had ever heard of and who vanished a century ago. But they did, and for that and their continued support for my work, I'm enormously grateful.

Rounding out the superb team at Penguin Random House Canada, I must further thank our managing editor Alanna McMullen, whose steady hand at the wheel keeps everything running smoothly despite any unanticipated changes in the forecast (of which for this book there were many). Zainab Mirza, the editorial assistant, played a valuable role in keeping things on track and getting the book ready for publication, as did Brittany Larkin, the production manager. Dylan Browne is the talented designer who created the book's layout and cover, while the typesetter was Erin Cooper. For all their excellent work, I am much in their debt. On the sales side of things, I once again had the good fortune to benefit from the expertise of a talented trio: Bonnie Maitland, Sales Director; Catherine Knowles, Director of Marketing and Publicity; and Stephen Myers, the book's publicist, who deserves an award just for putting up with my schedule. I again must thank all of them for their hard work.

Crissy Boylan was the book's excellent copy editor. Her wonderfully sharp eye helped catch mistakes and improve the manuscript. I also again had the benefit of Catherine Dorton's expertise as a proofreader. Both of them do great work for which I am thankful. Any mistakes that may remain are entirely my own.

The maps featured in the book came about through the work of a couple of talented individuals I happen to know personally: Ocean Shoalts and Aleksia Shoalts. Ocean drew the illustrated overview map of Darrell's major travel routes. When I say she drew it, I mean she really drew it the old-fashioned way, entirely by hand. The eight black and white maps featured in the book were all drawn by Aleksia, again by hand. I thank them both for their excellent work. Aleksia further read over the book before it was published and made many helpful suggestions to improve it, as did Mark and Catherine Shoalts. I am very lucky to have had all their help.

Lastly, I must thank Aleksia for other things as well. First, she encouraged me to follow Darrell's footsteps and tell his story, and more than that, she has looked after our two little boys, Thomas and Adrian, while I was away in the wilderness. For that, and much else, I am very lucky and grateful.